Foreign Direct Investment and the World Economy

Foreign Direct Investment (FDI) occupies a special place in the connection between economic development and globalization. FDI brings scarce capital and technology from rich to poor countries. The prospect is enticing: companies in rich countries can earn high returns while accelerating growth in poor countries. In the capital-hungry nations of the developing world, the possibilities appear endless. But is that how it works in practice?

Foreign Direct Investment and the World Economy posits that the real test of "integration" should be whether FDI has helped the convergence of per capita incomes across countries. In a series of papers, Ashoka Mody and several expert co-authors critically assess the extent to which FDI is, in this sense, "integrating" the world economy. The findings are negative. The forces driving FDI are strong and they lead FDI to flow to select, attractive destinations; this selectivity is reinforced by the tendency of investors to follow each other. In such settings, FDI appears to have its most beneficial effects. Elsewhere, however, the flows of FDI are weaker and so too are the benefits, and in this FDI follows rather than leads the development process.

Ashoka Mody is Assistant Director at the European Department, International Monetary Fund.

T0346562

Routledge Studies in the Modern World Economy

Foreign Direct Investment and the World Economy

Ashoka Mody

Routledge
Taylor & Francis Group

LONDON AND NEW YORK

First published 2012
by Routledge
2 Park Square, Milton Park, Abingdon, Oxon OX14 4RN

Simultaneously published in the USA and Canada
by Routledge
711 Third Avenue, New York, NY10017

Routledge is an imprint of the Taylor & Francis Group, an informa business

First issued in paperback 2014

Typeset in Times New Roman by
RefineCatch Limited, Bungay, Suffolk

British Library Cataloguing in Publication Data
A catalogue record for this book is available from the British Library

Library of Congress Cataloging in Publication Data
Mody, Ashoka.
Foreign direct investment and the world economy / Ashoka Mody.
   p. cm.
Includes bibliographical references and index.
ISBN 0–415–70192–9 (hb)
1. Investments, Foreign–Case studies. 2. International economic
integration. I. Title.

HG4538.M587 2006
332.67'3–dc22   2006017955

ISBN13: 978–0–415–70192–1 (hbk)
ISBN13: 978–0–415–65487–6 (pbk)
ISBN13: 978–0–203–96614–3 (ebk)

Contents

Figures

Tables

Acknowledgements

Foreign Direct Investment (FDI) occupies a special place in the connection between economic development and globalization. FDI brings scarce capital and technology from rich to poor countries. The prospect is enticing: companies in rich countries can earn high returns while accelerating growth in poor countries. In the capital-hungry nations of the developing world, the possibilities appear endless. But is that how it works in practice?

In this book, I ask if FDI is "integrating" the world economy. While the term "integrating" is often used, I propose in the opening chapter that the real test should be whether FDI has brought per capita incomes across countries closer together. By this yardstick, the answer is "no." The forces driving FDI are strong and they lead FDI to flow to select, attractive destinations; but even stronger is the tendency of investors to follow each other. In such settings, FDI appears to have its most beneficial effects. In other words, FDI goes and does best where the conditions are already propitious. Elsewhere, the benefits are meager. FDI follows rather than leads the development process.

This book brings together papers written with a wonderful set of colleagues, starting in the early 1990s. The papers are presented in two parts: determinants and benefits.

The earliest paper, with David Wheeler, which appeared in the *Journal of International Economics* in 1992, was intended to examine the host country features that attract FDI. It is one of the most cited papers in FDI literature, having set off many subsequent explorations of the determinants of FDI. Its surprising finding was that country characteristics may matter less than the strong tendency for U.S. investors to "herd" into a country. Later research with Krishna Srinivasan concluded that Japanese investors were similarly motivated and then, with Yuko Kinoshita, we concluded that this "herd" behaviour reflected not just the benefits of agglomeration but, importantly, the expectation that early investors in a country have an informational advantage. The examination of the role of information and scale economies continued with Prakash Loungani and Assaf Razin. Throughout, my co-authors and I were also interested in specific economic policies to attract FDI and the paper with Susmita Dasgupta and Sarbajit Sinha reflects, in particular, the importance of a skilled labour force in the host country.

The research on benefits has focused on the conditions under which FDI is effective. In an early paper, Fang-Yi Wang and I examined the role of heavy FDI inflow into southern China. We concluded that domestic absorptive capacity was important in generating benefits from FDI. More recently, Antu Murshid and I found that the surge of foreign investment flows in the 1990s was, on average, associated with only a modest increase in domestic investment rates, explained possibly by the portfolio nature of FDI; however, where domestic policies were strong, the relationship between FDI and domestic investment was tighter. In the paper with Maria Soledad Martinez, we found that the benefits of foreign bank entry required a competitive environment. With Shoko Negishi, the conclusion was that mergers and acquisitions helped restructuring following the Asian crises, though once again we emphasized the role of domestic competition policy and corporate governance.

The author and publishers would like to thank the following for granting permission to reproduce material in this work:

1: "Is FDI integrating the world economy?" *World Economy* 27(8): 1195–1222, 2004.

2: "International investment location decisions: the case of U.S. firms." *Journal of International Economics* 33: 57–76, 1992. With David Wheeler.

3: "Japanese and U.S. firms as foreign investors: do they march to the same tune?" *Canadian Journal of Economics* 31: 778–799, 1998. With Krishna Srinivasan.

4: "Private information for foreign investment in emerging economies." *Canadian Journal of Economics* 34 (2): 448–64, May 2001. With Yuko Kinoshita.

5: "The global disconnect: the role of transactional distance and scale economies in gravity equations." *Scottish Journal of Political Economy* 49 (5): 526–43. With Prakash Loungani and Assaf Razin.

6: "Japanese multinationals in Asia: drivers and attractors." *Oxford Development Studies* 27(2): 149–164, 1999. With Susmita Dasgupta and Sarbajit Sinha.

7: "Explaining industrial growth in coastal China: economic reforms ... and what else?" *World Bank Economic Review* 11(2): 293–325, 1997. With Fang-Yi Wang.

8: "Growing up with capital flows." *Journal of International Economics* 65(1): 249–266, 2005. With Antu Panini Murshid.

9: "How foreign participation and market concentration impact bank spreads: evidence from Latin America." *Journal of Money, Credit and Banking*, 36(3, part 2): 511–538, 2004. With Maria Soledad Martinez Peria.

10: "The role of cross-border mergers and acquisitions in Asian restructuring." In Stijn Claessens, Simeon Djankov, and Ashoka Mody (eds.), *Resolution of Financial Distress: An International Perspective on the Design of Bankruptcy Laws*. WBI Development Studies, The World Bank, Washington D.C., 2001. With Shoko Negishi.

1 Is FDI integrating the world economy?

Introduction

At first pass, the answer to the question posed in the title of this chapter is a resounding "yes." Foreign direct investment—or FDI—has spread rapidly through the world economy in the past two decades. More countries and more sectors have come become part of the international FDI network. The high level and diverse forms of FDI represent an important force generating greater global economic integration.

However, this is not a complete, nor even the right, conclusion since it is necessary to define the term "integration" more precisely. Markets for goods and assets are regarded as integrated when their prices across nations converge. More trade may be symptomatic of global links but price convergence is the true evidence of integration. When considering FDI, however, no easy market price is identifiable. The presumption is that the flow of FDI brings closer together the returns to capital and labor across nations. A test, therefore, of global integration through FDI is whether it acts to facilitate the process of per capita income convergence across the nations.

There is good reason to put FDI to this somewhat severe test. FDI is thrice blessed. It brings scarce capital where capital is needed and productive. It stimulates the domestic market for corporate control and hence serves to discipline managers. It is the bearer of knowledge to enhance productivity, potentially to the levels of international best practice.

There is also reason to believe that FDI could have acted in the past two decades, through each of its three attributes, to foster income convergence: the spectacular growth in FDI raised capital flows in relation to global productive capacity; the increasing importance of the mergers and acquisitions component of FDI put corporate laggards on notice; and the spread of FDI to non-tradable service sectors generated the possibility that these sectors with traditionally low productivity would be brought closer to the standards of international efficiency.

The answer to the question in this chapter's title flips if integration is assessed in terms of income convergence. That promise of FDI is yet to be fulfilled. There is little evidence that FDI served to speed up convergence despite the important trends in its levels and composition. This was so for two reasons. First, FDI flows remained highly concentrated and second, the benefits from FDI appear to have accrued principally where conditions were already conducive to investment and growth. FDI can, at least temporarily, draw a country's resources from domestic entrepreneurs who are unprepared to deal with the competition.

The policy and regulatory agenda at the domestic and international levels has focused on the need to further reduce barriers to foreign investment without creating undesirable tax competition among nations. By necessity, progress has been incremental and, even if the current efforts are successful, there is no reason to believe that the role of FDI will change significantly. I suggest, somewhat speculatively, that FDI that is associated with greater labor mobility could prove to be more of an integrating force.

This chapter is a selective survey of the literature, with an attempt to highlight results from recent and ongoing research. Inevitably, the selection of research reported is biased towards my own interests and analyses. The rest of this chapter is organized around three objectives: first, to provide an overview of the *trends* in the levels and composition of FDI flows; second, to consider the *analytical* basis for the high concentration of FDI and the mechanisms through which FDI has an impact on domestic economies; and third, to describe the policy and regulatory issues faced at the level of the host country and in bilateral, regional, and multilateral forums.

The spread of FDI

Ostensibly, FDI has been an integrating force in several ways. The first, and most obvious, indicator is the rapid—indeed, explosive—growth in FDI. Figure 1.1 shows these global trends. From about \$55 billion in the early

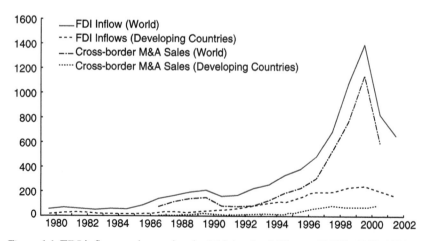

Figure 1.1 FDI inflows and cross-border M&A sales (billions of US\$), 1980–2002.

1980s, annual worldwide FDI rose to just over $200 billion in 1990 and then rose dramatically over six-fold to almost $1.4 trillion in 2000. While much of this increase represented a recirculation of capital within developed countries, developing countries also benefited from the huge expansion during this period. In the 1990s, FDI flows to developing countries rose from just under $40 billion in 1990 to over $240 billion in 2000, again a more than six-fold increase.

The large absolute rise in FDI also implied that FDI grew faster than world production and trade, especially during the 1990s. Figure 1.2 shows that the ratio of FDI to GDP rose steadily for developing countries from less than a quarter percent in 1970 to under 1 percent in 1990 and then to over 4 percent in 2000. This was a major transformation reflecting both the push of investors seeking high return opportunities and the pull from developing countries seeking needed investment and technology.

A second feature of FDI flows was the importance of international mergers and acquisitions. FDI may be in the form of "greenfield" projects (those projects where new investments are undertaken) and mergers and acquisitions (which entail the acquisition by foreign investors of ongoing domestic operations). Mergers and acquisitions were always important in developed-country transactions but their significance grew also for developing economies following the crises of the mid-1990s, as Figure 1.1 shows. In turn, these mergers and acquisitions reflected privatization of public sector assets in a number of developing countries in Latin America, and the international purchase of distressed banking and corporate assets in several Asian economies in the wake of the crisis triggered in July 1997.

A third important characteristic of FDI flows in the past decade was a massive shift into the services sector. Traditionally, FDI was directed to the

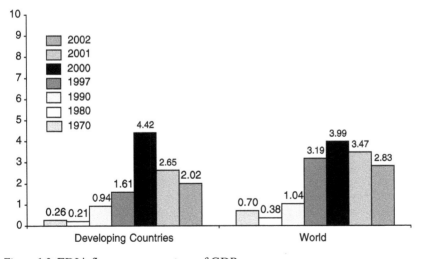

Figure 1.2 FDI inflows as a percentage of GDP.

development of natural resources and to manufacturing enterprises. In particular, during the 1980s, FDI flows increased to take advantage of lower costs of product assembly in developing economies, typically for exports to world markets. However, in the 1990s, increasingly larger shares of FDI went to service production and delivery—into such sectors as finance and telecommunications and more recently into wholesaling and retailing. The high level of mergers and acquisitions reported above and increased entry of foreign investors in service sectors were related. Figure 1.3 shows the transformation over time in the sectoral composition of mergers and acquisitions from a gradually declining share of the primary and manufacturing sectors and a rise of business services, finance, and communication; the trend applies to all of FDI, destined both for developed and developing countries.

Thus, at least in these three respects FDI flows acted to integrate developing countries into the world economy: there was substantially more FDI, it appeared increasingly in the form of mergers and acquisitions, and in a new range of service sectors. The reasons to celebrate these trends were clear. First, FDI brought in capital to capital-scarce economies. Second, in the form of mergers and acquisitions, it played an increasingly important role in generating competitive discipline in the domestic market for corporate assets. And, finally, by expanding its reach into service sectors, FDI promised to bring productivity gains to those non-tradable sectors where productivity growth has traditionally lagged and where the gaps between developed-country best practice and developing country efficiency levels are large.

Before turning to the assessment of the benefits that FDI did bring, it is useful to consider briefly what may have caused the huge upsurge in FDI and whether trends witnessed in the past two decades are likely to continue. We can presume that the promise of high returns drove FDI, but was that promise based on real prospects or did FDI follow the bubble in asset markets? This question has not been carefully analyzed and one can only speculate. An important observation in this context is the massive flow of FDI that occurred into the United States. To steal a phrase from Ross Perot, the erstwhile U.S. Presidential candidate, if there was "a giant sucking sound", it was into the U.S. not away from it, as he had feared. Much of this investment went into the booming U.S. telecommunications and finance sectors. It is likely that the same euphoria was influential in driving FDI to other countries. With disappointment in the returns to that investment, it is not surprising that FDI has slowed down. While I have described in some detail the run-up in FDI in the 1980s and 1990s, Figures 1.1 and 1.2 conspicuously point to a sharp decline thereafter. From a high of about $1.3 trillion, worldwide FDI was down to $820 billion in 2001 and to $650 billion in 2002. For developing countries also, FDI flows fell sharply in 2001 and 2002.

While a formal forecasting exercise is not appropriate in the context of this chapter, consider some sources of future FDI growth—some suggesting an optimistic outlook, others less so. First, an UNCTAD survey of multinationals suggests that despite the disruption following from the events of

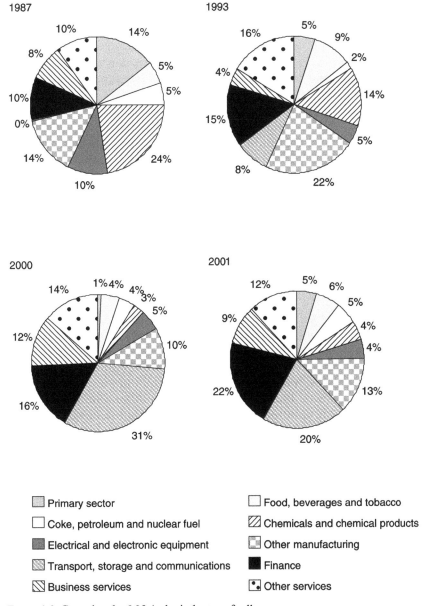

Figure 1.3 Cross-border M&As by industry of seller.

September 11 FDI trends will not be affected on that account (UNCTAD 2002). Only a very small fraction of firms reported a postponement of their plans. This is consistent with the view that FDI investors take a long-term view and, hence, FDI flows tend to be more stable than other forms of foreign capital flows (see, for example, Lucio Sarno and Mark Taylor 1999). Second, with declining scope for privatization, will FDI to developing countries be especially hurt? The answer depends on whether the decline in mergers and acquisitions activity will be offset by new investment. Recently acquired firms may benefit from continued foreign funding of new investment. Both econometric and survey findings, in this respect, are encouraging. Cesare Calderon, Norman Loayza, and Luis Serven (2002) find that mergers and acquisitions are followed by new "greenfield" investments. The UNCTAD survey is consistent with these findings and reports, for example, that Brazilian firms acquired by foreign companies do expect new foreign funding. Finally, a more potent force on FDI prospects is likely to be the slowdown in world growth. As discussed below, econometric results strongly suggest that high growth rates attract foreign investment. FDI's decline in 2001 and 2002 was, in large measure, a consequence of the worldwide deceleration in growth (Rui Albuquerque, Norman Loayza, and Luis Serven 2002 conclude that "world factors" rather than domestic factors drove the volume of FDI in the 1990s). If world economic growth remains subdued, then FDI flows are also likely to remain flat.

Why FDI flows remain concentrated

Robert Lucas (1990) laid out the challenge in his famous paper: "Why Doesn't Capital Flow from Rich to Poor Countries?" Poor countries, with scarce capital, should provide much higher marginal returns to capital than rich countries. That, in turn, should result in virtually all new investment occurring in the poor developing nations. Of course, the reality is not even close to that prediction. Figure 1.4 shows that over 80 percent of the world's population resides in developing nations and, at reported exchange rates, they produce just over 20 percent of the world's GDP (the share of developing country GDP is higher when allowance is made for differences in purchasing power). By these benchmarks, developing country share of world FDI has been modest. In the mid-1990s, when flows to developing countries were most buoyant, the developing country share reached around one-third, but for most of the past three decades, the share has averaged around one-fifth.

Further, within developing countries, the richer pull in the bulk of the FDI. Figure 1.5 shows that the middle-income countries had a significantly higher FDI/GDP ratio than low-income countries and that this gap grew over the 1990s.[1] Moreover, the 10 largest recipients of FDI—accounting for 80 percent of developing country FDI in the 1990s—all fell in the middle-income group and their FDI/GDP ratio was even higher.[2] The top three recipients, Brazil, China and Mexico (with about a third of developing country GDP), absorbed just over half of developing country FDI. Moreover, as the lower panel of Figure 1.5 shows, during this period, middle-income countries grew faster than low-income countries and the top ten grew even faster, suggesting a synergistic relationship between growth and FDI. Further, the positive relationship between the FDI–GDP ratio appears even within each of these

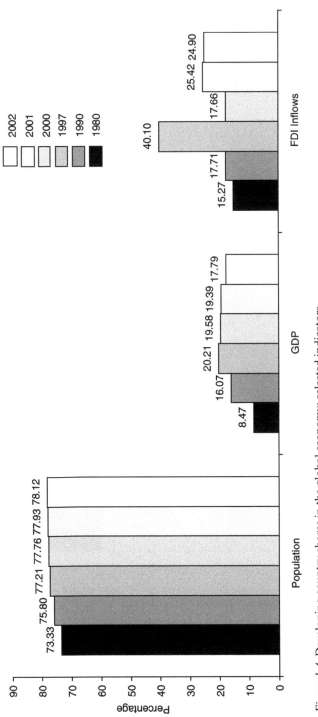

Figure 1.4 Developing country shares in the global economy: selected indicators.

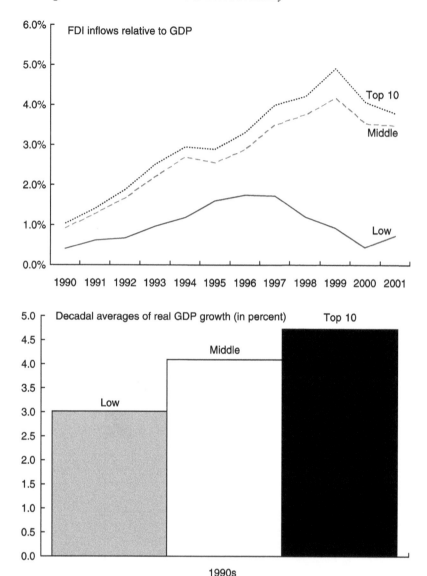

Figure 1.5 FDI flows and real GDP growth: low-income, middle-income, and Top 10 FDI recipients, 1990–2001.

country groups, though to varying degrees (Figure 1.6). Thus, higher level of development (reflecting institutional maturity) and higher country growth rate explain much of the cross-country allocation of FDI in the 1990s.

Finally, Michael Clemens and Jeffrey Williamson (2000) find that the "Lucas Paradox" was also operative in the late 19th and early 20th century with respect to British export of capital. They define such a paradox to exist

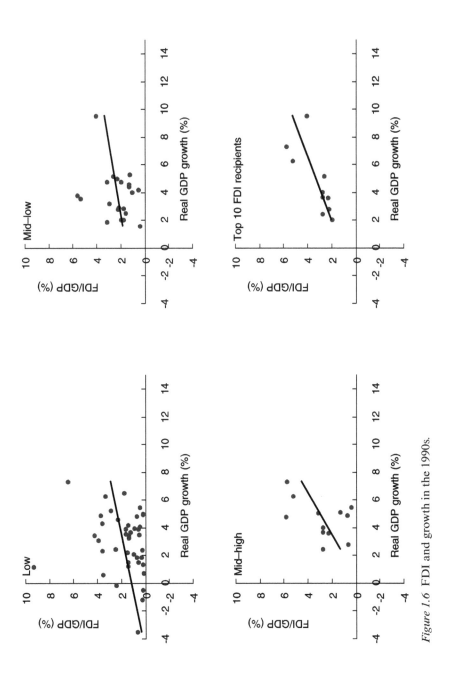

Figure 1.6 FDI and growth in the 1990s.

when a host country's GDP per capita exercises a "powerful positive affect" on the share of international capital flows received. In analyzing the reasons for the Lucas paradox, then and now, Clemens and Williamson (2000) propose that two sets of factors are at work. First, despite its scarcity, capital may be unproductive in poorer countries because of the absence of needed complementary inputs. Second, capital markets may fail for a variety of reasons to allocate capital efficiently. They conclude that market failure was unimportant and that the dominant reason for the Lucas paradox was differences in country fundamentals that made capital more productive in rich countries. The fundamentals they find to be of importance are: the fraction of children enrolled in primary schools, share of primary products in exports, immigration, and population growth. To represent possible misallocation of capital, Clemens and Williamson (2000) considered colonial status and adherence or otherwise to the gold standard, a proxy for commitment to macroeconomic discipline. Neither proved statistically significant.

Similar analyses for the more recent decades also find evidence for the importance of operating conditions that reduce capital productivity but, in addition, scale economies and informational gaps are found to play a significant role. David Wheeler and I found in an early paper that domestic country attributes mattered for U.S. foreign investors (Wheeler and Mody 1992; also Ch. 2 this book). Of particular significance was infrastructure availability. A subsequent paper with Krishna Srinivasan also considered Japanese foreign investment decisions and found further evidence for the importance of infrastructure and human capital (Mody and Srinivasan 1998; also Ch. 3 this book).[3] In addition, higher levels of country risk deterred foreign investors. Significantly also, the past stock of foreign investment was extremely important in explaining new inflows of FDI.

The finding that past stock of foreign investment matters in determining new flows is subject to various interpretations, including omitted country variables. In Wheeler and Mody (1992) and Mody and Srinivasan (1998), we proposed that the presence of agglomeration economies attracted foreign investors but offered no direct evidence to support that conjecture. Using a survey of Japanese investors, Yuko Kinoshita and I focused on informational gaps and found evidence consistent with a significant value attached to private information (Kinoshita and Mody 2001; also Ch. 4 this book). Investors who already had a presence in a particular host country were likely to have more ambitious investment plans in that country rather than in alternative locations. At the same time, when contemplating investment in a country that was "new" to them, investors were strongly influenced by the behavior of other investors, i.e., their likelihood of investing in the new country increased considerably if they perceived that others found it a desirable location. In other words, the evidence suggested a "herd-like" movement over and above that explained by country and industry characteristics.

More recently, Prakash Loungani, Assaf Razin and I have approached this question from a different perspective (Loungani, Mody, and Razin 2002; also

Ch. 5 this book). In so-called "gravity" models of bilateral investment, distance between the two countries appears with a large and negative sign. However, economic theory does not necessarily predict that greater distance between two countries should reduce the FDI that flows between them. Indeed, the opposite is predicted for "horizontal" foreign investment, which is investment undertaken as a substitute for trade when distance creates high transportation costs. We test the possibility that physical distance between countries proxies, among other things, for "informational distance," which we represent by bilateral telecommunications capability. Better information capability does stimulate more bilateral investment. Moreover, when such an informational variable is introduced into the regression, the coefficient of physical distance actually becomes positive for developed countries, suggesting that horizontal investment may be the dominant motive for FDI flows among developed countries. For developing countries, the coefficient on physical distance remains negative and significant, but better informational capacity reduces the disadvantage of physical distance.

Finally, econometric evidence typically supports the positive relationship between growth and FDI suggested in Figures 1.5 and 1.6. Robert Lipsey and Zadia Feliciano (2002) consider the factors that attract foreign investment into the United States. They find that high rates of U.S. growth lead to both acquisitions and new establishments. Firms are also acquired when they suffer from low profitability and are faced with high costs of capital, lending support to the role that foreign investors play in the market for corporate control. Foreign investors who establish new firms come from countries that have a comparative advantage in that activity.

To summarize, the Lucas paradox—i.e., the high correlation between per capita incomes and FDI flows—stems from three, possibly related, causes. High-income countries have better fundamentals, such as infrastructure and human capital. Moreover, poorer countries are also associated with higher measures of corruption: Beata Smarzynska and Shang-Jin Wei (2002) find that corruption lowers FDI, especially the FDI with high intellectual property content. At the same time, agglomeration economies and informational gaps have the effect of creating clusters of investors in more favorable operating conditions. And, finally, growth and FDI can have a mutually reinforcing relationship. The suggestion is that FDI is largely reactive to prevailing conditions and is not principally a source of entrepreneurship and creativity but rather is able to exploit favorable host country conditions. In the next section, I examine more directly the conditions under which FDI benefits the host economy.

Has FDI helped income convergence?

FDI can benefit the host economy by boosting domestic investment and by raising productivity. The evidence suggests that the investment effect applies in a broad range of conditions, though over time a dollar of FDI has been associated with less than a dollar of investment. Productivity benefits are more controversial. While anecdotal evidence of knowledge transfer through training and turnover of employees is often cited, the econometric evidence— using either firm-level data or aggregate data—offers much weaker support for productivity benefits. To the extent such benefits exist, they accrue where economic conditions are already favorable: FDI thus operates to support and enhance an existing growth dynamic.

FDI and domestic investment

Barry Bosworth and Susan Collins (1999) conducted an extensive analysis of the effect of foreign capital flows on domestic investment and found that a dollar of FDI to developing economies translated into a dollar of domestic investment; in contrast, bank loans and bond funds were less effective in generating investment in the host economy. This was an important finding but one that was not surprising. Most FDI up until the end of their sample period, i.e., 1995, was in the form of greenfield projects, which, by definition, involve new establishments. In contrast, bank loans and bond issuance may not be related to new investment. Extending their analysis in several ways, Antu Murshid and I find that marginal impact of FDI flows declined in the 1990s, especially in the second half of the decade (Mody and Murshid 2005; also Ch. 8 this book). This may have resulted from the larger share of mergers and acquisitions in FDI flows.

FDI and productivity spillovers

While the problem of attributing causation to foreign inflows is hard enough when analyzing short-term movements in domestic investment, it is especially difficult in considering the impact on productivity. Productivity growth is inherently a more medium-term phenomenon and hence, over that period, is likely to influence the level of foreign inflows. Research results remain ambiguous and, if anything, an increasing number of results point to limited productivity gains from FDI. Richard Caves (1999) has suggested that the ambiguity in the research findings with respect to the existence of productivity spillovers from foreign investment could reflect differences in host country absorptive capacity.

A number of possible mechanisms exist through which foreign investment can generate spillovers, i.e., increase or decrease the productivity of domestic firms. Consider, first, the so-called "horizontal" spillovers. In the empirical literature, these have been defined as the productivity benefits accruing to domestic firms with the same sector. Through informal contacts and turnover of workers trained by foreign investors, domestic firms can enhance their productivity, if—and this is an important if—they are capable of absorbing the knowledge available.[4]

In the analysis based on firm-level data, the charge has been led by Ann Harrison who, with several colleagues over the years and using data from different countries, has presented evidence that suggests that, at least in the short-run, FDI actually hurts local entrepreneurs rather than raising their level of productivity through "spillovers" of knowledge. In Mona Haddad and Harrison (1993) and Brian Aitken and Harrison (1999), the evidence is that a larger foreign presence in the sector is associated with lower domestic productivity. Domestic firms that compete directly with the foreign investor may lose market share and, left stranded with excess capacity, experience a decline in the productive use of their resources.

Negative externalities may also arise where foreign investors increase the demand for scarce resources, such as skilled labor and domestic credit, and hence raise production costs. Robert Feenstra and Gordon Hanson (1996 and 1997) argue that foreign investors will use a more skill-intensive technology than the typical domestic investor and hence raise the wages of skilled workers, a proposition for which they find support in Mexican data. Harrison and Margaret McMillan (2003) highlight a different channel of influence. They note that "foreign" investors often finance their investments by borrowing in domestic markets. Where, as in many developing economies, domestic companies are already credit rationed, foreign firms aggravate the degree of rationing. They find evidence for preemption of domestic credit by foreign investors in Cote d'Ivoire.

Firm-level evidence for positive externalities from FDI typically come from high absorptive capacity settings such as Taiwan, China, the coastal provinces of China, the German and U.K. manufacturing sectors, and smaller European economies such as Ireland and Belgium (World Bank 2001). Jonathan Haskel, Sonia Pereira, and Matthew Slaughter (2002) undertake an extensive analysis of a panel of U.K. firms and reach several interesting conclusions. They find evidence for productivity spillovers within a given sector; in magnitude the spillover would account for about 5 percent of U.K. productivity growth and, the authors conclude, was insufficient to justify the subsidies provided to foreign investors. Lee Branstetter (2000) finds that Japanese firms investing in the United States enhanced their knowledge while at the same time benefiting U.S. firms—another example suggesting that knowledge spillovers are most active when firms have strong absorptive capacity. For the Chinese coastal provinces, for example, the finding is that FDI does help growth, but particularly so in locations with good infrastructure and superior human capital (Mody and Fang-Yi Wang 1997; also Ch. 7 this book). Moreover, FDI and the supporting infrastructure and human capital appear to stimulate each other.

Vertical spillovers

Early case-study research on spillovers from FDI had focused on backward linkages developed by foreign investors (e.g., Sanjaya Lall 1980) but firm-level panel data studies shifted attention to horizontal spillovers. With the continued finding of limited horizontal spillovers in most developing economies, interest in "vertical" spillovers has been renewed. Is productivity enhanced in sectors that supply to foreign investors? In a vertical relationship, the foreign investor has an incentive to transfer technology and provide training to raise the supplier's productivity. Thus, where vertical relationships exist, we should expect spillovers to be significant—and, indeed, the limited evidence supports that presumption. However, in assessing the overall impact of FDI, it is necessary to also determine the fraction of FDI that generates significant backward linkages into the domestic economy. The evidence suggests that local infrastructure and capabilities are important for the establishment of backward linkages.

For firms in Lithuania, Smarzynksa (2002) finds no horizontal spillovers from foreign investors, in line with research reported above, but she does find that "upstream" producers (suppliers) have increasingly higher productivity as the share of foreign investors in the "downstream" (customer) sectors increases. This is consistent with spillovers through backward linkages. However, she notes that the evidence is also consistent with the possibility of increased competition among upstream producers that weeds out low productivity producers—and, hence, the higher observed productivity is an artifact arising from firm exit rather than a genuine rise in productivity. She further notes that, while it is difficult to distinguish between the two competing possibilities, such a distinction is critical since the policy implications arising from the alternatives are quite different. Garrick Blalock and Paul Gertler (2003) address this question. They also find evidence of spillovers in backward linkage relationships. Moreover, they find supplier sectors have a lower, not higher, degree of concentration as the foreign presence increases in downstream sectors. They argue that foreign investors have an incentive to enhance productivity of multiple suppliers to minimize the risk of being held hostage, even though some of the benefits of upgraded suppliers may accrue to their competitors.

Of interest, then, are the factors that contribute to the development of backward supply linkages. It is likely that economic activities that require strong backward linkages also imply costly investment in training. When this is so, the potential investor may choose not to invest at all (Andres Rodriguez-Claire 1996). Thus, in low income economies with weak institutions, FDI is likely to be directed towards "enclave" sectors, such as extractive industries, that generate few backward linkages. The empirical evidence supports this conjecture. Rene Belderbos, Giovanni Capannelli, and Kyoji Fukao (2001) examine the extent of backward linkages established by Japanese investors in different countries. They find, for example, that while 80 percent of inputs are sourced domestically when they operate in the United States, the share of domestic inputs is considerably lower in developing economies. A more formal examination of the determinants of the share of local inputs shows that the quality of local infrastructure and capabilities of local suppliers is crucial in determining the extent of backward linkages. They note, further, that imposition of local content requirements either has the effect of Japanese producers establishing their own input supply factories or of dissuading firms from investing in that country.

Thus, whether we consider horizontal or vertical spillovers, the role of domestic capabilities appears to be crucial. Studies using aggregate data also conclude that the effectiveness of FDI depends on the country circumstances. Eduardo Borensztein, Jose De Gregorio, and Jong-Wha Lee (1998) find that FDI spurs growth where complementary human capital is of high quality and V.N. Balasubramanyam, M. Salisu, and David Sapsford (1991) find that the benefits of FDI accrue in countries with a strong export-orientation and not where import-substitution is the dominant strategy. Laura Alfaro, Areendam Chanda, Sebnem Kalimbli-Ozcan, and Selin Sayek (2003) find complementarity with financial development. However, Maria Carkovic and Ross Levine (2002) are skeptical even of these more nuanced findings. Using an econometric technique that controls for country fixed-effects and simultaneous determination of FDI and growth, they conclude (p. 3) that "the data do not suggest a strong independent impact of FDI on economic growth."

Mergers and acquisitions

Finally, in view of the importance of cross-border mergers and acquisitions, consider briefly their impact on productivity. The evidence, unfortunately, is limited. Business academics are "dubious" with respect to the benefits of the megamergers that drove FDI flows in the later part of the 1990s (see, for example, Pankaj Ghemawat and Fariborz Ghadar 2000). Though, in line with the general literature on domestic mergers and acquisitions, most studies remain inconclusive, one study does argue that the international competition for corporate control in the U.S. has helped discipline managers (Jun-Koo Kang 1993).

In developing countries, potential gains arise from the foreign purchase of state-owned assets, where domestic residents and entrepreneurs do not have sufficient financial resources and/or management experience to operate large-scale enterprises. Stanislaw Uminski (2001) reports significant gains from privatization in Poland, for example. Benefits, in the form of lower spreads charged, have also been documented following foreign ownership of domestic banks (see, for example, a review of earlier literature and new findings in Peria and Mody forthcoming; also Ch. 9 this book). However, aside from the one-time gain, which is undoubtedly important, further improvements in productivity will require an appropriately competitive and regulatory environment and foreign ownership is unlikely to be sufficient.

The opposite concern has, however, been sometimes expressed—i.e., foreign ownership through mergers and acquisitions may be harmful. Based on research by Assaf Razin and his colleagues, Loungani and Razin (2001) are concerned that foreign investors may "skim the cream":

Through FDI, foreign investors gain crucial inside information about the productivity of the firms under their control. This gives them an informational advantage over "uninformed" domestic savers, whose buying of shares in domestic firms does not entail control. Taking advantage of this superior information, foreign direct investors will tend to retain high-productivity firms under their ownership and control and sell low-productivity firms to the uninformed savers. As with other adverse-selection problems of this kind, this process may lead to overinvestment by foreign direct investors.

Paul Krugman (1998) expressed concern about "fire sales" of domestic assets in the context of the Asian crises. He suggested that domestic owners are likely to be better informed about their businesses and, hence, about how to revive them following the sharp downturn experienced. However, because of the severe credit constraints faced by them, they would, in some instances, be forced to sell their assets at "fire sale" prices, an outcome that would not only be to the detriment of the sellers but also inefficient for the economy. Shoko Negishi and I, however, found little empirical support for this hypothesis (Mody and Negishi 2001; also Ch. 10 this book) and conclude that the sectoral and country pattern of mergers and acquisitions following the crisis was likely prompted by the opportunities arising from the policy reform efforts.

This review of the micro evidence on the role of FDI is consistent with the preceding discussion on macro trends of FDI destinations. As the data showed, FDI flows have been directed towards environments with higher per capita incomes and better growth opportunities. The micro level studies bear out that productivity gains from FDI are greater the better the absorptive capacity of the domestic economy.

Policy and regulatory matters

Removing the obstacles to operations by foreign investors without going overboard in favoring them is the challenge that faces those who regulate FDI today. This is an evolution from the 1970s and 1980s when national authorities required foreign investors to undertake activities with possible developmental spillovers—sourcing of domestic inputs, exporting output to generate scarce foreign exchange, and training domestic workers. Such performance requirements (see Table 1.1) came to be viewed as onerous by investors and, along with other entry barriers in the manufacturing sector, are being voluntarily phased out, with commitments codified under the WTO's agreement on Trade-Related Investment Measures (TRIMs). In the 1990s, attention shifted to entry barriers that foreign investors faced in the services sectors and these are being gradually lowered primarily through the General Agreement on Trade in Services (GATS). But as deterrents to FDI have been scaled back, concerns have also arisen about the spread of fiscal and regulatory incentives to attract FDI. Today, a patchwork of FDI policy exists through bilateral and

Table 1.1 International FDI policies: from old to new concerns

Concerns	Deterrents to FDI	FDI incentives
Old	• Performance requirements (TRIMs) • Threat of expropriation (bilateral treaties)	
New	• Lack of market access (GATS) • Insufficient transparency of rules	Regulatory and tax concessions: • Race to the bottom • Transferring rents to foreigners

multilateral agreements: deterrents and incentives are not typically dealt under a unified framework or a coordinated policy or institutional initiative.

To the extent progress on the FDI policy agenda is achieved, will that progress change the fact that half of all developing country FDI goes to three countries? Or, will productivity benefits of FDI increase? The forces described above, leading to the concentration of FDI in host economies with high absorption capacity, are powerful—and appear to have been only marginally influenced by the huge liberalization of FDI policy that did occur in the last two decades.

In this section, I discuss policy and regulatory matters with respect to FDI under three headings: (a) current cross-country disciplines on FDI; (b) host country incentives to attract FDI; and (c) a forward-looking multilateral agenda on FDI.

Cross-country disciplines on FDI

Cross-country policy measures to channel FDI include bilateral tax and investment treaties, regional agreements, and multilateral rules; the multilateral rules at the present time operate principally under the auspices of the World Trade Organization (WTO). In common, they seek to create a level playing field for foreign investors. In particular, "national treatment" implies that foreign firms should have the same rights of establishment and operation as do national firms.

Bilateral treaties are, perhaps, by far the most prevalent form of FDI regulation. In a recent analysis of tax treaties (also referred to as double-tax treaties), Bruce Blonigen and Ronald Davies (2002) note that more than 2000 such treaties are in existence (an update of the numbers of treaties is provided by UNCTAD's *World Investment Report* (2003)). Blonigen and Davies find, for the period 1982–1992, that U.S. firms undertook *less* not more FDI in countries with which the U.S. had recently concluded a treaty. The implication is that, where no tax treaties exist, multinationals use concessions and loopholes in foreign tax systems to their advantage. Tax treaties reduce the possibilities of tax evasion through, for example, transfer pricing and the use of "tax havens." The study thus lends credence to the view that multinational firms can and do bypass national tax systems and that bilateral treaties are desirable from a revenue perspective and, possibly, for the efficient allocation of investment.

Bilateral investment treaties have investor protection as their goal. These have also proliferated, especially in the 1990s, rising, as Mary Hallward-Driemeier (2003) notes from 470 in 1990 to almost 2000 in number by the year 2000, covering half of all FDI flows from OECD to developing economies. In an econometric study, she finds, however, that such treaties have had virtually no influence on increasing the flow of FDI to signatory hosts. Investment treaties, therefore, are not a substitute for domestic laws protecting property rights. Countries in Sub-Saharan Africa, for example, have entered into several agreements to protect investors but have had limited success in attracting FDI; in contrast, Brazil, a major FDI recipient, has not ratified a single investment treaty. Cuba does not have a treaty with either Canada or Mexico, its main foreign investors—almost two-thirds of the countries with which it does have a treaty make no investment in that country. Gaetan Verhoosel (2003) points out the investment treaties typically refer to, an often vaguely defined, "international law" as the standard by which possible expropriation is to be assessed and investors have recourse to various international dispute resolution forums. Drawing on several examples, Hallward-Driemeier (2003, p. 7) suggests that foreign investors could misuse the treaties to protect themselves even against normal commercial risks.

Beyond bilateral treaties lie regional agreements, which have also proliferated in recent years. Regional rules for investment could bolster investment flows in the short-run by committing countries to stable policy regimes (Raquel Fernandez and Jonathan Portes 1998) and by providing access to larger markets, but they are also likely to divert FDI from non-participating countries. It has been observed that FDI typically increases when a country joins a regional common market (see, for example, John Dunning 1997 and Ray Barrell and Nigel Pain 1998 for evidence on Europe, and Anne Krueger 2000 for Mexico following its entry into North American Free Trade Agreement (NAFTA)). The difficulty, however, arises in attributing the observed increase to the regional agreement. In the case of Mexico, for example, a 1993 foreign investment liberalization law that just predated NAFTA, the ongoing worldwide boom in FDI, and the general shift in Mexico's economic policies all contributed to increased foreign investment received (see Krueger 2000). UNCTAD (2003, p. 58) concludes that "the definitive study of NAFTA's impact on FDI has yet to be done." Even careful econometric analysis will find it difficult to disentangle the various effects. Eduardo Levy Yeyati, Ernesto Stein, and Christian Duade (2002) find that a host country receives more FDI if it is a member of a regional trading arrangement, not only from source countries under the same arrangement but also from other source countries presumably attracted by the larger market size that can be accessed.

At the same time, countries that are not members of regional arrangements receive somewhat lower FDI, suggesting a diversion of FDI. However, V.N. Balasubramanyam, David Sapsford, and David Griffiths (2002) conclude that when a full range of explanatory variables reflecting host and source country considerations is included, the regional agreement is found to have no independent effect. Thus, the evidence is, at best, inconclusive.

Finally, on the multilateral front, the World Trade Organization (WTO) remains the primary forum for advancing multilateral disciplines in investment. These include reduction of subsidies that favor exports, less discrimination against foreign firms with respect to rights of establishment and market access, and protection of investors against expropriation. Export processing zones that offer subsidies not available for other domestic activities are inconsistent with WTO standards and such subsidies are to be phased out over the coming years. John Mutti (2002) notes that this is a complex exercise with the phasing out to occur more rapidly where a country accounts for more than 3.25 percent of world market share in particular product categories; at the other end, the least developed countries (countries with an annual per capita income of less than $1000) will be allowed to retain their subsidies for the present.

The General Agreement on Trade in Services (GATS) promotes greater international trade in services and forms the umbrella for enhancing the rights of foreign firms to, among other things, national treatment. Investment regimes with respect to manufacturing establishments have been largely liberalized and hence it is in service sectors, with their myriad regulatory barriers to entry, that a more open environment is needed. However, as Pierre Sauve and Christopher Wilke (2000) note and as was discussed above, despite the remaining barriers, international investment flows to the services sectors have already been large. Thus, Sauve and Wilke (2000) conclude that there is no compelling case for a more aggressive approach to achieving multilateral disciplines for investment regime.

To summarize, the international regime governing investment flows remains a patchwork of bilateral, regional, and multilateral treaties and rules. While this is apparently an undesirable state of affairs—undesirable because investment is likely to be misallocated in the attempt to conform to the patchwork—policy makers are not overly concerned. This is largely attributable to a strong unilateral drive on the part of a large majority of countries to reduce entry barriers (see UNCTAD 2003, which documents the continued reduction of barriers to FDI). Looking ahead, multilateral rules may have a unifying role to play in the investment arena. However, both because the gains from the pursuit of an active multilateral agenda are unclear and because the various interested parties have differing views on priorities, multilateral efforts in the area of foreign investment have not been and are not expected to be forcefully pursued. Not surprisingly, the Doha round, even before it was set back, had a modest agenda for investment flows.[5] The more ambitious OECD-sponsored Multilateral Agreement on Investment failed because in terms of investment

protection it offered less than the existing bilateral investment treaties, potential signatories worried about free-riding by non-signatories (who would gain
from the most favored nation status through WTO disciplines), and labor
and environmental groups worried about the growing power of multinational
corporations (World Bank 2003, Box 4.2).

Host country incentives

Much of an earlier debate on policy towards FDI centered on the desirability
of "performance requirements," or obligations, such as export targets and
training of domestic nationals, that the foreign investor was required to
fulfill. The premise was that an active government effort was required to
realize the externalities from foreign investment. Thus, part of the FDI
folklore was Singapore's success in having its nationals trained by multinational firms, including large numbers not directly employed in those
firms. However, multinationals themselves never favored performance
requirements and, as the competition for FDI increased, such requirements
have gradually been phased out in many countries. Interestingly, despite
declining in policy respectability, the analytical case for performance
requirements has not disappeared. James Markusen (1998), for example,
argues that foreign investment flows from market distortions generate significant rents and it is legitimate for the host country to extract some part of
these rents.[6]

The policy pendulum, however, has swung to the other end. The concern
now is with excessive subsidies to attract foreign investors. To assess this
concern, we need answers to three questions: (a) Are governments indeed in a
race to attract foreign investors? (b) If they are, do incentives work? And (c)
how, if at all, should public policy respond to the possibility of excessive
competition for foreign investment?

A comprehensive measure of incentives is difficult to compile and, to my
knowledge, does not exist. Considerable effort has, however, been devoted
recently to one, possibly significant, element of the incentive package, namely,
the effective tax obligation of a foreign investor. A July 2000 study by the
United Nations Conference on Trade and Development (UNCTAD 2000)
surveyed 45 countries from all regions of the world and concluded: "Nearly
all countries surveyed offer incentives that target specific sectors. Regional
incentives aimed at assisting the economic development of rural or underdeveloped areas are also prevalent in 70 percent of the countries surveyed."
The incentives, the UNCTAD study reports, are offered principally through
various tax breaks, including tax holidays, accelerated depreciation, and
allowances for training and R&D.

The most plausible way to aggregate these tax incentives is to consider the
effective corporate tax paid by foreign firms. It is not straightforward to
obtain such rates and Mutti (2002) surveys several alternative measures. He
reaches three conclusions of interest:

- Between 1984 and 1996, statutory corporate tax rates typically declined around the world. Effective tax rates (tax collected/GDP) also declined but to a smaller extent as tax bases broadened.
- Tax rates fell especially in countries with higher rates. Rates were reduced by about 15 percentage points in countries with high rates (statutory rates greater than 45 percent) and by 4 percentage points in countries with low rates.
- Much of the tax reduction during this period occurred between 1984 and 1992 and slowed down thereafter. After 1992, rate reduction in high rate countries (statutory rates higher than 35 percent after 1992) was only of the order of 4 percentage points, while rates remained broadly unchanged in low rate countries.

Thus, the finding is that rates fell sharply mainly to bring effective rates across countries closer to each other and have since stabilized. One explanation for the sharp decline in the years immediately following 1986 is a change in that year in U.S. policy towards multinationals that significantly reduced their tax burden. International tax competition then made high rates untenable.

How relevant is tax competition for location decisions by foreign investors? The evidence on this score is mixed and Mutti's (2002) recent discussion of the literature and his new results help clarify the reasons for the ambiguities in the econometric results. He points out that the implications of tax rates will vary with the nature of the foreign investment. An important difference in this regard is whether the investment is directed to serving the domestic market in the host country or is intended to produce goods for the world market. Mutti (2002) finds that export-oriented investment is most sensitive to tax rates. This conclusion is consistent with early results reported in Wheeler and Mody (1992), where we showed that though tax rates were not especially relevant for location decisions when the manufacturing sector as a whole was considered, they were influential in guiding investors in the electronics industry, a "footloose" industry in the terminology of those years seeking low cost production sites for assembling products destined for world markets. As countries have vied for such export-oriented foreign investment, tax competition has become a more salient policy issue.

What, then, is the advice to policy makers? An OECD study offers some useful pointers (OECD 2001).[7] Since poor operating conditions act as the fundamental deterrents to foreign investment, improving those conditions should be the first order of business. Policymakers may be concerned that the fundamental structural reforms required to improve infrastructure and human capital will take too long and tax incentives offer a quick mechanism for bringing in needed foreign investment. Adoption of such an approach, however, requires credible evidence of positive externalities from foreign investment. Where such evidence does exist and is credible, the alternative of generally low tax rates, with a broader tax base, must be considered against selective incentives for foreign investors.

A forward-looking agenda

So is there reason to pursue a bolder international approach? One possibility is to revive and give greater attention to the consideration of labor mobility, such as that already tabled under the GATS. The premise is that investment flows *to* developing countries will increase if migration—particularly of skilled workers—*from* developing countries increases. On that relationship between migrants and investment, I believe, the empirical evidence is quite strong. A further, more speculative, assertion is that the *quality* of the capital flows, and hence their productivity, will also improve when accompanied by more mobile developing country workforce.

Arvind Panagariya (1999) has argued that developing countries should only agree to an international agreement on investment if there is a corresponding willingness on the part of developed nations to open their borders to migrants from developing countries. He offers two arguments in favor of this proposal. First, citing a study by Hamilton and Whalley (1984), he notes that worldwide gains from greater labor mobility are huge and they dwarf gains from other forms of liberalization. Second, the benefits of labor mobility will accrue principally to poorer countries and, hence, are desirable from an equity perspective. Panagariya (1999) is also not persuaded by claims that no political appetite exists for such initiatives. He interprets the history of the multilateral agreements, particularly recent agreements that have moved beyond the traditional trade agenda, as having evolved in an incremental fashion. He suggests, therefore, that an initial focus on the mobility of professionals is likely to be attractive to all, and will also allay fears of some developing countries who may be concerned themselves about supporting large numbers of unskilled migrants from less developed neighbors. Panagariya notes that such a vision is already reflected in the deliberations associated with GATS.[8]

More recently, Dani Rodrik (2002) has echoed Panagariya's analysis. Rodrik notes that even though goods and financial markets are not fully integrated, price differentials in those markets rarely exceed the ratio of 2 : 1. In contrast, wage differentials across countries are often of the order of 10 : 1. His "back-of-the-envelope" calculation for immigration equaling about 3 percent of the developed-country workforce produces an annual gain of $200 billion a year, almost all of it to developing countries. On the political economy of greater international mobility of labor, Rodrik also concludes, as Panagariya does, that political constraints are "malleable." He notes that those who oppose greater mobility of labor also oppose imports of labor-intensive products from developing countries but adequate mobilization of interested parties has been effective in reducing trade barriers. He proposes a *temporary* work visa scheme, though he would apply that to both skilled and unskilled workers.[9]

I would add one further consideration to this discussion. There is considerable evidence that labor flows will complement trade and investment flows.

Hence, though the argument is sometimes stated in terms of "this" *or* "that," I believe that need not be the case. The political bargaining may still be conducted in terms of a "quid pro quo"—a more liberal investment regime only in return for greater labor mobility. However, the economic argument should consider the complementarities.

Recent research shows that international networks of mobile specialists facilitate trade and investment. Jim Rauch (1999) and Rauch and Vitor Trindale (2002) have found that networks of Chinese migrants boost trade especially in differentiated goods. Such goods are characterized by high transactions costs on account of the product-specific knowledge necessary to complete such trades and migrant networks, with their traditional mechanisms of communication and trust built on repeated transactions, reduce those transactions costs. Evenett (2001) analyzes the level of mergers and acquisitions completed by U.S. firms in different countries around the world. He finds that mergers and acquisitions are significantly higher in those countries where a leading U.S. law firm has a substantial and long-standing presence. He infers that the local knowledge acquired by these lawyers helps bridge the gap between their U.S. clients and the regulatory requirements of the host country. Finally, in my own ongoing work with Antonio Spilimbergo, international students are found to precede both trade and investment. We find, controlling for traditional determinants, that a country imports more and receives more foreign direct investment from a partner country if, in the preceding decade, the host had sent a larger number of students to that partner. Moreover, in line with Rauch's research, trade in differentiated goods is especially lifted by the flow of students.

In sum, this evidence is consistent with a view that large informational gaps exist when trading and investing across borders and direct human intervention is particularly effective in overcoming this barrier. The implication is that information deficiencies cannot be overcome in a mechanical manner by applying routine rules of decision-making. Rather, the ability of skilled individuals to solve complex problems in real time is necessary to strengthen trade and investment links. Thus, the movement of traders, skilled professionals, and students (who may either return to their home country or continue to work as professionals in the destination economy) helps negotiate and reconcile the cultural and institutional variance across nations and thus reduces transaction costs.

Conclusions

The dramatic spread of FDI in the 1990s was an important development that will have long-term value. The immediate benefits in the form of higher levels of domestic investment have largely materialized but other expected benefits—more rapid productivity growth and better corporate governance—have been slow to accrue in a broad range of settings and appear to have been significant mainly where domestic absorptive capacity is already high.

However, FDI has been a trusted source of capital during the turbulent nineties. During a period when portfolio flows boomed and then crashed, FDI remained a resilient form of external finance. Lipsey (2000) notes that during the Mexican and Asian crises, foreign investors maintained their capital expenditures and were able to redirect their sales from domestic to international markets, transferring the benefits of their own flexibility to the stressed domestic economies. This has prompted some to suggest that FDI should be bolstered, not by providing fiscal incentives, but by reducing the disadvantages it faces in relation to other forms of external capital. Kenneth Rogoff (1999), for example, argues that the current domestic and international policy regime favors debt over equity capital and measures to redress the balance would be beneficial to host countries and the world economy.

Substantial challenges remain in harnessing the true value of FDI for raising growth rates in developing economies, especially among the least developed (Sanjaya Lall 2000 and World Bank 2002). However, the aggressive use of subsidies is unlikely to be the route through which that objective is achieved. Cross-country disciplines through bilateral, regional, and multilateral efforts are important in reducing the distortions that lead to misallocation of capital but ultimately domestic efforts to raise absorptive capacity will be critical. Efforts to increase labor mobility, as forseen, for example, under GATS, could have a significant effect in raising the benefits from FDI as the more mobile labor serves to bridge the cultural, institutional, and contractual differences across nations.

Notes

1   The analysis in Figures 1.5 and 1.6 excludes small countries (those with population less than 1 million) and transition countries (which had limited data for the 1990s and volatile behaviour of both investment and output). See the Appendix for the list of countries in various country groups.
2   In order of FDI received, these included: China, Brazil, Mexico, Argentina, Malaysia, Poland, Chile, Thailand, Venezuela, and Colombia.
3   In Mody, Susmita Dasgupta, and Sarbajit Sinha (1999) we found that in their investment decisions, Japanese investors were more concerned about labor quality than about lower wages.
4   In principle, such spillovers need not be restricted to firms with the same sector since general techniques, such as management methods, quality control, worker training, packaging, and marketing and distribution, could be useful to any firm. Indeed, the value of such general techniques may be large and Jane Jacobs (1969) argues that cities are efficient production agglomerations precisely because they facilitate such knowledge diffusion. However, we know little about such knowledge transfers, since the literature has focused on within-sector effects.
5   A potentially useful initiative of the Doha round is the effort to increase transparency in rules and regulations governing FDI, including procedures for consultation and notification.
6   Markusen (1998) refers specifically to the host country's obligation to protect a foreign investor's intellectual property but the right also to bargain for the rents

from such property. This is an important policy issue in the context of life-saving drugs. Whether a host country could bargain for the more typical commercial technologies is an open question, but seems unlikely.

7 See also Gordon Hanson (2001) for similar advice.
8 Allison Young (2000) describes these deliberations.
9 To enforce the temporary nature of the migration, he suggests that a portion of the migrant's earnings be withheld until return to the home country.

Appendix: Data sources and country coverage in Figures 5 and 6

Data on FDI inflows, GDP, and population were obtained from the World Bank's *World Development Indicators*. M&A sales statistics were obtained from the United Nations Conference on Trade and Development (UNCTAD). Countries' income groups used in Figures 5 and 6 correspond to the World Bank's GNI per capita classification.

While Figures 1–4 use global or country-group totals, the more country-specific analysis in Figures 5 and 6 dropped small countries (with a population of less than 1 million inhabitants) and transition economies (which had limited data in the 1990s and, moreover, experienced large fluctuations in both FDI and GDP). The list of the countries used in the country-specific analysis, by country-group (income and Top 10 FDI recipients), is provided below.

Low		*Mid–low*	*Mid–high*	*Top 10 (ranked)*
Angola	Madagascar	Algeria	Argentina	China
Bangladesh	Malawi	Bolivia	Botswana	Brazil
Benin	Mali	Brazil	Chile	Mexico
Burkina Faso	Mauritania	China	Costa Rica	Argentina
Burundi	Mongolia	Colombia	Malaysia	Malaysia
Cambodia	Mozambique	Dominican Rep	Mauritius	Poland
Cameroon	Nepal	Ecuador	Mexico	Chile
CAR	Nicaragua	Egypt	Oman	Thailand
Chad	Niger	El Salvador	Panama	Venezuela
Congo	Nigeria	Guatemala	Poland	Colombia
Cote D'Ivoire	Pakistan	Honduras	Uruguay	
Ethiopia	Papua New G.	Iran	Venezuela	
Gambia	Rwanda	Jamaica		
Ghana	Senegal	Jordan		
Guinea	Sierra Leone	Morocco		
Guinea-Bissau	Tanzania	Paraguay		
Haiti	Togo	Peru		
India	Uganda	The Philippines	*(continued overleaf)*	

Low		Mid–low	Mid–high	Top 10 (ranked)
Indonesia	Viet Nam	Sri Lanka		
Kenya	Zambia	Swaziland		
Lao		Thailand		
Lesotho		Tunisia		
Liberia		Turkey		

References

Aitken, Brian J. and Ann E. Harrison (1999) "Do Domestic Benefit from Direct Foreign Investment? Evidence from Venezuela." *American Economic Review* 89(3): 605–618.

Albuquerque Rui, Norman Loayza, and Luis Serven (2002) "World Market Integration Through the Lens of Foreign Direct Investors." Presented at "The FDI Race: Who Gets the Prize? Is It Worth the Effort?" Washington D.C.: Inter-American Development Bank and the World Bank. Available on the web at http://www.iadb.org/res/publications/pubfiles/pubs-FDI.pdf

Alfaro Laura, Areendam Chanda, Sebnem Kalimbli-Ozcan, and Selin Sayek (2003) "FDI Spillovers, Financial Markets, and Economic Development." IMF Working Paper WP/03/186, Washington D.C.: International Monetary Fund.

Balasubramanyam, V.N., M. Salisu, and David Sapsford (1991) "Export Promotion, Import Substitution and Direct Foreign Investment in Less Developed Countries." In A. Koekkok and L.B.M. Mennes (eds.) *International Trade and Global Development: Essays in Honour of Jagdish Bhagwati.* London: Routledge.

Balasubramanyam, V.N., David Sapsford, and David Griffiths (2002) "Regional Integration Agreements and Foreign Direct Investment: Theory and Preliminary Evidence." *The Manchester School* 70(3): 460–482.

Barrell, Ray and Nigel Pain (1998) "Real Exchange Rates, Agglomerations and Irreversibilities: Macroeconomic Policy and FDI in EMU." *Oxford Review of Economic Policy* 14(3): 152–167.

Belderbos, Rene, Giovanni Capannelli, and Kyoji Fukao (2001) "Backward Vertical Linkages of Foreign Manufacturing Affiliates: Evidence from Japanese Multinationals." *World Development* 29(1): 189–208.

Blalock, Garrick and Paul Gertler (2003) "Technology from Foreign Direct Investment and Welfare Gains through the Supply Chain." Available on the web at: http://aem.cornell.edu/faculty_sites/gb78/wp/vfdi_04_27.pdf

Blonigen, Bruce and Ronald Davies (2002) "Do Bilateral Treaties Promote Foreign Direct Investment?" National Bureau of Economic Research Working Paper 8834, Cambridge, MA.

Borensztein, E., J. De Gregorio, and J-W. Lee (1998) "How Does Foreign Direct Investment Affect Growth?" *Journal of International Economics* 45(1): 115–135.

Bosworth, Barry and Susan Collins (1999) "Capital Flows to Developing Economies: Implications for Saving and Investment." *Brookings Papers on Economic Activity* 1: 143–169.

Branstetter, Lee (2000) "Is Foreign Direct Investment a Channel of Knowledge

Spillovers? Evidence from Japan's FDI in the United States." NBER Working Paper 8015, Cambridge MA.

Calderon, Cesar, Norman Loayza, and Luis Serven (2002) "Greenfield FDI vs. Mergers and Acquisitions: Does the Distinction Matter?" World Bank, Washington D.C.

Carkovic, Maria and Ross Levine (2002) "Does Foreign Direct Investment Accelerate Economic Growth?" University of Minnesota.

Caves, Richard (1999) "Spillovers from Multinationals in Developing Countries: The Mechanisms at Work." William Davidson Institute Working Paper 247. Ann Arbor, Mich.

Clemens, Michael A. and Jeffrey G. Williamson (2000) "Where Did British Foreign Capital Go? Fundamentals, Failures, and the Lucas Paradox." National Bureau of Economic Research Working Paper 8028, Cambridge, MA.

Dunning, John H. (1997) "The European Internal Market Programme and Inbound Foreign Direct Investment." *Journal of Common Market Studies* 35: 1–30.

Evenett, Simon J. (2001) "Do All Networks Facilitate International Commerce? The Case of US Law Firms and the Mergers and Acquisitions Wave of the Late 1990s." Available at www.ssrn.com

Feenstra, Robert and Gordon Hanson (1996) "Foreign Investment, Outsourcing and Relative Wages." In R.C. Feenstra, G.M. Grossman, and D.A. Irwin (eds.) *Political Economy of Trade Policy: Essays in Honor of Jagdish Bhagwati*, Cambridge: MIT Press.

Feenstra, Robert and Gordon Hanson (1997) "Foreign Direct Investment and Relative Wages: Evidence from Mexico's Maquiladoras." *Journal of International Economics* 42: 371–394.

Fernandez, Raquel and Jonathan Portes (1998) "Returns to Regionalism: An Analysis of Non-Traditional Gains from Regional Trade Arrangements." *World Bank Economic Review* 12(2): 197–220.

Ghemawat, Pankaj and Fariborz Ghadar (2000) "The Dubious Logic of Global Megamergers." *Harvard Business Review* 78(4): 64–74.

Haddad, Mona and Ann Harrison (1993) "Are There Spillovers from Direct Foreign Investment?" *Journal of Development Economics* 42: 51–74.

Hallward-Driemeier, Mary (2003) "Do Bilateral Investment Treaties Attract FDI? Only a Bit . . . And They Could Bite." Washington D.C.: World Bank. Available on the web at http://econ.worldbank.org/files/29143_wps3121.pdf

Hamilton, B. and John Whalley (1984) "Efficiency and Distributional Implications of Global Restrictions on Labor Mobility: Calculations and Policy Implications." *Journal of Development Economics* 14(1): 61–75.

Hanson, Gordon H. (2001) "Should Countries Promote Foreign Direct Investment?" G-4 Discussion Paper Series 9, United Nations, New York and Geneva.

Harrison, Ann E. and Margaret S. McMillan (2003) "Does Direct Foreign Investment Affect Firms' Credit Constraints?" *Journal of International Economics* 61(1): 73–100.

Haskel, Jonathan E., Sonia Pereira, and Matthew Slaughter (2002) "Does Inward Foreign Direct Investment Boost the Productivity of Domestic Firms?" NBER Working Paper 8724, January 2002.

Jacobs, Jane (1969) *The Economy of Cities*, New York: Random House.

Kang, Jun-Koo (1993) "The International Market for Corporate Control: Mergers and Acquisitions of U.S. Firms by Japanese Firms." *Journal of Financial Economics* 34(3): 345–371.

Kinoshita, Yuko and Ashoka Mody, 2001, "Private Information for Foreign Investment in Emerging Economies." *Canadian Journal of Economics* 34(2): 448–464, May 2001.

Krueger, Anne (2000) "NAFTA's Effects: A Preliminary Assessment." *World Economy* 23(6): 761–775.

Krugman, Paul (1998) "Fire-Sale FDI." Available on the web at http://web.mit.edu/Krugman/www/FIRESALE.htm

Lall, Sanjaya (1980) "Vertical Inter-Firm Linkages in LDCs: An Empirical Study." *Oxford Bulletin of Economics and Statistics* 42: 203–226.

Lall, Sanjaya (2000) "Evaluation of Promotion and Incentive Strategies for FDI in Sub-Saharan Africa." Oxford University.

Levy Yeyati, Eduardo, Ernesto Stein, and Christian Duade (2002) "Regional Integration and the Location of FDI." Presented at "The FDI Race: Who Gets the Prize? Is It Worth the Effort?" Washington D.C.: Inter-American Development Bank and the World Bank. Available on the web at http://www.iadb.org/res/publications/pubfiles/pubS-FDI-11.pdf

Lipsey, Robert (2000) "Foreign Direct Investors in Three Financial Crises." National Bureau of Economic Research Working Paper 8084, Cambridge, MA.

Lipsey, Robert and Zadia Feliciano (2002) "Foreign Entry into U.S. Manufacturing by Takeovers and the Establishment of New Firms." National Bureau of Economic Research Working Paper 9122, Cambridge, MA.

Loungani, Prakash and Assaf Razin (2001) "How Beneficial is Foreign Direct Investment for Developing Countries?" *Finance and Development* 38(2).

Loungani, Prakash, Ashoka Mody, and Assaf Razin (2002) "The Global Disconnect: The Role of Transactional Distance and Scale Economies in Gravity Models." Forthcoming in the *Scottish Journal of Political Economy*.

Lucas, Robert (1990) "Why Doesn't Capital Flow from Rich to Poor Countries?" *American Economic Review* 80: 92–96.

Markusen, James R. (1998) "Multilateral Rules on Foreign Direct Investment: The Developing Countries' Stake." Department of Economics, University of Colorado, Boulder.

Mody, Ashoka and Fang-Yi Wang (1997) "Explaining Industrial Growth in Coastal China: Economic Reforms . . . and What Else?" *World Bank Economic Review* 11(2): 293–325.

Mody, Ashoka and Krishna Srinivasan (1998) "U.S. and Japanese Investors: Do they March to the Same Tune?" *Canadian Journal of Economics* 31: 778–799.

Mody, Ashoka, Susmita Dasgupta, and Sarbajit Sinha (1999) "Japanese Multinationals in Asia: Drivers and Attractors." *Oxford Development Studies* 27(2): 149–164.

Mody, Ashoka and Shoko Negishi (2001) "The Role of Cross-Border Mergers and Acquisitions in Asian Restructuring." In Stijn Claessens, Simeon Djankov, and Ashoka Mody (eds.) *Resolution of Financial Distress: An International Perspective on the Design of Bankruptcy Laws*. WBI Development Studies, The World Bank, Washington D.C.

Mody, Ashoka and Antu Murshid (2005) "Growing Up with Capital Flows." *Journal of International Economics* 65(1): 249–266.

Mutti, John (2002) *Foreign Direct Investment, Taxes, and Tax Competition*. Department of Economics, Grinnell College, Grinnell, IA.

OECD (2001) *Corporate Tax Incentives for Foreign Direct Investment*. OECD Tax

Policy Studies 4, Organization for Economic Co-Operation and Development, Paris.

Panagariya, Arvind (1999) "The Millenium Round and Developing Countries: Negotiating Strategies and Areas of Benefits." University of Maryland, College Park. Can be found at: http://www.bsos.umd.edu/econ/panagariya/apecon/polpaper.htm

Peria, Maria Soledad Martinez and Ashoka Mody. Forthcoming. "How Foreign Participation and Market Concentration Impact Bank Spreads: Evidence from Latin America." *Journal of Money, Credit and Banking.*

Rauch, James (1999) "Networks Versus Markets in International Trade." *Journal of International Economics* 48: 7–35.

Rauch, James and Vitor Trindale (2002) "Ethnic Chinese Networks in International Trade." *Review of Economics and Statistics* 84: 116–130.

Rodriguez-Clare, Andres (1996) "Multinationals, Linkages, and Economic Development." *American Economic Review* 86(4): 852–873.

Rodrik, Dani (2002) "Feasible Globalizations." Centre for Economic Policy Research Discussion Paper 3524, London.

Rogoff, Kenneth (1999) "International Institutions for Reducing Global Financial Instability." *Journal of Economic Perspectives* 13(4): 21–42.

Sarno, Lucio and Mark P. Taylor (1999) "Hot Money, Accounting Labels and the Permanence of Capital Flows to Developing Countries: An Empirical Investigation." *Journal of Development Economics* 59: 337–364.

Sauve, Pierre and Christopher Wilke (2000) "Investment Liberalization in GATS." In Pierre Sauve and Robert M. Stern (eds.) *GATS 2000: New Directions in Services Trade Liberalization.* Center for Business and Development, Harvard University, and Brookings Institution Press, Washington D.C.

Smarzynska, Beata (2002) "Does Foreign Direct Investment Increase the Productivity of Domestic Firms? In Search of Spillovers through Backward Linkages." World Bank Policy Research Paper 2923, Washington D.C.

Smarzynska, Beata and Shang-Jin Wei (2002) "Corruption and Cross-Border Investment: Firm-Level Evidence." Presented at "The FDI Race: Who Gets the Prize? Is It Worth the Effort?" Washington D.C.: Inter-American Development Bank and the World Bank. Available on the web at http://www.iadb.org/res/publications/pubfiles/pubS-FDI-7.pdf

Uminski, Stanislaw (2001) "Foreign Capital in the Privatization Process of Poland." *Transnational Corporations* 10(3): 75–94.

United Nations Conference on Trade and Development (2000) "Tax Incentives and Foreign Direct Investment: A Global Survey." New York and Geneva.

United Nations Conference on Trade and Development (2002) "FDI Downturn in 2001 Touches Almost All Regions." UNCTAD Press Release TAD/INF/2850. Available at: http://www.unctad.org/en/press/pr0236en.htm

United Nations Conference on Trade and Development (2003) *World Investment Report.* Geneva.

Verhoosel, Gaeten (2003) "The Use of Investor-State Arbitration Under Bilateral Investment Treaties to Seek Relief for Breaches of WTO Laws." *Journal of International Economic Law* 6(2): 493–506.

Wheeler, David and Ashoka Mody (1992) "International Investment Location Decisions: the case of U.S. Firms." *Journal of International Economics* 33: 57–76.

World Bank (2001) *Global Development Finance: Building Coalitions for Effective Development Finance.* Washington D.C.

World Bank (2002) *Global Development Finance*. Washington D.C.

World Bank (2003) "Global Economic Prospects 2003: Investing to Unlock Global Opportunities." Washington D.C.

Young, Allison (2000) "What Next for Labor Mobility under GATS?" In Pierre Sauve and Robert M. Stern (eds.) *GATS 2000: New Directions in Services Trade Liberalization*. Center for Business and Development, Harvard University, and Brookings Institution Press, Washington D.C.

Part I
FDI determinants
Agglomeration, information, and policy

2 International investment location decisions

The case of U.S. firms

With David Wheeler

Introduction

With international capital increasingly perceived as footloose, many countries have accelerated their entry into what David (1984) has termed "location tournaments" policy adjustments, promotional campaigns, and incentive programs designed to attract investment by multinational firms. Their participation reflects the belief that history matters; that locational advantage, once gained, tends to perpetuate itself. Some location theorists support this view by stressing the importance of agglomeration economies in industrial location. Others, however, contend that location decisions are dominated by classical sources of comparative advantage such as relative wages, market size, and transport costs. Some also suggest that international investors may discount agglomeration benefits, preferring multiple sites as a hedge against risk.

Qualitative discussion of these possibilities is common, but careful empirical work has been greatly hindered by data scarcity. This chapter combines two extensive data sources to take a new look at investor preferences. The first, published annually by the U.S. Department of Commerce, is a comprehensive report on manufacturing investment by U.S. multinationals. The second has been generously provided by the Country Assessment Service of Business International, Inc. (BI). This service provides corporate clients with annual country rating scores for many social, political, and economic factors which might be relevant for investment decisions. To our knowledge, ours is the first systematic attempt to utilize this rich data base for econometric work.

We begin this chapter with a review of the relevant theoretical considerations and the current state of the empirical art. We then develop and estimate a non-linear capital expenditure model for U.S. multinationals which incorporates measures of agglomeration economies and risk as well as the classical factors. In the concluding sections we present our results and summarize their apparent message for would-be participants in location tournaments.

The economics of investment decisions

Why should governments choose to compete so vigorously in location tournaments? Many government planners believe that locational advantage, once gained, will be self-perpetuating. Arthur (1986, 1990) provides a useful generalization of this view by recalling the fundamental distinction between ergodic and non-ergodic systems. An ergodic system returns to its initial state when initial conditions are replicated, whatever the interim history. A non-ergodic system, by contrast, can exhibit strikingly different and irreversible evolutionary responses to small changes in initial conditions. Non-ergodicity underlies much recent work on international trade, economic growth, and industrial development.[1]

For location theorists, non-ergodicity resides in agglomeration economies, or increasing benefits to co-location by economic units [Englander (1926), Palander (1935), Hoover (1937), Maruyama (1963)]. A specific example is provided by regional groupings of specialized service suppliers [Markusen (1990), drawing on Ethier (1979, 1982)]. More suppliers (each providing a different service) create finer divisions of labor in intermediate input markets, thereby lowering unit costs for final producers. Markusen (1990) demonstrates that a firm's early decision to invest in a region (for a variety of reasons, including an "accident of history") can promote the creation of such specialized services, reinforcing the area's attractiveness for other investors. Arthur (1986) demonstrates that this factor can translate a minor regional advantage into a major concentration of industrial activity. Important agglomeration economies therefore imply big rewards for the winner of a location tournament.[2]

A contrasting, ergodic view runs through the work of von Thunen (1826), Predohl (1925) Losch (1941) and Isard (1956). Here industry location patterns are essentially pre-ordained by geographical endowments, relative prices, and transport costs. From any initial point the spatial distribution of industrial activity evolves, ceteris paribus, to a unique final pattern. In such an ergodic world, the notion of "winning" a locational tournament is quixotic: once the winner halts the subsidies, industrial location patterns will revert to their predetermined state.

Reduction in risk through geographical diversification may also be an important factor in international location decisions. Location tournament play will disappoint all participants if risk reduction dominates agglomeration benefits in investor thinking. In theory, capital market perfection eliminates the rationale for geographical diversification by multinationals; investors can create their own diversified portfolios, having no reason to use multinationals for financial intermediation [Hufbauer (1975)]. In the absence of such perfection, however, firms cannot invest unlimited amounts in high return but high risk assets. If they do not police themselves, their creditors will do so [for an early reference to this argument, see Kalecki (1938)]. In addition, as Caves (1970) points out, uncertainty avoidance may be important for managers.

Portfolio diversification is, of course, relevant only if events across countries do not move in a perfectly synchronous manner [Grubel (1979), Flamm (1984)]. Supporting evidence from Rugman (1979) suggests that firms with foreign operations do have more stable profit rates than firms that operate only domestically.

Previous empirical work

Several recent empirical studies consider the role of the "classical" variables which figure prominently in ergodic location theories. Kravis and Lipsey (1982) report positive impacts for host country market size and "degree of openness" on the location decision of U.S. multinationals in the 1960s, but a negligible role for relative labor costs. Their results suggest that the weights on location factors differ significantly across industries. Blomstrom and Lipsey (1986) find a significant size threshold effect for firms' decision to invest abroad, but no other apparent effect of scale. Grubert and Mutti (1989) find some evidence for sensitivity to relative tax rates in a study of U.S. multinational investment in Canada; Shah and Slemrod (1990) report a similar finding for Mexico. In a series of empirical papers, Lipsey and Kravis (1987) and Kravis and Lipsey (1989) find that U.S. multinationals have remained competitive in management and technology while adjusting their plant locations in response to the declining competitiveness of the United States as a production site. Their work does not attempt a detailed empirical analysis of locational economics.

A few studies attempt to incorporate risk factors as well. Flamm (1984) estimates an equation relating multinational electronics investments to relative wages, using country-specific dummy variables as proxies for differential risk. In their previously-mentioned paper, Shah and Slemrod (1990) find significant effects for perceived risk as measured by a general index of Mexico's creditworthiness.

Model specification and interpretation

This chapter attempts to broaden the scope of the existing empirical work on multinational investment by specifying a capital expenditure function which incorporates measures of agglomeration benefit as well as risk and classical location factors. We begin by assuming that investment I_i in the ith country responds to expected return π_i as well as risk σ_i, either because firms are risk averse or because of the irreversibility of fixed investment:

$$I_i = f(\pi_i, \sigma_i). \tag{1}$$

Since we have seen no compelling evidence to the contrary, we assume zero perceived covariance between rates of return in different locations. This permits straightforward panel estimation of an investment function.

If the intended investment is primarily for export production, the expected return π_i from a particular site will depend upon unit input costs. Although the productivity of specific inputs is relevant (low wages are not necessarily equivalent to cheap labor), we focus on (a) the general input-augmenting effects of differences in infrastructure quality (transportation, communications, and energy), and (b) the cost-reducing impact of local agglomeration economies, exemplified by differences in the availability of differentiated material and service inputs.

If the investment is intended to serve the local market (i.e. is import substituting), then the size and openness of that market will also be relevant in determining π_i. By openness, we mean the degree to which local producers are exposed to external competition. Ceteris paribus, closed markets should be more attractive for foreign investors because the profits of local producers will be enhanced by limitations on imports of competitive products. However, economies are rarely restrictive in this dimension alone; import controls are often accompanied by other restrictive measures which dampen profits. Only a multidimensional measure of openness can be expected to yield unambiguous empirical results.

For econometric estimation we employ a translog specification of eq. (1). This specification [eq. (2)] allows the marginal value of any characteristic to depend on its own current level and on the current levels of all other characteristics. It also permits nested tests of simpler specifications: the constant elasticity model [eq. (3)] and an intermediate specification [eq. (4)], which drops the quadratic terms of the translog form. Henceforth, we will refer to (3) and (4) as log-linear and log-interactive, respectively. Comparison of these forms also permits analyses of parameter stability:

$$\ln I_i = \beta_0 + \sum_k \beta_k \ln X_{ik} + \sum_k \sum_l \beta_{kl} \ln X_{ik} \ln X_{il} + \sum_k \beta_{kk} (\ln X_{ik})^2, \qquad (2)$$

where the X_{ik} are the determinants of risk and expected return,

$$\ln I_i = \beta_0 + \sum_k \beta_k \ln X_{ik}, \qquad (3)$$

$$\ln I_i = \beta_0 \sum_k \beta_k \ln X_{ik} + \sum_k \sum_l \beta_{kl} \ln X_{ik} \ln X_{il}. \qquad (4)$$

Our data are drawn from a panel of 42 countries for the period 1982–1988. The equations are estimated without country-specific dummy variables because much of the interesting variation in the data is across countries, reflecting conditions which change only slowly. The use of country-specific dummies would have the effect of removing this variation, leaving only short-run, within-country changes as the basis for parameter estimation. The results would tell us much less about how firms choose among countries when making investment decisions.

Not wishing to suppress useful information about within-country variation, however, we have retained the time-series dimension of our data set. This forces us to confront the possibility of spurious regression results, since the country series are non-stationary [see Nelson and Plosser (1982)]. Intertemporal first-differencing is inappropriate here because it would have the same effect as country-specific dummies—elimination of differences in the *levels* of variables across countries.

For estimation of eqs. (2)–(4) we deal with the time-series issue by translating to equations which determine investment in country i relative to investment in some numeraire (comparison) country j.[3] This eliminates the main source of the time-series problem—the common effect of annual fluctuations in the nominal values of aggregative investment.

Eq. (5) illustrates the appropriate translation for the translog form:

$$\ln (I_i/I_j) = (\beta_{0i} - \beta_{0j}) + \sum_k \beta_k (\ln X_{ik} - \ln X_{jk})$$

$$+ \sum_k \sum_l \beta_{kl} (\ln X_{ik} \ln X_{il} - \ln X_{jk} \ln X_{jl})$$

$$+ \sum_k \beta_{kk}[(\ln X_{ik})^2 - (\ln X_{jk})^2]. \tag{5}$$

Finally, to distinguish between annual effects which influence investment in all countries and investment in individual countries, we allow for fixed annual effects (i.e. dummy variables to control for common effects in each year).

Data

Our data are drawn from two principal sources. The first is the annual table, "Capital Expenditures by Majority-Owned Foreign Affiliates of U.S. Companies", which appears in the U.S. Department of Commerce Publication, *Survey of Current Business*. This table is based on surveys of actual and planned expenditures by U.S. companies, and is updated semi-annually. It includes capital expenditure estimates for a variety of sectors at approximately the two-digit level of industrial classification.

The second major source of information is an international database generously made available to us by the Country Assessment Service of Business International, Inc. (BI). The database includes country scores for many factors which may affect corporate operations and profitability. We define the relevant variables in Table 2.1 and provide illustrations of the BI scoring

Table 2.1 Country assessment factors—Business International, Inc.[a]

Variable	

Classical variables

1. Labor cost — Average hourly wage in manufacturing
2. Level of corporate taxation — Assumes no tax holiday, $1 million profit, 50 percent remitted
3. Market size — Market size as indicated by GDP

Agglomeration benefit indices

4. Infrastructure quality — Quality of transport, communications, energy infrastructure
5. Degree of industrialization — Based on manufacturing/mining as percent of GDP
6. Level of foreign direct investment

Risk: Geopolitical considerations

7. Relationship with West — Political, economic, commercial relations
8. Relationship with neighbors — Emphasis on probability of military conflict

Principal components from BI domestic risk and policy variables

9. RISK: first principal component from:

Political change—institutional	Likelihood, nature of government change
Attitude of opposition groups	Attitude toward foreign investment
Probability of opposition takeover	Probable impact on foreign investment
Stability of labor	Likely degree of disruption
Terrorism risk	Local terrorism risk factor
Desire for foreign investment	General attitude and policies of the government
Attitude toward private sector	Government support for private business activity
Cultural interaction	Problems from local cultural, business practices
Expatriate environment	Overall living environment for expatriates
Bureaucracy and red tape	Difficulty in obtaining approvals, permits
Corruption	Average payment requirements
Quality of legal system	Efficiency, integrity, as affects foreign firms
Distribution of wealth	Degree of inequality

10. OPEN, first principal component from:

Restrictions on imports	Impact on needed components, materials
Export requirements	Forced exports as an operating requirement
Price controls	Government imposition and enforcement
Local content requirements	Insistence on local components in manufacturing

Expropriation risk	Probability, with or without compensation
Currency convertibility	Degree of government regulation
Profit repatriation controls	Degree of restriction on free flow of capital
Ownership limits: existing investment	Foreign equity or size restrictions
Ownership limits: new investment	Initial local equity requirement

[a] More complete descriptions of the BI scoring system are provided in Appendix, Table A.2.

system in the Appendix (Table A.2). Although BI forecasts five years into the future, we have limited ourselves to one-year-ahead forecasts.

For econometric estimation, the BI information presents us with an unusual problem—too much data. We employ the translog specification to allow for possible non-linearity, but its complexity precludes the introduction of too many variables. We therefore limit our estimation exercise to the 10 variables which are numbered sequentially in Table 2.1.

We have taken eight factors directly from the BI data set. Three are classical—labor cost, corporate taxes, and market size. We would expect multinationals to be differentially attracted to sites with lower labor costs, lower taxes, and a larger domestic market, other things equal. The BI system scores countries on perceived desirability, so the "best" country from the perspective of labor cost is the lowest-wage site. We would therefore expect positive elasticities for all three indices.

Three variables are indices of perceived agglomeration benefits. The first, infrastructure quality, has a straightforward interpretation. The other two— degree of industrialization and level of foreign investment—are proxies for the relative availability of specialized support activities. Again we would expect positive elasticities.

Our inclusion of the existing stock of foreign investment as an explanatory variable provides a test of Markusen's (1990) hypothesis that first-mover advantage can lead to uneven development. The self-reinforcing impact of foreign investment can operate through a variety of channels, including promotion of specialized inputs (e.g. trained labor, marketing, and distribution services), reputational effects, etc. Our least squares estimates should not suffer from simultaneity bias in this case, since foreign investment and its determinants influence each other over periods considerably longer than a year (the time unit of our study).

Our main risk variable is a first principal component, extracted from a set of BI indices which are highly intercorrelated (Tables 2.1 and 2.2). Available measures of risk include indices of political stability, inequality, corruption, red tape, quality of the legal system, cultural compatibility, attitude toward foreign capital, and general expatriate comfort (including the risk of terrorism). From this group we have extracted the first principal component (named RISK), which accounts for 48 percent of total intragroup variation. It is highly correlated with all 13 indices in the data set (see Table 2.2). Since

Table 2.2 Principal component results

RISK		OPEN	
Socio-political conditions		Market intervention	
(240 observations)		(240 observations)	
(13 variables)		(9 variables)	
Variation proportion accounted for			
RISK	0.48	OPEN	0.56
2nd P.C.	0.15	2nd P.C.	0.16
Correlations with underlying variables			
RISK		OPEN	
Political change—institutional	0.46	Restrictions on imports	0.82
Attitude of major opposition groups	0.57	Export requirements	0.73
Prob. of opposition group takeover	0.48	Price controls	0.52
Stability of labor	0.50	Local content requirements	0.84
Likelihood of terrorism	0.55	Expropriation risk	0.70
Desire for foreign investment	0.62	Currency convertibility	0.70
Attitude toward the private sector	0.75	Profit repatriation controls	0.83
Cultural interaction	0.77	Limits on foreign ownership	0.74
Expatriate environment	0.73	Limits on new investment	0.77
Bureaucracy and red tape	0.86		
Corruption	0.88		
Quality of legal system, judiciary	0.84		
Distribution of wealth	0.83		

the BI scoring system assigns high scores to more desirable sites, we would expect RISK to enter with a positive sign. In addition to the RISK principal component, we also incorporate two BI geopolitical risk factors—relations with the West, and relations with neighboring states.

Another set of indices characterizes the degree of openness of the economy. These indices include nine measures of government intervention—import restrictions, export requirements, local content requirements, price controls, profit repatriation controls, exchange controls, foreign equity limitations for existing and new investment, and the risk of expropriation (see Table 2.1). The first principal component from this group (named OPEN) accounts for 56 percent of total variation. Again, we observe very high correlations with the underlying variables in Table 2.2.

In the BI system, "better" economies are those that are less restrictive. However, there is no a priori reason to be certain that this accurately reflects the perception of U.S. multinationals. It is true, of course, that investors would prefer fewer limits on equity participation and profit repatriation if it were possible to consider these factors in isolation. As Table 2.2 suggests, however, government restrictions tend to rise and fall together. Multinationals may perceive good opportunities for differential profit from import-substituting activities once they are established behind trade barriers. We are therefore agnostic about the sign on OPEN.

Estimation results

We have fitted translog capital expenditure equations with annual fixed effect controls to data for total manufacturing investment and electronics investment in 42 countries. We focus on electronics because the other sectoral data are plagued by missing values. In addition, the pattern of electronics investments seems likely to provide a particularly good sensitivity test for the BI risk variables. As Flamm (1984) notes, electronics is generally thought of as a mobile industry with high sensitivity to the risk of production disruption.

For our relative investment model, the Philippines has been arbitrarily chosen as the numeraire country.[4] Thus, the left-hand variable is, for a particular country, industry, and year, the log of U.S. multinational capital expenditure divided by the equivalent observation for the Philippines.[5] Right-hand variables are differences of logs, log-interactions, or squared logs of attribute scores for sample countries and the Philippines. All BI indices have been increased by one unit to avoid the zeros problem for logarithms. Our sample period is 1982–1988.

We begin with a summary of major findings, to be followed by an extensive discussion of the significance and stability tests which underlie our conclusions. For the present, we should note that appropriate F-tests on translog parameter restrictions suggest clear rejection of the log-linear model and mixed evidence about the log-interactive form.[6] Although quite plausible, these results present us with an expositional problem. A log-linear model yields constant elasticity estimates which are easy to interpret, while translog and log-interactive models yield a complex pattern of variation in elasticities. Our interpretation of the results relies principally on elasticities calculated at mean values for country groups at different per capita income levels [see Table 2.4]. We find, however, that straight log-linear estimates for all sample countries provide a useful and essentially accurate first approximation. We therefore present these estimates in Table 2.3, with more detailed highlighting of major interactive results in Table 2.4, parts (b) and (c).[7] These tables should be consulted while reading the following summary.

Summary of major findings

Agglomeration benefits and classical factors are dominant

All three agglomeration benefit indices exhibit a high degree of statistical significance and have large, positive impacts on investment. The same is true for the two classical variables, labor cost and market size, although the corporate tax rate does not appear to play much of a role. Geopolitical risk is apparently significant, but domestic socio-political considerations, as summarized by the principal component RISK, appear to have a very small effect.

Table 2.3 Log-linear capital expenditure function estimates

	Total manufacturing		Electronics	
F:	43.00		21.30	
R^2:	0.71		0.60	
Adj. R^2:	0.70		0.57	
N:	255		232	
K:	15[a]		16[a]	
Variable	Coef.	T	Coef.	T
Intercept	−1.33	−5.95	−2.07	−6.86
Relations with West			1.50	3.28
Relations with neighboring countries	0.16	0.75	0.46	1.71
Labor cost	0.21	1.49	1.02	6.00
Current foreign investment	1.56	5.77	1.86	5.49
Market size	1.24	9.16	0.58	3.02
Infrastructure	1.57	3.31	2.54	3.88
Industrialization	1.40	3.25	1.87	2.92
Corporate taxation	0.19	1.02	−0.31	−1.30
OPEN (principal component)	−0.13	−2.25	−0.11	−1.52
RISK (principal component)	0.08	1.12	0.03	0.34

[a] Includes fixed-effect dummies for years.

The degree of openness of the economy, summarized by the principal component OPEN, has, if anything, a negative impact on multinational investment. That is, controlling for factors such as market size, more restrictive economies seem somewhat more attractive to U.S. multinationals. Good examples during the sample period were provided by Brazil and Mexico, which attracted major investment despite very low OPEN ratings (see Appendix Table A.1 for representative scores). These countries were recipients of import-substituting investment, attracted by high trade barriers.

Investment responses can vary strongly by sector

Our results suggest that electronics is atypically sensitive to intersite differentials. With the exception of market size, the electronics elasticities are considerably larger than average elasticities as represented by the total manufacturing results. The difference is particularly striking for labor cost. We should note, however, that electronics *is* typical in exhibiting little or no sensitivity to differences in tax rates, domestic risk, and relative openness.

Elasticity patterns differ markedly by level of development

As we previously noted, a log-interactive function yields a pattern of variable elasticities: the magnitude of investment response to a particular site characteristic will depend on the other perceived qualities of the site.

Table 2.4 (a) Variable capital expenditure elasticities: summary of translog results—income groups

1	2	3	4	5
Egypt	Brazil	Argentina	Austria	Australia
India	Chile	Greece	Belgium	Canada
Indonesia	Colombia	Ireland	France	Denmark
Liberia	Ecuador	Israel	Hong Kong	Germany
Nigeria	Malaysia	Korea	Italy	Japan
Peru	Mexico	Spain	Netherlands	Norway
The Philippines	Panama	Taiwan	Singapore	Sweden
Thailand	Portugal	Venezuela	Trinidad	Switzerland
	Turkey		U.K.	

(b) Group median elasticities.

	Total manufacturing (a)	Electronics (b)	Ratio (b/a)
Labor cost	0.27	1.99	7.4
Foreign investment	1.42	2.60	1.8
Infrastructure	1.23	2.17	1.8
Industrialization	1.07	1.84	1.7
Market size	1.57	0.90	0.6

(c) Intergroup elasticity variations.

Electronics

Low-income countries (Group 1)		High-income countries (Group 5)	
	Elasticity		Elasticity
Infrastructure	2.65	Industrialization	6.41
Labor cost	2.20	Foreign investment	3.83
Foreign investment	1.59	Market size	1.77
Industrialization	0.37	Labor cost	1.10
Market size	0.24	Infrastructure	0.93

Total manufacturing

Low-income countries (Group 1)		High-income countries (Group 5)	
	Elasticity		Elasticity
Infrastructure	1.99	Foreign investment	4.28
Industrialization	1.54	Industrialization	2.30
Market size	0.74	Market size	1.86
Foreign *investment*	0.69	Labor cost	0.63
Labor cost	–	Infrastructure	–

For industrial and developing countries, typical values of our ten location factors are quite different (see Appendix Table A.1). Our results therefore imply that response elasticities vary considerably with level of development. To illustrate, we rank the major decision factors in Table 2.4, part (c), for the poorest (Group 1) and richest (Group 5) sample countries.

Developing countries   For electronics investment in developing countries, infrastructure quality and labor cost are dominant, followed by existing foreign investment. Degree of industrialization and market size play small roles. These results seem quite consistent with the view that U.S. electronics manufacturers have regarded developing countries primarily as export assembly platforms, giving most weight to the cost of basic labor and the quality of the local support base. For total manufacturing investment, the agglomeration measures as a group remain strongly dominant. Infrastructure quality retains its primacy, while the general level of industrialization takes on a greater weight. Between the two classical variables, we see labor cost clearly supplanted by market size as the dominant consideration. This seems quite plausible if we accept the view that electronics is atypically footloose.

Industrial economies   At the top of the international income distribution we see a clear pattern of convergence in the results. In the wealthiest industrial economies the two general agglomeration variables (foreign investment and industrialization) rank at the top for both total manufacturing and electronics, followed by market size.[8] Labor cost drops substantially in relative importance, although its reponse elasticity is still high for total manufacturing. Infrastructure ranks much lower, undoubtedly because most countries in this class already have high-quality infrastructure. Wealthier countries take precedence as sites for integrated production and marketing of relatively high-quality products. Domestic market size and the relative size of the industrial support base therefore loom larger in the calculations.

Significance and stability testing

As previously noted, we interpret the translog results by separating our sample countries into five income groups [see Table 2.4, part (a)], using 1984 as the sample midpoint. Estimates of per capita GNP are drawn from the World Bank's *World Development Report* (1986). From the translog and log-interactive results, we calculate group elasticities for each independent variable and look for evidence of gross instability, consistently perverse signs, or values constantly near zero. We conclude that three variables fail one or more of our tests: the corporate tax rate, RISK, and OPEN.

Our preliminary list of survivors includes two classical variables (labor cost and market size), the three agglomeration benefit measures (infrastructure quality, degree of industrialization, and level of foreign investment), and the two geopolitical control variables (relations with neighboring countries and relations with the West). We then re-estimate the translog and log-interactive capital expenditure equations with these variables, again checking for instability, sign problems, and estimates consistently near zero. All results are reassuringly stable. A few negatively-signed elasticities in otherwise-plausible sets of positive estimates apparently reflect local failures of the log-interactive and translog approximations to preserve asymptotic boundaries at zero.

Rejected variables

Among the rejected variables, the corporate tax rate presents the most difficult problem of interpretation. In the full translog equation for total manufacturing, its elasticities are consistently positive and very large. When the log-quadratic terms are dropped, however, all elasticity estimates collapse and three of the five take on a perverse sign. In the electronics equation, the results are much weaker to begin with and the same pattern of collapse and sign reversal is apparent. The log-linear results (Table 2.3) are also quite weak. In our view, this evidence weighs against any confident ascription of importance to relative corporate tax rates.

For the composite variable, OPEN, we note that the elasticities are always small and exhibit frequent sign changes in the translog and log-interactive results. The relative frequency of negative values does suggest a general pattern of import-substituting investment behind trade barriers, as we previously noted, and the strongly negative log-linear results in Table 2.3 reinforce the impression. While it is certainly plausible to suppose that openness encourages export investment, our results for electronics, which is highly export-oriented, do not differ significantly from the results for general manufacturing.

Our results also suggest little importance for RISK, the composite index for relevant socio-political conditions. In Table 2.3, the constant elasticity estimates are negligible. The group elasticity estimates have some consistently positive runs, but are seldom far from zero. Because RISK and OPEN are collinear, we have re-estimated our equations without OPEN and obtained a similar (indeed, weaker) pattern of results. We conclude that RISK should also be discounted, although it would not be implausible to assign it some small weight as a decision factor.

Admissible variables

All the remaining independent variables pass the tests with some degree of success. The infrastructure estimates are unstable in the transition from translog to log-interactive specification for total manufacturing, but considerably less so for electronics. The general pattern suggests a very substantial impact, particularly for poor countries. For both total manufacturing and electronics, the constant elasticity estimates (Table 2.3) are quite large and significant. Almost the same things can be said about degree of industrialization. It is unstable and has many perverse signs in the translog total manufacturing results, but emerges powerfully in the electronics results and in the constant elasticity estimates.

For labor cost, market size, and level of foreign investment, we see no problems on any front. The estimated elasticities are generally positive, large, and stable across all specifications. Finally, both of BI's geopolitical indices—relations with the West and relations with neighboring countries—have sufficient explanatory importance for admissibility as non-interactive controls.[9]

Conclusion

The expected payoff from participation in international location tournaments depends on the balance in investor thinking between agglomeration-related benefits on one side and some combination of risk and classical factors on the other. We find that U.S. investors give almost all the decision weight to agglomeration benefits and some classical variables. Among agglomeration-related factors, infrastructure quality clearly dominates for developing economies. Specialized support services are more important for industrial economies, all of which already have high-quality infrastructure. In the classical group, market size eclipses labor cost as national income level rises.

The importance of the existing stock of foreign investment as a proxy for agglomeration factors raises an important question: If past foreign investment is important, then how does an economy ever manage to attract some investment in the first place? Our results suggest that the self-reinforcing aspect of foreign investment begins to operate only after a certain development threshold has been reached. In the early phases of development, the important policy variables do not seem to involve incentives such as tax breaks. Investors seem to prefer good quality infrastructure to tax incentives, for example, since the latter have limited potency when transfer pricing and deduction of foreign taxes from U.S. tax liabilities provide alternative routes for minimizing taxes paid.

For developing countries, our results suggest the overriding importance of infrastructure development, stable international relations, rapid industrial growth, and an expanding domestic market. We conclude that those developing countries which are already doing well in these categories do not need location tournaments. The others are not likely to profit from them.

To our surprise, our results assign little importance to perceived risk, except for some modest weight attached to geopolitical considerations. Neither does adherence to open-market policies generate much investor response at any level of development. Again, however, we should stress the ambiguity in any single measure of openness. Alternative indices with very different implications for profitability are highly correlated, and openness can influence export-oriented investment and import-substituting investment in quite different ways.

Notes

1 The potential importance of non-ergodicity for trade policy is recognized by Grossman and Helpman (1989). It also underlies the new growth theory, which explores possibilities for multiple equilibria in an economy with one or more externalities at the macro-level [see Romer (1986), Lucas (1988) and Drazen and Azariadis (1990)]. Murphy et al. (1989) use non-ergodicity to rationalize a "big push" in industrial development.

2 Tournament play, of course, may be costly. The greater the perceived first-mover advantage the heavier the bidding, the higher the gains for prospective investors, and the fewer the net benefits for the competing locations.

3 Eq. (5) can also be derived from a model of discrete choice between alternative locations: pairwise site comparison reflects a translog valuation function; (I_i/I_j) estimates the probability ratio for unit investments in country i and the numeraire country j. Right-hand variables enter as logs of characteristics ratios [or, equivalently, as differences of logs of characteristics as in (5)].

4 Since all equations are estimated using relative investment flows, the choice of numeraire is entirely arbitrary and has no effect on the results.

5 There are occasional missing values for total manufacturing in the Department of Commerce data, and more frequent missing values for electronics manufacturing. The latter are generally due to enforcement of single-firm disclosure rules. For cases where the reported amount is greater than zero but less than $500,000, we arbitrarily assume investment to be $250,000.

6 The translog function becomes log-linear when all log-interactive and log-quadratic terms are dropped. It becomes log-interactive when all log-quadratic terms are removed. Complete results for all specifications are available from the authors on request.

7 As the reader can easily verify, the log-linear elasticities do provide a good sense of the typical translog-based values. Although we cannot rigorously prove this, we also think that the log-linear results provide a good first-order test of robustness. The burden of proof is certainly on any independent variable whose effect cannot be significantly differentiated from zero in a first-order approximation.

8 While we associate the existing foreign investment base with agglomeration economies, we recognize the possibility that it also proxies other attractions which are not captured by the BI scoring variables. Given the variety and apparent plausibility of the BI-assigned scores, however, we are inclined to favor the agglomeration hypothesis.

9 Relations with neighboring countries seem to have a modest impact for total manufacturing and some possible impact for electronics. Relations with the West show up only for electronics, perhaps reflecting the greater-than-average military sensitivity of this industry. Exclusion of both variables has no significant effect on the other results.

Appendix

Table A.1 Country ranks: Mean values from business international indices. Location factors: total manufacturing.

Group/ country	Manuf. inv.[a]	Lab. cost	Infr. qual.	Corp. tax	Mkt size	Deg. ind.	Lev. for. inv.	RISK	OPEN
1									
Canada	10	1	8	6	10	7	10	9	7
Germany	10	3	9	2	10	9	10	9	10
Japan	9	3	9	1	10	9	3	7	7
Australia	8	2	8	4	8	9	10	8	6
Sweden	7	1	9	1	8	9	4	8	8
Switzerland	6	3	8	10	7	9	7	10	9
Denmark	5	1	9	7	5	9	5	9	9
Norway	3	3	7	4	5	9	2	10	8
2									
France	10	4	9	2	10	9	6	7	6
U.K.	10	4	7	9	10	9	9	8	9
Italy	9	2	6	4	10	9	6	6	9
Netherlands	9	2	9	7	8	9	9	10	10
Belgium	8	1	9	2	7	9	8	7	8
Singapore	7	5	8	9	2	5	9	10	10

Group/ country	Manuf. inv.[a]	Lab. cost	Infr. qual.	Corp. tax	Mkt size	Deg. ind.	Lev. for. inv.	RISK	OPEN
Austria	5	3	9	3	6	7	9	8	7
Hong Kong	4	8	6	10	3	7	8	9	10
Trinidad	1	5	3	4	1	4	5	6	5
3									
Spain	8	4	5	9	8	6	9	5	5
Argentina	7	6	5	3	6	5	3	4	4
Ireland	7	4	5	10	2	7	7	7	7
Taiwan	7	7	7	8	5	7	6	7	5
Venezuela	6	6	4	7	6	4	3	4	2
Korea	5	7	7	6	7	5	4	5	4
Israel	4	5	6	1	2	4	8	6	6
Greece	3	6	4	5	4	1	1	4	5
4									
Brazil	9	8	6	8	10	5	9	4	1
Mexico	8	8	5	2	8	5	5	2	2
Malaysia	6	9	4	8	3	4	4	4	3
Colombia	5	4	3	7	3	3	5	2	2
Chile	4	9	4	5	3	2	2	5	7
Portugal	4	6	4	3	2	6	2	5	6
Ecuador	2	6	2	9	1	1	2	3	3
Turkey	2	5	2	4	5	3	2	3	2
Panama	1	8	6	7	1	1	6	6	8
5									
The Philippines	6	10	1	5	4	2	8	2	3

	Manuf. inv.	Lab. cost	Infr. qual.	Corp. tax	Mkt size	Deg. ind.	Lev. for. inv.	RISK	OPEN
India	4	10	3	1	9	4	4	3	1
Indonesia	3	10	1	5	7	2	2	1	2
Thailand	3	10	2	6	4	2	5	1	4
Nigeria	2	7	1	6	6	1	3	1	1
Peru	2	9	2	4	3	5	2	2	3
Egypt	1	9	2	9	3	2	1	3	4
Liberia	1	7	3	10	1	2	7	1	4

Manuf. inv. = Manufacturing investment; Lab. cost = Labor cost; Infr. qual. = Infrastructure quality; Corp. tax = Level of corporate taxation; Mkt size = Market size; Deg. ind. = Degree of industrialization; Lev. for. inv. = Level of foreign direct investment; RISK = Principal component for socio-political indices; OPEN = Principal component for government intervention indices.
[a] Investment data have been converted to 10 groups for easy comparison.

Table A.2 BI country assessment service rating systems: regression variables.

1. *Agglomeration benefits*

Infrastructure quality: Quality, dependability of transport, communications, energy infrastructure

10 Excellent transportation, communication, energy services readily available
 8 Normally good services but specific shortcomings
 6 Widespread shortcomings but basically adequate
 4 Inadequate infrastructure, only a fews adequate services
 2 Totally inadequate infrastructure overall
 0 Practically no infrastructure to support business activity

Level of foreign direct investment: Relative magnitude and breadth of foreign investment

10 Very high; large investments in many sectors
 8 High; broadly based
 6 Moderate; broadly based
 4 Moderate; selective sectors
 2 Low
 0 Very low

Degree of industrialization: Manufacturing/mining as percent of GDP. OECD countries are ranked as 10 even though their share is technically too low because of importance of services

10 Greater than 50 percent
 8 30–50 percent
 6 20–30 percent
 4 Significant, but less than 20 percent
 2 Low level of industrialization; only several key industries
 0 Little if any industry

2. *Geopolitical risk measures*

Relationship with West: Political, economic, commercial relations

10 Exceptionally strong, stable relations
 8 Generally favorable relations
 6 Independent, no clear-cut relationship
 4 Independent, sometimes antagonistic relationship
 2 Frequently in economic or political confrontation with Western nations
 0 Completely antagonistic to Western interests and policies

(*continued overleaf*)

Relationship with neighboring countries: Includes political, economic, and commercial relations with neighbors that may affect the conduct of business

10 Peaceful and cooperative relationship
 8 Generally favorable relationship
 6 Generally neutral relationship
 4 Selective competition and confrontation with neighboring countries
 2 Possibility of major economic or military confrontations
 0 Probability of military conflict

3. *Principal components*

RISK (representative indices):

Political change—institutional: Probability that institutional framework will be changed within the forecast period by elections or other means

10 Government virtually certain not to change
 8 Peaceful, orderly transition to opposition possible
 6 Relatively strong government but vulnerable to sudden changes
 4 Active and violent opposition; strong possibility of institutional disorder
 2 Active and violent opposition; strong possibility of anti-MNC regime
 0 Probability of overthrow, social revolution or civil war

Bureaucracy and red tape: Regulatory environment faced by foreign companies when they seek approvals and permits

10 Smoothly functioning; efficient bureaucracy
 8 Modest requirements for contract approvals; some delays
 6 Frequent requirements for governmental approvals
 4 Constant need for governmental approvals and frequent delays in getting them
 2 Disorganized and/or corrupt bureaucracy
 0 Bureaucracy extremely antagonistic to foreign business

OPEN (representative indices):

Local content requirements: Government requirement that a certain percentage or specific type of local components be used when setting up manufacturing operations

10 None
 8 Pressure to utilize local components and materials
 6 Specific selective requirements for local content
 4 General requirements for specified percentage of local content
 2 Strictly enforced requirements for fully utilizing local components and materials
 0 No outside components allowed

Limits on foreign ownership: New investment

10 No ceiling on foreign equity percentage
 8 Pressure, but no requirements for local equity
 6 Local majority required in many key industries
 4 Strict joint venture requirements
 2 Only foreign minority position tolerated and this on a limited basis
 0 No foreign equity allowed

References

Arthur, B. (1986) Industry location patterns and the importance of history, Stanford University, Center for Economic Policy Research, Paper no. 84.

Arthur, B. (1990) Positive feedbacks in the economy, *Scientific American* 262, 92–99.

Blomstrom, M. and R.E. Lipsey (1986) Firm size and foreign direct investment, NBER Working Paper no. 2092 (National Bureau of Economic Research, Cambridge).

Caves, R.E. (1970) Uncertainty, market structure and performance: Galbraith as conventional wisdom, in: J.W. Markham and G.F. Papanek, eds., *Industrial organization and economic development: Essays in honor of E.S. Mason* (Houghton Mifflin, Boston, MA).

David, P. (1984) High technology centers and the economics of locational tournaments, Stanford University, Mimeo.

Drazen, A. and C. Azariadis (1990) Threshold externalities in economic development, *Quarterly Journal of Economics* 105, 501–526.

Englander, O. (1926) Kritisches und positives zu einer allgemeinen reinen lehre vom standort. Zeitschrift fur Volkswirtschaft und Sozialnolitik, NeueFolae 5.

Ethier, W. (1979) Internationally decreasing costs and world trade, *Journal of International Economics* 9, 1–24.

Ethier, W. (1982) National and international returns to scale in the modern theory of international trade, *American Economic Review* 72, 389–405.

Flamm, K. (1984) The volatility of offshore investment, *Journal of Development Economics* 16, 231–248.

Grossman, G. and E. Helpman (1989) Comparative advantage and long-run growth, NBER Working Paper no. 2809 (National Bureau of Economic Research, Cambridge).

Grubel, H.G. (1979) Foreword, in: A.M. Rugman, *International diversification and the multinational enterprise* (Lexington Books, Lexington).

Grubert, H. and J. Mutti (1989) Financial flows versus capital spending: Alternative measures of U.S.–Canadian investment and trade in the analysis of taxes, Mimeo.

Hoover, E.M. (1937) *Location theory and the shoe and leather industries* (Harvard University Press, Cambridge, MA).

Hufbauer, G.C. (1975) The multinational corporation and direct investment, in: P. Kenen, ed., *International trade and finance* (Cambridge University Press).

Isard, W. (1956) *Location and space economy* (Wiley, New York).

Kalecki, M. (1938) The principle of increasing risk, in: *Essays in the theory of economic fluctuation* (George Allen and Unwin, London).

Kravis, I.B. and R.E. Lipsey (1982) Location of overseas production and production for export by U.S. multinational firms, *Journal of International Economics* 12, 201–223.

Kravis, I.B. and R.E. Lipsey (1989) Technological characteristics of industries and the competitiveness of the U.S. and its multinational firms, NBER Working Paper no. 2933 (National Bureau of Economic Research, Cambridge).

Lipsey, R.E. and I.B. Kravis (1987) Competitiveness and comparative advantage of U.S. multinationals 1957–1984, *Banca Nazionale del Lavoro Quarterly Review* 161, 147–165.

Losch, A. (1941) *The economics of location* (Yale University Press, New Haven).

Lucas, R.E., Jr. (1988) On the mechanics of economic development, *Journal of Monetary Economics* 22, 3–42.

Markusen, J.R. (1990) First mover advantage, blockaded entry, and the economics of uneven development, NBER Working Paper no. 3284 (National Bureau of Economic Research, Cambridge).

Maruyama, M. (1963) The second cybernetics: Deviation amplifying mutual causal processes, *American Scientist* 51, 164–179.

Murphy, K., A. Schleifer and R. Vishny (1989) Industrialization and the big push, *Journal of Political Economy* 97, 1003–1026.

Nelson, C. and C. Plosser (1982) Trends and random walks in macroeconomic time series, *Journal of Monetary Economics* 10, 139–162.

Palander, T. (1935) Beitrage zur standortstheorie, Almqvist and Wicksell.

Predohl, A. (1925) Das standortsproblem in der wirtschaftslehre, Weltwirtschaftliches Archiv 21, 294–331.

Romer, P. (1986) Increasing returns and long-run growth, *Journal of Political Economy* 94, 1002–1037.

Rugman, A.M. (1979) *International diversification and the multinational enterprise* (Lexington Books, Lexington).

Shah, A. and J. Slemrod (1990) Tax sensitivity of foreign direct investments: An empirical assessment, Policy, Research and External Affairs Working Paper no. 434 (The World Bank, Washington, DC).

Von Thunen, J.H. (1826) Der isolierte staat in beziehung auf landwirtschaft und national-okonomie (Hamburg).

World Bank (1986) *World Development Report* (The World Bank, Washington, DC and Oxford University Press, New York).

3 Japanese and U.S. firms as foreign investors

Do they march to the same tune?

With Krishna Srinivasan

1. Introduction

Japanese firms emerged as a major presence on the international scene with substantial new investments in the mid-1980s and have contributed in a significant way to the large investment flows since then (Figure 3.1). The flows of Japanese investment almost quadrupled between 1985 and 1988, stabilizing at those high levels in 1989 and 1990. Over the same period, U.S. investments also rose, approximately doubling between 1985 and 1988. The outstanding stock of Japanese foreign investment remains lower in absolute value than that of the United States—the dominant international investor—but has almost caught up in relative terms. According to the Japan External Trade Organization, one-fifth of production by Japanese firms is located overseas, compared with 25 percent for U.S. firms.

As the two principal investing nations, how do Japan and the U.S. allocate their investment host country destinations? We begin by analysing the differences in investment flows over time *within particular countries* and the investment allocations *across countries*. With that as background, we ask a series of questions. Do investors from Japan and the United States value the same country attributes? As late-comers to international investing, are Japanese investors more risk averse? Over time, is there a "convergence" in the factors driving U.S. and Japanese foreign investors?

Certain similarities exist in Japanese and U.S. allocations of investment: a heavy concentration of investment persists in developed or high-income countries, while middle-income countries receive a modest share of investment (Table 3.1).[1] The surge of investment in the second half of the 1980s was also accompanied by a further focus on high-income countries. For both Japanese and U.S. investors, interest in developing countries outside East Asia and Latin America is truly limited. However, certain important differences also exist in the patterns of Japanese and U.S. investment flows. Over half the Japanese investment flows have been to the United States, and the U.S. share of Japanese investment grew during the investment surge in the second half of the 1980s. In contrast, U.S. investments are concentrated in the major European countries. Japanese investors had a somewhat greater interest in

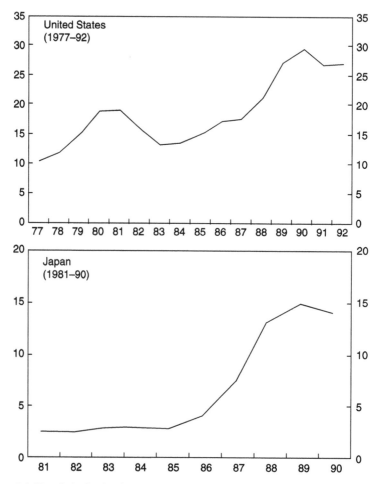

Figure 3.1 Trends in foreign investment outflows (billions of US$).

Sources: United States: Bureau of Economics Analysis, Department of Commerce. Japan: Ministry of Finance and Ministry for International Trade and Industry.

developing (middle- and low-income) countries in the first half of the 1980s. Within the set of developing countries, Japanese investors have had a strong interest in East Asia; U.S. investment in East Asia, though low, has steadily increased over the past two decades.

Research has focused on factors determining the outflow of U.S. investment rather than the *allocation* of such investment across a range of countries (Scaperland and Balough 1983; Lipsey 1988; Kravis and Lipsey 1992; Barrell and Pain 1996). In a study that examines investment allocation, Wheeler and Mody (1992; also Ch. 2 this book) found that good infrastructure, large market size, and an economy relatively closed to trade attracted U.S. investors. A particularly interesting feature of the analysis was the strong

Table 3.1 Allocation of foreign direct investment across country groups (percentage)

	1977–80	1981–85	1986–90
United States, 1977–92			
Developed countries	81.9	77.6	78.7
European Economic Community	57.3	53.9	54.7
Other high income	24.6	23.7	24.0
Developing countries	18.1	22.4	21.3
Latin America	12.9	14.4	11.3
East Asia	4.9	7.7	9.7
Other middle income	0.1	0.1	0.2
Other low income	0.2	0.2	0.1
Japan, 1981–90			
Developed countries		64.9	82.3
European Economic Community	–	10.6	15.1
Other high income	–	54.3	67.2
Developing countries		35.1	17.7
Latin America	–	18.1	4.0
East Asia	–	16.4	13.4
Other middle income	–	0.1	0.2
Other low income	–	0.4	0.1

Sources: United States: Bureau of Economic Analysis, Department of Commerce. Japan: Ministry of Finance and Ministry for International Trade and Industry.

persistence exhibited by U.S. investors—past investment in the country was a strong predictor of new investment. That persistence was attributed to the favorable effects of agglomeration, but it could include cascading effects due to observation of other investor decisions (Kinoshita and Mody 1997; also Ch. 4 this book). We examine whether this persistence carries over to Japanese firms. A growing literature also is concerned with the determinants of Japanese foreign investment. Recent examples include Kogut and Chang (1996), who show that past investment does indeed increase the probability of future investment. Belderbos and Sleuwaegen (1996) study the allocation of Japanese investment across North America, Europe, and East Asia and find that the Asian investment is driven by factors quite different from those of the "West-bound" investment. Using an approach similar to ours, Eaton and Tamura (1994) examine the factors driving Japanese and U.S. direct foreign investment; they, however, focus on a limited set of explanatory variables (population density, per capita income, human capital, regional dummies) and do not distinguish between the time-series and cross-sectional variations in the allocation decisions.[2]

In this chapter we exploit the panel features of the data (several observations on individual countries) to draw inferences on factors driving investments *within* countries over time (sometimes referred to as short-run estimates) and factors that cause investors to differentiate *between* countries (the long-run estimates). The goal is to explain the shares of foreign investment received by a set of host countries (thirty-five hosts for U.S. investment over the period 1977–92 and twenty-nine hosts for Japanese firms over 1981–90). A specially constructed data set on country attributes consistent over time and across countries is used. Careful attention is paid to the inefficiencies and biases that arise when panel data are used.

In section 2 we present a framework of analysis. The sources of variation in the data are highlighted in section 3 by an examination of four different estimates for the United States that are possible in a panel data setting; specifically, a distinction is made between country attributes that change significantly over time versus those that remain relatively unchanged. In section 4 the random-effects model is used to draw the principal contrasts between the determinants of U.S. and Japanese investment allocations. The estimates are repeated for the first and second half of the 1980s in section 5 to determine if factors influencing investment have changed over time and, in particular, if the two sets of investors are increasingly responding to the same country attributes. In a final section we summarize and conclude.

2. The framework of analysis

We define f_{it} as the *share* of host country i in the total investment flowing out of supplier country (which is either the United States or Japan) in year t. The basic equation estimated relates the host country's investment share to a set of attributes that characterize the country. The host countries are pooled in the analysis, but separate equations are estimated for the two supplier countries. The decision to pool the data across countries was inevitable, since the number of observations for any one country is too small. While pooling creates obvious limitations by forcing the regression coefficients across countries to be the same, pooled data also present opportunities for interesting and useful insights by allowing consideration of within-country and between-country dimensions.

Certain assumptions underlying the analysis need to be spelled out. Consider a (U.S. or Japanese) firm making the decision to invest abroad. We postulate a two-step process: the firm decides first on the extent of total investment abroad (Barrell and Pain 1996) and then on the allocation of that investment across countries. The allocation process is the one we focus on: in this second step, the investment shares of the various host countries are determined by the country attributes. Two apparently reasonable assumptions are required to facilitate the econometric estimation. First, like Wheeler and Mody (1992; also Ch. 2 this book), we assume that the factors determining the aggregate foreign investment (such as profitability in domestic operations) do not influence the allocation across countries and so can be omitted from the analysis; a weaker form of this assumption, consistent with our analysis, would be that these omitted factors are not correlated with host-country attributes.

Second, the decision to invest abroad is made by several individual firms, based on expected profits and the risks they face. Our data do not distinguish the individual investments but rather are the aggregate investment by a large number of U.S. and Japanese firms. A danger exists that heterogeneity among firms (of different sizes and in different industries) may lead in such aggregative analysis to biased conclusions. Most foreign investment studies implicitly assume that aggregation is, in fact, possible (Barrell and Pain 1996). Firm-level studies of foreign investment are becoming more common but are typically restricted in industry and host country coverage. Kogut and Chang (1996), for example, study investment by Japanese electronics firms in the United States. There is a trade-off, therefore, between a full analysis of firm heterogeneity and the ability to identify country attributes attractive to foreign investors. In this chapter, we continue with the assumption that the individual investments can be aggregated such that a country's share in U.S. or Japanese investment represents the decisions made by the firms. In effect, therefore, we assume that all firms are motivated by the same essential set of country characteristics. The share of a "representative" U.S. (or Japanese) firm's investment in country i is thus proxied by the share of all U.S. (Japanese) investment in that country. This may be thought of as a measurement error in the dependent variable, which we assume, once again, is not correlated with the country attributes, and hence no bias results.

The basic equation, estimated separately for the United States and Japan, may be characterized as follows:

$$f_{it} = \beta X_{it} + U_{it}, \qquad i = 1, 2, \ldots, n; t = 1, 2, \ldots, T,$$

where $i = 1, 2, \ldots, n$ is the list of host countries, and $t = 1, 2, \ldots, T$ are the years over which observations are available for each country. f_{it} represents the share of investment in country i in period t from either the United States or Japan. X_{it} is the ($K \times 1$) vector of regressors representing the values of the country attributes that potentially influence foreign investment. The important feature of this model is the error structure, which has two components:

$$U_{it} = \mu_i + v_{it}.$$

The first term, μ_i, represents a set of influences specific to a country, and the other, v_{it}, is white noise, the traditional error term in a regression equation with zero mean and variance σ^2_v and uncorrelated with the regressors.

As is well known, each of the different estimators for pooled data suffers from certain limitations. To recapitulate briefly, the ordinary least squares (OLS) estimator will lead to biased estimates where unobserved country effects, μ_i, are correlated with the observed explanatory variables. Panel data, in principle, provide a solution for this problem. The *within-estimator* (or the fixed-effects model) is obtained when, for each country, each variable is measured as the actual value in the different years *minus* the mean value of that variable (over time in the specific country). By thus "extracting" the mean value prevailing in a country over the time period under consideration, the variation in the data that arises from different mean levels across countries— and hence the influence of "fixed" and unobserved country characteristics— is eliminated. With the bias thus eliminated, the regression coefficients reflect responsiveness of foreign investment to changes within a country, over time. For this reason, within-estimates are sometimes referred to as *short-run* estimates (Baltagi and Griffin 1984; Caballero and Lyons 1991). While country attributes such as infrastructure do not change much between one year and another and so will not influence foreign investment in the short run, other attributes, such as labor and capital costs, are more likely to influence foreign investment from one year to the next. Besides potential biases of its own, such as the assumption of strict exogeneity[3] and the aggravation of measurement errors because of the differencing process,[4] the procedure entails substantial loss in cross-sectional information, since the differences between countries are ignored.

At the other extreme, only the variation across countries is considered in the *between-estimator*. Here, each variable is represented by the country's mean observed value over the years for which the data are available. Between-estimators, which relate a country's average investment share to its average attribute values over time, can be thought to reflect *long-run* investment decisions. The bias due to omitted variables, correlated with included variables, remains in the between-estimator. By ignoring the within-variation, this estimator fails to utilize all available information.

Thus, though both the within- and the between-estimators ignore certain information in the data, they provide different perspectives, and we use them initially, along with the OLS estimates, to describe the variation in the data. In a fully specified model and under equilibrium conditions, the within- and between-estimators should give the same estimates (Mairesse 1990). However, large shifts in investment during this period make it unlikely that the investment allocation process is in equilibrium. Equilibrium in this context would imply that the new investment is simply replacing the depreciation of the stock of past investment, which is clearly not the case, especially for Japan. Moreover, many equalitative country characteristics (such as the ease of doing business) can only be measured with error, and full model specification thus is difficult to achieve. In particular, any attempt to use the between, or cross-sectional, variation in the data implies the possibility of bias because of the correlation between the error term and the regressors; hence, it is useful to consider what the nature of this bias may be. Essentially, the concern arises from the possibility that the unchanging component of the error term, μ_i, represents an important omitted variable that is correlated with one or more the included regressors. The bias then occurs because the influence of this unobserved country feature on foreign investment may be wrongly attributed to the included country attributes. An obvious candidate for such a bias is infrastructure, which changes slowly from one year to another. If the unobserved μ_i reflects general business and operating conditions in the country, it is likely that μ_i and infrastructure will be correlated. Since the cross-sectional variation in the data is important, our approach here is not to ignore that variation but rather to interpret infrastructure more broadly to include the effects of country operating conditions.

To compare the U.S. and Japanese investment determinants, we use the *random-effects model*. The choice of this model stems essentially from its *composite* nature: reflecting both the influences across countries and within countries, the random-effect model estimates coefficients that are a weighted average of the between- and within-estimates (Maddala 1983; Hsiao 1986). Unlike the situation of the fixed-effects model, where the country effect, μ_i, is a pure admission of the investigator's ignorance, in the random-effects model a specific realization of μ_i for a country can be thought of as drawn from a normal distribution with mean zero and variance σ^2_μ, and independent of v_{it}. The random-effects model assumes that μ_i is not correlated with the included explanatory variables, and the Hausman test is used to determine the plausibility of that assumption.[5] The presence of μ_i in the error structure implies a strong serial correlation and renders the standard errors of ordinary least square (OLS) estimates incorrect. For this reason, a generalized least square (GLS) estimate is obtained based on transformation of the variables using the estimated variance-covariance matrix.

Where the model is correctly specified, the GLS estimate provides the right standard errors. The potential correlation between μ_i and the explanatory variable implies, however, that the potential of bias in the estimates remains. Tests to judge the seriousness of this bias require that the within-model lead to consistent estimates, which is not always possible. Tests are conducted, however, and are shown to provide a reasonable basis for using the random-effects model. More important, we maintain that each different type of estimate provides a specific perspective on the data and that the random-effects model, by combining the within and between perspectives, represents the best composite picture.

3. The sources of variation in the data: explaining U.S. investments

We use the different estimation techniques—the OLS, the within (or fixed-effects), the between, and the random-effects (or GLS or composite) estimators—to infer the sources of variation in the explanatory variables. The model estimates, based on the years 1977–92 for the United States are presented in Table 3.2. U.S. investment data was available for 35 countries (see the list of countries and their income and regional classification in Appendix A). The country attributes considered in explaining a country's share in foreign investment are, for expository convenience, divided into six groups:

1. The relevant price variables: here we consider the *price of labor* and *the cost of capital*; the cost of capital consists of two elements: an investment

price deflator, which measures the cost of investment goods in the economy, and the corporate tax rate.
2.   The *size of the domestic market*.
3.   The *trade propensity of the economy*.
4.   The degree of *country risk* (or, its inverse, *country "safety"*).
5.   Factors enhancing productivity of the investment undertaken, such as *infrastructure* and *education*; also relevant are domestic agglomeration effects for which we have no direct measure but for which the *accumulated stock of foreign investment* is used as a proxy (though, as we shall discuss, the stock of foreign investment may influence new investment for reasons other than agglomeration effects).
6.   Finally, certain unmeasured country characteristics can be controlled, for which we use *country group dummies*; for example, proximity in distance and methods of conducting business are captured by these dummies (Eaton and Tamura 1994).

Variables in any one group may condition the influence of variables in another group. For example, labor quality, as proxied by primary enrolment rates, conditions the reaction to wage costs. Potential omitted variables include the "incentives" provided to foreign investors through, for example, reduced taxes, special dispensation of land or infrastructure, and reduced tariffs on imported inputs. We have been unable to construct a panel data set on such incentives. The analysis below proceeds on the presumption that foreign investment incentives are not correlated with the variables included in the analysis and the omission thus does not bias the results obtained; an indirect inference on tax incentives is possible, however, through examining the effect of capital costs on investments. Also, we initially included an exchange rate variable, but found that its role in influencing investment flows was extremely sensitive to model specification, and that most diagnostic tests favored its exclusion. Hence, we converted all the relevant data into one common unit, the U.S. dollar, and excluded the explicit incorporation of the exchange rate as an explanatory variable.

The precise definitions of the variables and their sources are provided in Appendix B. The variables are measured in logarithmic values (except for the regional and country dummies) and so the coefficients can be interpreted as elasticities.

Two country attributes that have a distinctly within-country quality are the country risk measure and the labor costs (Table 3.2). The between-estimates suggest that investors do not discriminate between countries on the basis of this risk measure. In contrast, the within-estimates (as well as the random-effects estimates) have a strongly signficant coefficient. Recall that this measure is conventionally on a scale of 0 to 100, with a higher number indicating a safer country. Hence, the estimates clearly indicate that a rise in risk (or a fall in the degree of safety) reduces investment within a country. One interpretation of contrasting within- and between-estimates is that, while country risk

Table 3.2 Determinants of U.S. foreign investment, 1977–92 (dependent variable: host country share of foreign investment outflow)

Variable	OLS	Within	Between	Random	Random
Constant	−14.321	–	−16.309	−10.841	−9.529
Market size	0.601*(3.2)	1.312*(4.6)	1.876**(1.6)	1.093*(4.4)	1.254* (4.8)
Cost of investment	0.002(0.01)	−0.046(0.3)	−1.486(1.2)	−0.104(0.7)	−0.209(1.4)
Corporate tax rate	−0.094(1.3)	−0.077(0.8)	−0.023(0.1)	−0.054(0.6)	−0.101(1.2)
Cost of labor	−0.048(1.1)	−0.098*(2.3)	0.070(0.3)	−0.096*(2.5)	−0.082*(2.1)
Trade propensity	0.218(1.6)	−0.438*(2.1)	0.617(1.0)	−0.528*(3.4)	−0.588*(3.6)
Stock of past FDI	0.485*(12.3)	0.678*(7.5)	0.455*(2.9)	0.628*(8.8)	0.673*(8.8)
Country risk[a]	0.975*(6.4)	1.052*(6.9)	−1.131(0.8)	1.177*(8.9)	1.083*(8.2)
Infrastructure	0.775*(13.4)	0.131(1.1)	0.955*(3.7)	0.337*(4.1)	–
Primary school enrolment ratio	2.762*(4.5)	0.575(1.1)	3.730(1.0)	0.766**(1.6)	–
Latin America	0.117**(1.6)	–	0.014(0.04)	0.256**(1.6)	0.249(1.2)
East Asia	−0.067(0.9)	–	0.159(0.4)	0.251(1.4)	0.318(1.4)
Other high income	−0.349*(6.0)	–	−0.348**(1.6)	−0.368*(2.1)	−0.361**(1.6)
Other middle income	−0.500*(5.0)	–	−0.837**(1.8)	−0.580*(2.2)	−0.780*(2.4)
Other low income	−0.519*(3.6)	–	0.226(0.3)	−0.020(0.1)	0.235(0.8)
	Adj R^2 = 0.83	Adj R^2 = 0.94	Adj R^2 = 0.84	Adj R^2 = 0.93	Adj R^2 = 0.90

Number of Countries = 35
Number of Observations = 521
Tmax = 16 Tmin = 11
Hausman: Chi Sq(9) = 23.2

Hausman: Chi Sq(7) = 10.0

* Indicates statistical significance at the 5 percent level.
** Indicates statistical significance at the 10 percent level.
a The variable "country risk" is measured on a scale of 0 to 100, with an increasing value indicating a safer country.

measures do not affect the long-run choice of countries, they do affect the *timing* of the investment. In other words, investors do not abandon high-risk countries. Rather, they choose periods to enter, or expand in, such countries during years when they are perceived as relatively low risk.

Of interest also is the labor cost variable. It will be noted that labor costs do not show up as an important influence in either the OLS or the between results. In contrast, the within-estimates show the labor costs to be a negative influence on foreign investment. This influence also is seen strongly in the random-effects estimates, where the value of the coefficient is somewhat smaller. Recall that this coefficient is a weighted average of the small, positive between-estimate and the larger, negative within-estimate—virtually, the entire strength of the within-estimate is reflected in the random-effects model. Thus, we interpret that level of labor costs is not decisive in choosing between one country and another, but changing costs—or wage inflation—can influence investments from one year to another. This interpretation seems plausible, since in their cross-country decisions firms use capital-intensive techniques in high-wage countries and labor-intensive techniques in low-wage countries (U.S. Department of Commerce 1996). Within a country, however, changes in capital intensity are difficult to modulate over short periods of time and, hence, wage inflation has the effect of slowing investment. For U.S. investors, the market size of the host economy is both a within- and a between-country driver. Eaton and Tamura (1994) arrive at a similar conclusion, though they use a different approach. The within-effect is statistically stronger than the between-effects (in terms of the high *t*-values). Note that the between-coefficient value is actually much higher, however, indicating that market size is important in making country choices. Also, the trade propensity variable (trade volume divided by Gross Domestic Product) shows a significantly negative sign in the within-dimension, indicating that U.S. investors perceive trade and foreign investment as substitutes.

Finally, the one variable that is strongly present in both within- and between-country effects is past foreign investment in the country. Thus, whether making country choices or timing decisions, investors are guided forcefully by past investments in that country. Note that, though the within-effects appear somewhat stronger, the value of the coefficients across the different estimates is quite similar, creating confidence in the statistical validity of this influence. Various interpretations of this finding are possible. Agglomeration effects, for example, availability of components for assembly in the automobile and electronics industry, favors new investment where past investment has occurred. The recent decision by General Motors to base its Asia operations in Thailand rather than in the Philippines (which offered several incentives) was partly based on an existing agglomeration of suppliers (*Financial Times*, 30 May 1996). However, the within-effects also suggest the signaling influence of other investors is important. Where other investors are believed to have private information on the country or where oligopolistic rivalry is strong, there can be cascading effects leading to discontinuous increases in investment. An empirical examination of this idea, using survey data, has been articulated in Kinoshita and Mody (1997; also Ch. 4 this book).

In contrast, a country's infrastructure is a strong sorting variable for investors. The between, random-effects, and OLS estimates all show it to be a major influence in making country choices. Since the stock of infrastructure changes very little from one year to another, the within-effects are very weak. Thus, small increases in infrastructure from one year to the next have very little impact on foreign investors; major infrastructure investments over the years, however, signaling a sustained commitment to readily available services, can attract investors. Similarly, primary school enrolment rates show some tendency to differentiate investor interest between countries.

As discussed above, both infrastructure and primary enrolment rates could, in addition, be picking up the influence of other variables, such as country business operating conditions, and so these variables must be interpreted to include all slowly changing country characteristics. The extent of such bias is gauged through the Hausman test, which, in effect, measures the distance between the within-estimates and the random-effect estimates. The null hypothesis here is that the within-estimates are consistent (since the effect of the unobserved variables is eliminated). For the full model, the Hausman test rejects the random-effects estimates at the 5 percent level of significance. Since we suspect that the difference in the within-estimates and the random-effects estimates arises principally from the infrastructure and primary school enrolment rate variables, we report the random-effects model without these two variables. Now the random-effects model is accepted, with a *p*-value of 0.10. Note that the coefficients on the other variables change very little when infrastructure and primary enrolment rates are dropped.

The validity of the Hausman specification test, however, depends pivotally on whether the within-effects model does indeed lead to consistent estimates (Keane and Runkle 1992). While the between-estimates may be biased upward, equally the within-estimates may be biased downward (Mairesse 1990). For example, if variables are measured with error—and variables like infra-structure very probably are—then the within-estimate could magnify this error because it is based on the difference between a mismeasured variable and its mean, which itself is mismeasured. As a consequence, the within-estimates of the infrastructure coefficient could be downward biased, and hence, the distance between the within- and random-effects coefficient may be exaggerated. Thus, the validity of the random-effects model is likely to be greater than is suggested by the Hausman test.

4. Japanese investors: are they different?

Keeping in mind these sources of variation in the explanatory variables, we examine the similarities and differences between the U.S. and Japanese investment patterns on the basis of the composite or random-effects estimates. But first it is useful to note that, as may be expected, the within-country variation, σ^2_μ, is about four times higher for Japan than it is for the United States (0.20 compared with 0.05). By contrast, the between-country variation, σ^2_v, is about the same for both countries (0.10). This indicates that Japanese estimates are much more sensitive to choice of years. Hence, Japanese estimates are presented for 1981–90 and for 1981–88 (Table 3.3). For 1981–88, the random-effects model is accepted by the Hausman test (*p*-value equal to 0.25) but is rejected for 1981–90. Hence, in making the comparison with the U.S. estimates, we rely primarily on the 1981–88 estimates, although it will be noted that the 1981–90 estimates are not very different. Also, while our pre-ferred model includes dummies for countries grouped by regions (as for the U.S. estimates), alternative models with different country group dummies are presented, since the Japanese estimates are sensitive to the specific country dummies used.[6]

Table 3.3 Determinants of Japanese foreign investment: random effects estimates (dependent variable: host country share of foreign investment outflow)

Variable	1981–88		1981–90	
	Regional dummies	*Income dummies*	*Regional dummies*	*Income dummies*
Constant	−14.203	−15.259	−11.508	−13.524
Market size	0.395(0.5)	0.201(0.3)	−0.191(0.3)	0.488(0.8)
Cost of investment	0.147(0.3)	0.627(1.1)	−0.106(0.2)	0.217(0.2)
Corporate tax rate	−0.103(0.3)	−0.296(0.9)	−0.316(1.3)	−0.498*(1.8)
Cost of labor	−0.314*(2.0)	−0.427*(2.7)	−0.057(0.5)	−0.122(1.0)
Trade propensity	0.047(0.1)	0.793*(1.9)	0.210(0.5)	0.958*(2.5)
Stock of past FDI	0.540*(3.2)	0.582*(3.1)	0.488*(3.2)	0.523*(3.0)
Country risk	2.208*(4.3)	2.189*(4.4)	2.460*(5.3)	2.320*(5.2)
Infrastructure	0.689*(3.0)	0.738*(3.3)	0.718*(3.3)	0.673*(3.2)
Primary school enrolment ratio	2.932**(1.6)	3.775*(2.0)	1.321(0.8)	2.231(1.3)
Latin America	0.352(1.2)	–	0.375(1.3)	–
East Asia	1.097*(3.1)	–	1.001*(3.1)	–
Other high income	−0.197(0.8)	–	−0.205(0.8)	–
Other middle income	−0.492(0.9)	–	−0.486(1.0)	–
Other low income	−0.243(0.4)	–	−0.622(1.1)	–
Middle income	–	0.244(0.6)	–	0.299(0.9)
Low income	–	−0.389(0.6)	–	−0.277(0.70)
	Adj R^2 = 0.71	Adj R^2 = 0.71	Adj R^2 = 0.72	Adj R^2 = 0.70
	Hausman: Chi Sq(9) = 11.3	Hausman: Chi Sq(9) = 15.0	Hausman: Chi Sq(9) = 22.0	Hausman: Chi Sq(9) = 27.7
	Number of countries = 29		Number of countries = 29	
	N = 199　Tmax = 8　Tmin = 1		N = 247　Tmax = 10　Tmin = 1	

* Indicates statistical significance at the 5 percent level.
** Indicates statistical significance at the 10 percent level.

A formal test of the equality of coefficients for the Japanese and U.S. equations is rejected strongly. An *F*-test was conducted to measure the difference in residual sum of squares between the "pooled" estimates—that is, when coefficients for the two investor groups were assumed equal—and the estimates with no restrictions on the coefficients. The large difference in the residual sum of squares led to a rejection of the hypothesis that coefficients are equal in size. We note below, however, several similarities in the signs of the coefficients.

4.1. Country dummies

The use of these dummies controls for certain omitted variables that characterize the country groups. Consider the regional dummies, which capture influences such as proximity and other geographical or historical connections that are not measured directly by the country attributes used in the analysis. Here, the countries of the European Economic Community (EEC) serve as the benchmark and the question of interest is whether U.S. and Japanese investors show any preference for specific country groups once the measured country attributes are accounted for. For U.S. firms, the finding is that no country group has investment shares higher than that of the EEC after controlling for country attributes, but "other" middle- and high-income countries have a significantly lower share (Table 3.2). Japanese firms show a special preference for East Asia and also, though to a smaller extent, for Latin America (Table 3.3). These results reflect the descriptive statistics presented in Table 3.1, which showed that Japanese firms had a relatively high focus on East Asia and correspondingly low interest in European destinations.

4.2. Labor and capital costs

A certain ambiguity exists in the impact of labor costs on foreign investment. Low labor costs usually are thought to attract foreign investors. Where labor costs are high, however, capital may be substituted for labor, raising the level of investment undertaken. Also, high labor costs may reflect superior labor productivity, which would be attractive to foreign investors. While we make no direct "correction" for labor productivity, the regression includes a proxy for labor quality—the level of primary school enrolment—which, in part, conditions the labor cost variable and hence reduces the ambiguity.

The finding is that low wage inflation is attractive to Japanese investors (for the period 1981–88) and to U.S. investors throughout. As noted above for the United States, labor costs do not discriminate between countries, but where wage inflation is high, investors are likely to be deterred. That labor costs do not help to distinguish between countries suggests that labor and capital are substitutes: since foreign investors can substitute capital for labor, low labor costs result in labor-intensive production requiring relatively little capital (see discussion above and U.S. Department of Commerce 1996). Thus, capital inflows in low-wage countries are small, even though the level of activity—especially employment—under foreign management may be large. Moreover, to the extent that firms locate specific categories of production in specific country groups (e.g., hi-tech production in high-income countries and the more rudimentary production in low-income countries), wages are unlikely to be a consideration.

The effect of cost of capital is generally weaker. Note that we split the capital costs component into two: an internationally comparable price for investment goods and the tax rate. We do not find price for investment goods to be influential in the investment decision. Both U.S. and Japanese investors react negatively to the corporate tax rate prevailing in the host economy but the effects are not statistically significant.

4.3. Domestic market size and trade propensity

Domestic market size (the Gross Domestic Product) has the expected positive and statistically strong influence on foreign investment for U.S. investors but not for Japanese investors. Thus, it would appear that Japanese investors are less interested in the home market than are their U.S. counterparts (see also Eaton and Tamura 1994, 507).

At first, it also appears that U.S. and Japanese investors differ in their overall response to the trade propensity of the host economy, which is measured here as the sum of exports and imports divided by the country's Gross Domestic Product. U.S. investors respond negatively to increases in trade-intensities, irrespective of the country dummies used. Japanese investors take a clearly positive view of trade intensity (significant at the 5 percent level) when country dummies are by income group (or when no dummies are included). When regional dummies are used, however, the Japanese response, though still positive, becomes insignificantly different from zero. Thus, the positive sign on trade intensity (whenever regional dummies are not included) reflects the preference for East Asian economies (which also happen to have higher trade propensities); elsewhere, Japanese investors have a more ambiguous relationship with trade intensity.

The conclusion for U.S. investors seems clear: larger Gross Domestic Product and low volumes of trade (in relation to the Gross Domestic Product) encourage these investors. Japanese investors show a weaker interest in the domestic market size and display a greater keenness for in economies with a greater trade propensity, especially in East Asia. In interpreting these results, we should note that though the trade propensity of an economy is not necessarily equivalent to the extent of its "openness," there is a correlation between the two and the interpretations are similar. Openness refers to import restrictions and tariffs and is one factor that will determine the trade propensity of an economy. Reduced openness lowers trade propensity and protects investors from import competition. A recent report notes: "For foreign investors in hugely expensive chemical plants, tariff protection has been a prerequisite for entry into southeast Asia. However, Trade liberalization is now threatening such supports, leaving some of the region's biggest investments looking precarious" (Young 1995). Tariff protection offers an important incentive and compensates, in part, for high costs resulting from inadequate infrastructure. The ambiguity in the results for Japanese investors suggests that this is not always a critical decision factor.

4.4. Productivity enhancement through infrastructure
and educated labor

We have measured infrastructure as the availability of electric power (in kilowatt hours per dollar of GDP produced) and find that such infrastructure has a strongly positive influence on attracting investors. Japanese investors are more responsive to better availability of infrastructure. Similar, though statistically weaker, differences arise in the case of educational differences between countries. The variable that best distinguished countries in this regard was the primary school enrolment rate, which may be thought to reflect the "trainability" of the labor force. For U.S. investors, the coefficient on enrolment rate significant at the 10 percent level; for Japanese investors, the significance level is lower. The lack of statistical significance stems partly from the correlation between infrastructure and enrolment rates. Examining only the magnitudes of the coefficients, however, we find that Japanese investors are more sensitive to primary enrolment rates than U.S. investors are.

4.5. Persistence of investment

As noted in the introductory remarks, an important finding of the Wheeler and Mody (1992; also Ch. 4 this book) study was the strong persistence displayed by U.S. investors as reflected in the large and significant influence of the accumulated stock of foreign investment in the country on new investment. In the analysis here, the accumulated stock of foreign investment refers to invest-ment from all countries and in all sectors of the economy. As such, the variable measures the general attractiveness of the economy to foreign investors, over and above that implied by the directly measured variables in this analysis.

The finding is that both U.S. and Japanese investors are strongly con-ditioned by past investment in the country.[7] The coefficient values on past investment are somewhat higher for U.S. investors. While this difference is not large, recall that for other key variables—tax rates, infrastructure, and enrol-ment rates—Japanese investors showed greater sensitivity. Thus, U.S. investors display greater persistence, relying more on past investment as an indicator of investment possibilities and less on certain important country attributes.

4.6. Country risk

Country risk deters both groups of investors. Risk is much more influential in conditioning timing of Japanese investment within a country rather than in discriminating between countries. However, the effect of risk is clearly much greater on Japanese investors. Note that the coefficient on the country risk variable is about one for U.S. investors, but it is over two for Japanese inves-tors. Thus, Japanese investment is likely to be much more volatile than U.S. investment. This finding is once again consistent with the evidence above on the greater persistence of U.S. investors.[8]

5. Is there convergence over time?

Comparing the first half of the 1980s with the second, we see considerable stability in the determinants of U.S. investments (Table 3.4). This is consistent with the other evidence in this chapter, the generally greater persistence of U.S. investment, and the relatively low within-country variance. We do see some important changes in the determinants of foreign investment, especially in the influences on Japanese investment. These changes, the evidence suggests, moved U.S. and Japanese firms closer to each other in certain respects.

The Japanese firms showed a clear preference for East Asian locations throughout the 1980s, as reflected in the dummy variable for East Asia. Domestic market size was not an important consideration for Japanese

Table 3.4 Determinants of foreign investment: estimates from the random effects model (dependent variable: host country share of foreign investment outflow)

Variable	*United States*		*Japan*	
	1981–85	1986–90	1981–85	1986–90
Constant	−12.889	−4.570	−17.966	−7.949
Market size	1.419*(3.5)	0.073(0.2)	0.042(0.04)	1.171(1.3)
Cost of investment	−0.187(0.9)	0.592(0.2)	0.508(0.7)	−1.243**(1.6)
Corporate tax rate	−0.159(1.0)	−0.022(0.2)	0.114(0.3)	−0.041(0.1)
Cost of labor	−0.124(1.4)	−0.082**(1.7)	−0.144(0.7)	0.357(0.2)
Trade propensity	−0.499**(1.7)	−0.820*(3.7)	−0.193(0.3)	−0.066(0.1)
Stock of past FDI	0.604*(4.8)	0.457*(4.3)	0.516*(2.3)	1.246*(5.3)
Country risk	0.464*(2.1)	1.701*(5.4)	1.571*(2.5)	1.174(1.3)
Infrastructure	0.330*(2.8)	0.252*(2.5)	0.786*(3.0)	0.270(0.8)
Primary school enrolment ratio	1.996*(1.9)	−0.847(1.0)	5.274*(2.0)	0.633(0.3)
Latin America	0.042(0.2)	0.057(0.3)	0.230(0.7)	0.580**(1.8)
East Asia	0.273(1.2)	0.099(0.5)	1.215*(2.7)	1.668*(4.5)
Other high income	−0.305(1.5)	−0.444*(2.3)	−0.411(1.2)	0.361**(1.6)
Other middle income	−0.864*(2.8)	−0.727*(2.4)	−0.193(0.3)	0.248(0.5)
Other low income	0.091(0.3)	−1.063*(2.9)	−0.322(0.4)	0.248(0.7)
	Adj R^2 = 0.95	Adj R^2 = 0.98	Adj R^2 = 0.73	Adj R^2 = 0.69
	Hausman: Chi Sq(9) = 14.0	Hausman: Chi Sq(9) = 37.6	Hausman: Chi Sq(9) = 8.5	Hausman: Chi Sq(9) = 20.0
	N = 175	N = 171	N = 125	N = 122
	TMax = 5	TMax = 5	TMax = 5	TMax = 5
	TMin = 5	TMin = 3	TMin = 1	TMin = 1
	Number of countries = 35		Number of countries = 29	

* Indicates statistical significance at the 5 percent level.
** Indicates statistical significance at the 10 percent level.

investors in either the first half or the second half of the 1980s. An indication of convergence is the reduced U.S. investor interest in domestic market size in the second half of the 1980s. However, U.S. investors continued to move contrary to a country's trade intensity—if anything, this effect has increased over time. Japanese investors continued their somewhat ambiguous stance towards openness to foreign trade.

Notice that for Japanese investors the strong effect of past stock of foreign investment in the second half of the 1980s. As Japanese investment surged, investors strongly preferred locations that already had significant stocks of past investments; all other effects were consequently muted. The sensitivity to infrastructure fell for both groups of investors in the second half of the 1980s, but especially for the Japanese. The magnitudes of the coefficients in the second half of the 1980s consequently were closer to each other, but for the Japanese are not significant at conventional levels. For both groups of investors, the interest in primary school enrolment seems to have fallen sharply (suggesting possibly a greater interest in more highly qualified workers). Investors react quite sharply to country risk in the second half of the 1980s. For U.S. investors, we see an increase in the coefficient on the country risk measure (from 0.46 to 1.7); for Japanese investors, there was some decline in the country risk effect, and coefficient is no longer statistically significant, but the magnitude of the coefficient continues to be high. Thus, the lower overall sensitivity of U.S. firms to country risk reflects primarily a difference from the first half of the 1980s.

In sum, while differences in the investment determinants remained, reduced effects of market size on U.S. investments, greater responsiveness of U.S. investors to country risk, similar coefficient magnitudes on infrastructure, and reduced emphasis on primary education all suggest some movement towards similarity in response to country attributes. It is important to caution again, however, that since the Japanese investments during this period were clearly in a transitional stage, the evidence on convergence must await data covering a longer time span.

6. Conclusions

Some similarities exist in the factors that drive U.S. and Japanese investments, though the two groups of investors vary in the degree of responsiveness to specific factors. Low wage inflation attracts foreign investors, but is more of a consideration for the Japanese; the Japanese also appear to attach greater value to labor quality. Neither the costs of investment goods nor the corporate tax rates have a major influence on investment; the latter generally has the expected negative sign. A larger stock of (electricity) infrastructure attracts investors. High country risk discourages them.

There are also some contrasts. Japanese investors seek more trade-intensive economies, though doing so reflects their predilection for investment in East Asia. U.S. investors, by contrast, tend to changes in trade intensity. Viewed over the entire period, U.S. investment tends to be much more persistent, as reflected in the strength of past investment in determining new investment in a country. Again, from the perspective of the entire period, past investment is important also for Japanese investment, but the relationship is not as strong. Japanese investment is seen to be more sensitive to the other important influences (wage inflation, infrastructure, school enrolment, and country risk). Thus, Japanese investment was for at least the first half of the 1980s, and perhaps until 1988, characterized by greater fluidity, reflecting, perhaps, the more recent emergence of the Japanese as foreign investors. In the last few years of the decade, however, most influences were weakened and a strong preference was expressed for countries in East Asia and countries with large stocks of foreign investment. There is some suggestive evidence that during this period the determinants of investment for both groups of investors converged in certain respects.

Notes

1   The defenitions of country-groups are based on World Bank categories, defined in the annual *World Development Report*. See Appendix A.
2   Other relevant studies examine specific determinants of foreign investment flows; see, for example, Slemrod (1990) and Cummins and Hubbard (1995), who test the reaction of investment flows to host-country tax rates.
3   Although the country-specific component of the error term disappears, potentially, a new problem is created. The error term now is $\varepsilon_i - \frac{1}{n} \Sigma^n_{j=1} \varepsilon_j$. Subtraction of the mean of the white-noise term from its realization in period t, in effect, creates a series of error terms. Consistent estimation—"strict exogeneity"—now requires that each realization of this error term, in past and future periods, be uncorrelated with the regressors (see Keane and Runkle 1992). Future realizations can safely be assumed to be uncorrelated with the regressors (as is typically assumed), and even past realizations are unlikely to influence major host-country characteristics. Where plausible correlations do, in fact, exist, as in the case of perceived country risk, we discuss the implications.
4   The extent of such aggravation depends upon whether the measurement error changes over time. See Mairesse (1990).
5   Where the assumption holds, the OLS estimates are also consistent, though the standard errors are not.
6   Since the United States dominates the Japanese investment allocation, estimates also were obtained after dropping the United States as an observation. Those results, however, were quite similar and are not reported here.
7   For reasons outlined in footnote 3, the coefficient is actually biased downwards. Also, the estimates obtained are the result of two competing factors: the bias on account of the endogeneity and the correlation of the stock variable with other included variables (e.g., infrastructure). In the fixed-effect estimates, because the infrastructure variable virtually drops out, that correlation is not important. In the OLS and RE estimates, however, that correlation is important and reduces the effect of the past stock of FDI.
8   If past realizations of foreign investment share influence the estimate of the country risk measure, then an endogeneity will exist. This will result in a downward bias of the estimated coefficient for the country risk measure.

Appendix A: List of host countries for U.S. and Japanese investment

Country	Region	Data available for
Argentina	Latin America	U.S., Japan
Australia	Other high income	U.S., Japan
Austria	Other high income	U.S., Japan
Belgium	EEC	U.S., Japan
Brazil	Latin America	U.S., Japan
Canada	Other high income	U.S., Japan
Chile	Latin America	U.S., Japan
Colombia	Latin America	U.S., Japan
Denmark	EEC	U.S.
Ecuador	Latin America	U.S.
Egypt	Other low income	U.S.
France	EEC	U.S., Japan
Germany	EEC	U.S.
Greece	EEC	U.S., Japan
India	Other low income	U.S., Japan
Ireland	EEC	U.S., Japan
Italy	EEC	U.S., Japan
Japan	East Asia	U.S.
Korea	East Asia	U.S., Japan
Malaysia	East Asia	U.S., Japan
Mexico	Latin America	U.S., Japan
Netherlands	EEC	U.S., Japan
Nigeria	Other low income	U.S., Japan
Norway	Other high income	U.S., Japan
Panama	Latin America	U.S., Japan
Peru	Latin America	U.S., Japan
the Philippines	East Asia	U.S., Japan
Singapore	East Asia	U.S., Japan
Spain	EEC	U.S., Japan
Sweden	Other high income	U.S.
Thailand	East Asia	U.S., Japan
Trinidad	Other middle income	U.S.
Turkey	Other middle income	U.S., Japan
UK	EEC	U.S., Japan
USA	Other high income	Japan
Venezuela	Latin America	U.S., Japan

Appendix B: Data description and sources

1. Dependent variable

The dependent variable in all the regressions is the host country share of foreign investment outflow from the United States or Japan. In the case of the United States, foreign investment is measured as the capital expenditure of majority-owned affiliates in the host country. These data have been obtained from the Bureau of Economic Analysis, Department of Commerce. For Japan, we obtained data on actual flows (disbursements) of foreign investment from the Ministry of Finance and the Ministry for International Trade and Industry (MITI).

2. Independent variables

2.1. Market size

Per capita gross domestic product in constant dollars expressed in international prices. Summers and Heston (1993). Also see Summers and Heston (1991).

2.2. Cost of investment

We use the price deflator for investment in the host country to measure the cost of investment. The data have been obtained from the Penn World Tables (Summers and Heston 1991, 1993).

2.3. Corporate tax rate

Tax revenue collected as a share of gross domestic product is used as a measure of the corporate tax rate. To be consistent, data on both, tax revenue and GDP, were retrieved from the International Financial Statistics data base of the International Monetary Fund (IMF). The IFS data are published by the IMF on a monthly basis.

2.4. Cost of labor

Measured as earnings per employee in the manufacturing sector. Data on total worker earnings in the manufacturing sector and total number of employees, obtained from the United Nations Industrial Development Organization (UNIDO), have been used to calculate earnings per worker. Data in local currency units were converted to U.S. dollar units by using the average exchange rate tabulated by the International Financial Statistics, IMF.

2.5. Trade propensity

We use a measure of exports plus imports as a share of Gross Domestic Product to measure trade propensity. Data have been obtained from the Penn World Tables.

2.6. Stock of past FDI

Measured as the sum of all previous FDI in the host country irrespective of its origin (millions of U.S. dollars). Data have been obtained from the DEC analytical database of the World Bank. The DEC analytical database is a subset of the data compiled by the socio-economic data division of the International Economics Department at the Bank.

2.7. Country risk

Country risk is measured as a composite measure of economic, political, and social uncertainty in the host country. The index is compiled and published by Institutional Investor (II) in March and September each year and takes a value between 0 and 100 for each country, with higher values indicating lower risk.

2.8. Infrastructure

We use production/output of electricity per dollar gross domestic product as a measure of infrastructure availability. Data on the production of electricity are obtained from the *Year Book of Energy Statistics* published by the United Nations, while data on GDP are obtained from the Penn World Tables.

2.9. Primary school enrolment ratio

The ratio measures the gross enrolment of all ages at the primary level as a percentage of children in the country's primary school age group. The data have been obtained from the World Tables compiled by the World Bank.

References

Baltagi, B.D., and J.M. Griffin (1984) "Short and long run effects in pooled models," *International Economic Review* 25, 631–45.

Barrell, R., and N. Pain (1996) "An econometric analysis of U.S. foreign direct investment," *Review of Economics and Statistics* 78, 200–7.

Belderbos, R., and L. Sleuwaegen (1996) "Japanese firms and the decision to invest abroad: business groups and regional core networks," *Review of Economics and Statistics* 78, 214–20.

Caballero, R.J., and R.K. Lyons (1991) "Short and long run externalities," NBER Working Paper No. 3810, Cambridge, MA.

Cummins, J.G., and R.G. Hubbard (1995) "The tax sensitivity of foreign direct investment: evidence from firm-level panel data," In *The Effects of Taxation on Multinational Corporations*, ed. Martin Feldstein, James R. Hines, Jr, and R. Glenn Hubbard (Chicago: University of Chicago Press).

Eaton, J., and A. Tamura (1994) "Bilateralism and regionalism in Japanese and U.S. trade and direct foreign investment patterns," *Journal of the Japanese and International Economies* 8, 478–510.

Greene, W.H. (1993) *Econometric Analysis*, 2nd ed. (New York: Macmillan),

Hackett, S., and K. Srinivasan (1998) "Do supplier switching costs differ across Japanese and US multinational firms?" *Japan and the World Economy* 10, 13–32.

Hsiao, C. (1986) *Analysis of Panel Data* (Cambridge: Cambridge University Press).

Keane, M.P. (1996) "On the estimation of panel-data models with serial correlation when instruments are not strictly exogenous," *Journal of Business and Economic Statistics* 10, 1–9.

Keane, M.P., and M.P. Runkle (1992) "On the estimation of panel data models with serial correlation when instruments are not strictly exogenous," *Journal of Business and Economic Statistics* 10, 1–9.

Kinoshita, Y., and A. Mody (1997) "The usefulness of private and public information in foreign investment decisions," Policy and Research Working Paper 1733, World Bank, Washington, DC. Also (2001) "Private information for foreign investment in emerging economies," *Canadian Journal of Economies* 34(2), 448–464.

Kogut, B., and S.J. Chang (1996) "Platform investments and volatile exchange rates: direct investment in the U.S. by Japanese electronic companies," *Review of Economics and Statistics* 78, 221–31.

Kravis, I.B., and R.E. Lipsey (1992) "Sources of competitiveness of the U.S. and of its multinational firms," *Review of Economics and Statistics* 74, 193–201.

Lipsey, R.E. (1988) "Changing patterns of international investment in and by the United States," In *The United States in the World Economy*, ed. Martin Feldstein (Chicago: University of Chicago Press).

Maddala, G.S. (1983) *Limited Dependent and Qualitative Variables in Econometrics* (New York: Cambridge University Press).

Mairesse, J. (1990) "Time-series and cross-sectional estimates on panel data: Why are they different and why should they be equal?" In *Panel Data and Labor Market Studies*, ed. J. Hartog, G. Ridder, and J. Theeuwes (Amsterdam: North-Holland).

Raff, H., and K. Srinivasan (1998) "Tax incentives for import-substituting foreign investment: Does signaling play a role?" *Journal of Public Economics* 67, 167–93.

Scaperland, A., and R.S. Balough (1983) "Determinants of U.S. direct investment in the EEC," *European Economic Review* 21, 381–93.

Slemrod, J. (1990) "Tax effects on foreign direct investment in the United States: evidence from a cross-country comparison." In *Taxation in the Global Economy*, ed. Assaf Razin and Joel Slemrod (Cambridge, MA: National Bureau of Economic Research).

Srinivasan, K. (1993) "Three essays on foreign investment," unpublished Ph D thesis, Indiana University.

Summers, R., and A. Heston (1991) "Penn World Table (Mark 5): an expanded set of international comparisons, 1950–1988," *Quarterly Journal of Economics* 106, 327–68.

—— (1993) "Penn World Tables, Version 5.5," available on diskette from the National Bureau of Economic Research, Cambridge, MA.

United States Department of Commerce (1996) *Survey of Current Business* 76(12) (Washington, DC: Bureau of Economic Analysis).

Wheeler, D., and A. Mody (1992) "International investment location decisions: the case of US firms," *Journal of International Economics* 33, 57–76.

Young, I. (1995) "Companies ponder the end of investor protector," *Financial Times*, 15 September, 6–7.

4 Private information for foreign investment in emerging economies

With Yuko Kinoshita

[E]ither he should discover the truth about them for himself or learn it from some one else; or if this is impossible, he should take the best and most irrefragable of human theories and make it the raft on which he sails through life.

Plato

Introduction

Almost by definition, emerging market economies are characterized by limited information on business operating conditions and economic prospects. Under conditions of limited public information, private information can be extremely valuable and can lead, in turn, to correlation and/or persistence in investor behavior.[1] This chapter is motivated by the following empirical questions. Is privately acquired information important in the decision to undertake foreign investments in emerging market economies? If so, is the private information acquired mainly through direct experience, that is, through the firm's own investment in the country? Or is potential for economic returns inferred from actions undertaken by others who may have private information? What is the relationship between private information and publicly available information on a country? Finally, can correlated investment outcomes generated by private information be distinguished from those generated by industrial agglomerations or by strategic behavior of investors?

In this chapter, we use a specially designed data set to answer these questions. We find that a firm's investment decisions are positively correlated to its *own* previous investment in the country. We interpret this as a learning effect. Investment decisions are also correlated with current/planned investments by competitors, implying the possibility that the private information held by others signals investment potential. In addition, it is found that these two channels are primarily substitutes, that is, investment by competitors comes less important when the firm already has experience in the market. These findings support the idea that private information is valuable. In reaching this conclusion, we control for firm and country characteristics and also for industrial clustering effects. However, it is not possible to rule out alternative interpretations of the evidence. A firm expanding on its base may be benefiting from economies of scale and also from agglomeration economies. More difficult to distinguish is whether competitors' actions signal privately held information or stimulate a strategic response. The absence of differentiated effects across industrial sectors favors an informational interpretation. Strategic positioning, for example, should be more prominent in specific industrial sectors where a "first mover" advantage has a high payoff; however, no such differentiated response is found.

The setting for the empirical examination is investment by Japanese manufacturing firms in a number of key Asian countries in the early 1990s. To deal with scaled responses by firms, an ordered logit model is used to estimate the relationships. The stated likelihood of planned investments in a country is the dependent variable that is explained by whether the firm is already present in the country and by its perceptions of the likelihood of investments by competitors in that country. Since the results obtained may be consistent with alternative interpretations, we attempt to control for several other information sources and investment drivers that may influence the foreign investment decisions. Specifically, we control for firm, country, and industry characteristics. Firm dummies (or firm characteristics) are included in the estimated equation to determine if the "private information" merely reflects firm attributes. The influence of public information on investment decisions is dealt with by introducing country dummies, which are assumed to embody information available to all. Finally, dummies for industrial sectors (and their interactions with past presence, expectation of rivals' actions, and country dummies) seek to isolate the influence of industry-specific factors, including agglomeration effects.

The chapter is organized as follows. In the next section we review the literature, focusing on the sources of public and private information relevant for foreign direct investment decisions. This is followed by a description of the questions asked in the survey, the data, and the analysis methodology. We then present our benchmark model, which allows for the possibility of substitution or complementarity between the two sources of private information and controls for publicly available information through the use of country dummies. To help to distinguish the informational interpretation favored in this paper from agglomeration and strategic rivalry effects, we control for industry characteristics. Before concluding, we summarize several extensions (detailed in Kinoshita and Mody 1997) to highlight the robustness of the findings.

The literature and hypotheses

Physical agglomeration of foreign investment is commonly observed, as for example in the southeastern provinces of China and in northern Mexico close to the U.S. border. In studies of aggregate foreign investment flows the stock of existing investment has been found to have a significant influence on new investment into that area. For example, Wheeler and Mody (1992; also Ch. 2 this book) found that U.S. investments into a country were strongly conditioned by existing stocks of foreign investment in that country (after controlling for a variety of factors, including market size). Subsequent analysis showed that new Japanese investment was equally influenced by the stock of past investment (Mody and Srinivasan 1998; also Ch. 3 this book). The authors of these studies speculated that agglomeration benefits, relevant for industrial sectors relying heavily on intermediate inputs from suppliers in close proximity or those able to gain through labor or informational spillovers between firms, may drive the persistence.

Kogut and Chang (1996) used firm-level data for Japanese multinationals investing in the United States and found past presence to be an important predictor of new investments, consistent with the aggregate studies. However, the evidence has alternative interpretations. It may reflect agglomeration economies: firms in specific agglomerations may seek to grow as they experience the benefits of proximate location. Alternatively, the evidence can be interpreted as the consequence of a foreign investor's learning experience in a country. As greater familiarity with operating in the country is acquired, and the specific opportunities for expansion are revealed, more investment is committed.

Not only may firms rely on their own experience, but they may also be directed by the current/planned investments of their competitors. Where information on competitors' behavior is important, cascading of foreign investment may be observed. Persistence, punctuated by significant discontinuities, is commonly found for investments into specific countries. China has attracted a rush of investment not only from overseas Chinese but also from U.S., Japanese, and European investors, starting quite abruptly in the late 1980s and growing explosively into the mid-1990s. China receives about $40 billion a year of foreign investment despite cumbersome procedures and uncertainty surrounding property rights and contract enforceability; in contrast, India, even after rolling back restrictions and despite a longer tradition of a market economy, chalks up $3–4 billion a year. During the early 1990s there also was a discontinuity for Vietnam as competing investors staked out positions.

Such evidence of synchronized investment is consistent with two alternative hypotheses. Strategic rivalry may be inferred where firms are staking out positions to obtain early-mover advantages. However, where firms mainly "follow the leader," they are driven less by strategic concerns than by the interpretation that the leader's investment decisions indicate the potential for profitable operations in the targeted location. Knickerbocker (1973) examined the response by firms to the investment decisions of competitors. Supporting the strategic interpretation in that pioneering study, he showed that the more oligopolistic an industry, the greater was the likelihood that foreign investments would be concentrated into a short period of time and hence display spikes or discontinuities in foreign investment flows.

Head, Ries, and Swenson (1995) have shown that Japanese investors in the

United States tend to "follow the leader," affirming that decisions by other investors have a signaling value. Privately held information—or private beliefs—can have a significant impact on investment flows, even in the absence of a change in economic fundamentals, since a *perception* of change can drive a critical mass of investors, with a consequent snowballing effect. The "herd" behavior—actions based on others' actions—can be quite rational in as much as it economizes on the gathering of scarce information (see Scharfstein and Stein 1990; Bikhchandani, Hirshleifer, and Welch 1992; and Lee 1993 for models of information cascades, and Calvo and Mendoza 1998 for a model in the context of emerging markets). Arthur (1995) discusses several examples from economics and finance in which private beliefs play an important role. Kuran (1995) explains the persistence of certain social institutions as well as their abrupt breakdown on the basis of privately held but publicly concealed preferences.

Private information may be important, especially in the context of emerging economies, where investors seek information on a variety of operational conditions which are not publicly available, including the functioning of labor markets, industrial literacy of the workforce (as distinct from educational attainments), the practical implementation of foreign investment polices, and the timely availability of inputs. The importance of such information on operating conditions in a country is notably illustrated by General Motors' decision to locate its Asian hub in Thailand: "the fact that 11 car manufacturers already operate in Thailand was a sign that the country's infamous physical infrastructure and labor bottlenecks could be overcome" (Bardacke 1996). The General Motors' investment decision, however, could also be consistent with strategic positioning for growth in the Thai and Asian markets.[2]

Data and methodology

The survey questionnaire was mailed by the Japanese Ministry of International Trade and Industry (MITI) to several hundred Japanese firms, of which 173 returned usable responses in March 1993. The sample thus obtained cannot be treated as representative of all Japanese firms—we do not know the characteristics of firms who did not respond. There is, however, sufficient heterogeneity among the respondents to permit a statistical analysis of their foreign investment behavior. The firms in our sample are relatively large. The average annual sales are 330 billion yen (over $3 billion), the largest firm in the sample has sales of $70 billion and the smallest has sales of $2 million. This is also a set of firms that is prone to making significant foreign investments—in the three years prior to the survey, over a fifth of their investment was undertaken outside Japan.

Our dependent variable is based on the following question regarding the firm's expectation that it will invest in specific Asian countries: "In each of the following countries, how likely are you to invest in the next three years?"

Respondents were asked to check a space on a 1–7 scale provided, ranging from "very unlikely" to "very likely."

VERY   VERY
UNLIKELY   LIKELY

The question was answered for the following seven countries: China, Thailand, Malaysia, Indonesia, Vietnam, the Philippines, and India. These countries constitute the principal developing country recipients of foreign investment in Asia. Their level of economic development is substantially lower than the level in the so-called Asian Tigers—South Korea, Taiwan, Hong Kong, and Singapore—with Malaysia being the closest to the Tigers by most development measures. For each of the seven countries, we have 173 responses, potentially creating 1,211 (173 × 7) observations (however, since all respondents did not answer all questions, for certain estimations fewer usable observations are available and, where appropriate, we have tested for selection bias).

Our two key independent variables are PAST and RIVAL. The questionnaire asked whether the firm already had a presence in each of the seven countries being studied. For each firm and each country, the PAST variable was coded 1 if the firm was present in the country and 0 if it was not. Recall that we infer a learning effect if past presence leads to a high likelihood of future investment. The other key variable referred to the information obtained from competitors. The question asked was: "Are your competitors making investments in the following Asian countries?" Once again, the response allowed ranged on scale of 1 (very little) to 7 (very substantial).

The average value of the responses for the seven countries (and the standard deviations) are reported in Table 4.1. Respondents to our survey were most likely, by far, to invest in China, the average measure on the 1–7 scale for China being 4.08; the perceived level of rivals' interests in China was also high, second to Thailand. However, only 20 percent of the firms had existing investments in China, limiting the influence of past experience. Following China, four countries had similar likelihoods of investment: Thailand, Malaysia, Indonesia, and Vietnam. Of these, Malaysia and Thailand have traditionally attracted substantial Japanese interest, with 25 and 30 percent of firms, respectively, reporting existing presence in those countries; and rivals were also reported to be strongly interested. In contrast, Vietnam had a low existing Japanese presence and also a relatively low level of interest from rivals. The least attractive sites were the Philippines and India, with low expected investment, low initial presence, and low rivals' activity. Thus, a simple comparison across countries indicated a positive correlation between expected investment by the firm and its perception of the strength of rivals' interest in the country. Since past presence is indicated only in 15 percent of the possibilities, information provided by behavior of rivals was likely to be valuable where the firm was entering new countries.

Table 4.1 Firm characteristics by sector and future investment plans

	Past presence (Yes = 1, No = 0)	Rivals' activity (Scale: 1–7)	Automobiles	Building materials	Chemicals	Food	Electrical equipment	Non-electrical equipment	Light manufacture[a]	All
Number of firms			22	20	33	14	27	34	23	173
Average size of firms (billion yen)			3623	2870	2940	494	9820	767	1649	3289
R&D/sales (%)			3.05	2.72	3.63	3.64	4.08	3.13	2.56	3.32
Exports/sales			0.13	0.04	0.09	0.15	0.30	0.12	0.03	0.13
Future investment plans (Scale: 1–7)										
China	0.20	3.67	3.18	3.79	4.60	5.21	4.38	3.53	4.25	4.08
India	0.03	1.94	1.59	2.37	1.55	1.58	2.54	1.26	1.32	1.72
Indonesia	0.18	3.31	2.24	3.39	3.59	2.77	3.20	2.16	2.53	2.84
Malaysia	0.25	3.53	2.50	2.89	3.37	3.00	3.70	2.22	2.37	2.85
The Philippines	0.06	2.54	2.14	2.06	2.07	2.17	2.50	1.61	1.74	2.02
Thailand	0.30	4.10	2.52	3.33	3.40	3.46	4.04	2.71	2.68	3.16
Vietnam	0.01	1.92	1.91	3.60	2.67	2.46	2.75	1.81	2.89	2.53
All	0.15	3.02	2.30	3.07	3.04	3.00	3.32	2.19	2.55	2.75

a Light manufacture contains garments, electronics and other light manufactured products.

An ordered logit model was used to investigate these relationships more precisely. The ordered logit is an extension of the binomial logit and deals with situations where there exist multiple ordered choices (see Greene 1993). For the purpose of the regression, the likelihood of investment (LFDI) variable was rescaled to create three ordered choices. As illustrated above, the original data is on a scale of 1 through 7. The three rescaled categories are: 2 (highly likely to invest where the response was 6 or 7), 1 (moderately likely, where the response was 3, 4, or 5), and 0 (unlikely to invest, where the response was 1 or 2). As in the binomial logit model, we assume a latent regression model of the following form:

$$y^* = \beta x + \varepsilon. \tag{1}$$

A vector of variables, x, which includes PAST and RIVAL, and the vector of coefficients, β, determine a latent variable, y^*. Though y^* is not observed, the response indicating the likelihood of investment is observed. The observed responses are related to the latent variable in the following manner:

$$y = 0 \text{ if } y^* < 0$$
$$y = 1 \text{ if } 0 < y^* \leq \mu$$
$$y = 2 \text{ if } \mu \leq y^*. \tag{2}$$

Then, for the logistic cumulative distribution function, λ, the model predicts the following probabilities for each of the responses:

$$\text{Prob}(y = 0) = \lambda(-\beta x)$$
$$\text{Prob}(y = 1) = \lambda(\mu - \beta x) - \lambda(-\beta x)$$
$$\text{Prob}(y = 2) = 1 - \lambda(\mu - \beta x). \tag{3}$$

The joint probability or likelihood function is:

$$L = \prod_{i=1}^{n} [\text{Prob}(Y_i = 0)]^{d_{i0}} [\text{Prob}(Y_i = 1)]^{d_{i1}} [\text{Prob}(Y_i = 2)]^{d_{i2}}. \tag{4}$$

where d_{ik} ($k = 0,1,2$) is an indicator function equal to 1 if $y_i = k$ and zero otherwise. The number of observations is n, where the observational unit is a firm's investment plans for each country, implying up to seven observations per firm. The parameters, β and μ, are estimated by maximizing the log of the likelihood function.

The value of private and public information: the benchmark model

In the benchmark model, we regress the firm's likelihood of investing in a particular country on its past presence (or absence) in that country (PAST), perceptions about competitors' interest in that country (RIVAL), the inter-action between PAST and RIVAL, firm and country dummies (Table 4.2, column 4). Both the firm's past presence and its perception of competitors' behavior have a strong influence on its plans to invest in a country. The inclusion of the PAST*RIVAL variable improves the log-likelihood and from the likelihood ratio test we can conclude (at the 2.5 percent significance level)

Table 4.2 The base model: value of private information

	Dependent variable: LFDI (likelihood of FDI)			
	[1]	[2]	[3]	[4]
Intercept	−3.29***	−3.46***	−7.32***	−7.59***
	(0.17)	(0.18)	(0.49)	(0.57)
Past	1.55***	2.79***	3.11***	3.46***
	(0.21)	(0.46)	(0.64)	(0.69)
Rival	0.37***	0.42***	0.61***	0.56***
	(0.03)	(0.04)	(0.06)	(0.07)
Past*rival	–	−0.27***	−0.29**	−0.29**
		(0.09)	(0.12)	(0.13)
μ	1.54	1.55	2.25	2.65
Firm dummies	no	no	yes	yes
Country dummies	no	no	no	yes
China	–	–	–	1.52***
				(0.35)
India	–	–	–	−2.03***
				(0.40)
Indonesia	–	–	–	−0.25
				(0.34)
Malaysia	–	–	–	−1.03***
				(0.38)
The Philippines	–	–	–	−1.64***
				(0.37)
Thailand	–	–	–	−0.79**
				(0.38)
n	875	875	875	875
log likelihood	−686.74	−682.30	−494.30	−430.66

Notes
*** and ** indicate 1 percent and 5 percent significance level, respectively.
Figures in parentheses are standard errors. μ is the second intercept defining the threshold for the transition from LFDI equal to 1 to 2.

that the interaction term belongs to the model. The negative sign on the interaction term (PAST*RIVAL) indicates that the two channels of private information are primarily substitutes for each other.

Inclusion of firm dummies is possible because we have multiple observations on each firm (with a maximum of seven observations where a likelihood was reported for each country). If firm j's unobserved characteristics (h_j), which are part of the composite error term ($e_{ij} = h_j + g_{ij}$), are correlated with PAST and RIVAL, then the coefficients will be biased. By adding firm dummies to the regression, the unobserved served characteristics become part of the set of regressors and the error term now has only the white-noise component, g_{ij}.[3] The results show that adding the firm dummies improves the statistical fit in standard ways (Table 4.2, column 3).

The country dummies capture, in summary form, the relative attractiveness of the different countries. An alternative specification would include specific country features, such as infrastructure, market size, and labor costs. As Head, Ries, and Swenson (1995) have argued, a full elaboration of country characteristics is difficult, and hence a country dummy, which reflects the country's attractiveness to the "average" investor, is preferred in this situation. In the final section of the paper, we do examine the effects of specific country features. The regression leaves out Vietnam, which is consequently the reference against which the attractiveness of other countries is measured.

The robustness of the PAST and RIVAL effects is evident. However, these effects are complemented by publicly available information: widely held perceptions of a country's potential, as summarized by the dummy variable representing the country, are influential in driving investment flows. The significantly improved log-likelihood indicates that important information is contained in these country dummies. With Vietnam as the reference, investors, on average, express a strong preference for China. The Indonesian coefficient is not significantly different from that of Vietnam. Malaysia and Thailand come next in the country dummy rankings. Thus, the surveyed Japanese firms indicated a shift from their previously favored destinations, Malaysia and Thailand, to China, Indonesia, and Vietnam, countries with lower wage labor and potentially large domestic markets. Agglomeration diseconomies in Malaysia and Thailand reflected, for example, in high land prices, could also be factors inducing the shift.[4] However, note from Table 4.1 that despite the shift in general sentiment, the average likelihood of investment in Malaysia and Thailand continues to be high because the sample firms with presence in the two countries remain committed to further investments, and also because perception of relatively high competitor interest further drives investment into the two countries. The countries lowest on the preference list are the Philippines and India, where past presence, competitor interest, and a perception of untapped country potential all are at low levels.

Basing our calculations on Greene (1993, 675–6), we compare the model's predictions with the actual stated likelihood of foreign investment. The model correctly predicts 78 percent of the firms' investment plans (Table 4.3,

Table 4.3 Model predictions: "hits and misses"

A: Model: lfdi = f(past, rival, past*rival, and firm dummies)

	Predicted			
	Very likely	Likely	Unlikely	Total
Observed				
Very likely	81 (0.57)	47	15	143
Likely	24	105 (0.54)	65	194
Unlikely	6	54	478 (0.89)	538
Total	111	206	558	875 (0.76)

B: Model: lfdi = f(past, rival), past*rival, firm dummies, and country dummies)

	Predicted			
	Very likely	Likely	Unlikely	Total
Observed				
Very likely	89 (0.62)	46	8	143
Likely	29	107 (0.55)	58	194
Unlikely	4	51	483 (0.90)	538
Total	122	204	549	875 (0.78)

Notes
In parentheses are the percentage of observations that are correctly predicted. For example, in Panel A, 81 out of 143 (57 percent) reported "very likely" observations are correctly predicted. Also in Panel A, (81 + 105 + 478) out of 875 or 76 percent of all observations are correctly predicted.

panel B). The "very unlikely" declarations are almost fully predicted. In the "likely" category the prediction rate is about 55 percent. The addition of country dummies especially improves the prediction rate for the "very likely" category. The model's predictive power of about three-fifths in the "likely" and "very likely" categories (as against 90 percent in the "very unlikely" category) indicates that a number of firms with PAST and RIVAL equal to zero have aggressive foreign investment plans—possibly, high production costs in Japan have the general effect of pushing firms to seek lower cost production locations.

How important are agglomeration and strategic effects?

In our discussion above, we have implied that the variables PAST and RIVAL represent information flows that influence the decisions of foreign investors. However, both these variables have alternative interpretations. If particular industrial sectors within a country are favored on account of agglomeration benefits, then a firm's past investment in that country may reflect the agglomeration potential; moreover, new investments would result from the validation of that potential. Private information, proxied by past investment, in that case would be collinear with agglomeration benefits. Similarly, the variable RIVAL may be collinear with strategic reactions to the actions of competitors.

In this section we examine if the alternative interpretations can be empirically distinguished. We do so by controlling for the industrial sectors of the firms in our sample. First, we control simultaneously for country and industry effects to allow for the possibility that firms within an industrial sector in a particular country act differently from firms in other sectors investing in that country.[5] If these sectoral differences are important, then their omission could be responsible for incorrectly attributing significance to the PAST and RIVAL variables. Second, we interact PAST and RIVAL with industry dummies to test if these effects are especially pronounced for particular sectors. Specifically, if the influences of the PAST or RIVAL are associated with certain sectors, then, respectively, the agglomeration and strategic rivalry effects are likely to be important. The benefits of agglomeration apply where firms value co-location with producers of high-quality intermediate inputs or if they rely on knowledge spillovers from similar firms (through, for example, high labor turnover). Strategic effects are important, as noted by Knickerbocker (1973), in oligopolistic sectors where the advantage gained from preemptive positioning is significant. In such sectors, a first mover advantage can be significant if, for example, brand-name recognition creates customer loyalty. Note, however, that these tests are suggestive rather than conclusive. To appropriately test for agglomeration economies, we would need to know the extent of investment by all other firms in the same industrial sector in the same location (rather than only the firms in our sample). Moreover, our sectoral characterization may be too broad: agglomeration and strategic effects may well operate in more finely defined sectors.

The first column in Table 4.4 shows the basic model with only the industry dummies, which are reported, and the second column includes also the country dummies, which are not reported.[6] In either case, the PAST, RIVAL, and the PAST*RIVAL variables remain highly significant, as before. The industry that was used as the base was garments and footwear (and other light manufacturing firms that could not be elsewhere classified). Relative to this base, industrial sectors that expect similar levels of foreign investment are building materials, chemicals, and food. Sectors for which the industry coefficient is negative and significantly different from zero (and that therefore have a lower

Table 4.4 Industry effects on investment plans

	Dependent variable: LFDI (likelihood of foreign investment)				
	[1]	[2]	[3]	[4]	[5]
Intercept	-3.16***	-2.79***	-2.77***	-2.73***	-2.82***
	(0.36)	(0.31)	(0.58)	(0.32)	(0.44)
Past	2.82***	2.94***	2.92***	2.41***	2.94***
	(0.47)	(0.48)	(0.50)	(0.89)	(0.49)
Rival	0.44***	0.42***	0.44***	0.43***	0.42***
	(0.04)	(0.04)	(0.04)	(0.04)	(0.11)
Past*rival	-0.26***	-0.27***	-0.28***	-0.29***	-0.29***
	(0.09)	(0.09)	(0.10)	(0.10)	(0.09)
Industrial sectors				Industry dummy* past	Industry dummy* rival
Automobile	-0.66**	-0.69**	-1.47*	1.15	0.35**
	(0.32)	(0.28)	(0.89)	(0.91)	(0.17)
Building materials	0.25	0.26	0.86	-0.18	-0.17
	(0.30)	(0.31)	(0.74)	(1.02)	(0.15)
Chemical	-0.29	-0.24	-0.17	1.28	0.02
	(0.27)	(0.28)	(0.70)	(0.84)	(0.13)
Food	-0.13	-0.14	-0.27	0.23	0.06
	(0.33)	(0.34)	(0.79)	(1.08)	(0.16)
Electrical equipment	-0.52*	-0.49	-0.78	-0.07	-0.13
	(0.29)	(0.31)	(0.77)	(0.84)	(0.14)
Non-electrical equipment	-0.81***	-0.85***	-1.12	0.73	0.03
	(0.27)	(0.29)	(0.73)	(0.86)	(0.14)
μ	1.58	1.69	1.73	1.70	1.71
Industry dummies	No	Reported above	Reported above	Yes	Yes
Country dummies	No	Yes	Yes	Yes	Yes
Country/industry interactions	No	No	Yes	No	No
n	875	875	875	875	875
Log likelihood	-671.30	-634.69	-622.55	-630.56	-627.52

Notes

Parentheses are standard errors.***, **, and * indicate 1 percent, 5 percent, and 10 percent significance level, respectively.

μ is the second intercept defining the threshold for the transition from LFDI equal to 1 to 2.

For industry dummies, light manufacture was used as base.

For country dummies, Vietnam was used as the base.

propensity for foreign investment than the base) include electrical equipment, non-electrical equipment, and automobiles and auto parts. The significant differences in industry dummy coefficients could imply either the existence of agglomeration economies in specific host locations or rising costs of production in Japan for those sectors. However, while agglomeration economies possibly exist, PAST is not a proxy for agglomeration, since the effect of past presence remains an additional and important investment driver.

Industry dummies are also interacted with country dummies (column 3). The estimates continue to show that past investment has an effect that is independent of any agglomeration benefits: after the introduction of country and industry interactions, the coefficient on past investment remains positive and highly significant. Similarly, the coefficients on the RIVAL variable and the PAST*RIVAL retain their signs and statistical significance. Also, the country and industry interactions are not statistically significant.[7]

Table 4.4 also reports the interactions between PAST and industry dummies (column 4) and between RIVAL and industry dummies (column 5).[8] Once again, the variables of interest to us, PAST, RIVAL, and PAST*RIVAL, remain highly significant, and, moreover, the interactions, with one exception, are not significant. These results, therefore, imply that PAST investment is not associated with any specific industry characteristic. Since, as discussed above, agglomeration effects are likely to be more pronounced for some industrial sectors than others, we infer that past presence is important in and of itself and is, therefore, a plausible proxy for learning about operating conditions in the economy. Similarly, the value of observing competitors is also independent of the sector, with automobiles and auto parts being the exception. Note that Japanese auto firms have a low propensity to invest relative to other sectors; however, those who do invest appear driven by strategic concerns.

Robustness tests

To test the robustness of the findings, several extensions were examined. To conserve space, only the main results are reported here (details are available in the working paper version of this paper, Kinoshita and Mody 1997). Replacing firm dummies with specific firm characteristics left our principal results unchanged. Larger firms have higher expected foreign investment. R&D has only a weak positive relationship to expected investment; since R&D and size are correlated, once size is taken into account, any independent influence of R&D is not discernible. Finally, firms with a high likelihood of investment in Asia have a low export propensity (for further discussion, see Mody, Dasgupta, and Sinha 1999).

Instead of using country dummies in a pooled regression, we also ran regressions for individual countries. Again, while the basic results remain unchanged, some interesting country variations are worth highlighting. For India, the Philippines, and Vietnam, where the PAST variable is not statistically significant, the extent of past presence is also very small, limiting the statistical predictive power of that coefficient. For Vietnam, the coefficient on RIVAL is very large, suggesting that firms are very sensitive to perceived actions of rivals, hence the possibility of a cascading effect. Though the effect is smaller, a similar force may well be operative for India. At the other extreme, in Malaysia, where significant past presence exists, the effect of RIVAL is negligible for those who are already operating in that country (PAST = 1); however, even in Malaysia, new entrants are significantly guided by the actions of rivals. In this respect, Thailand is different from Malaysia: though a significant past presence exists there, existing investors in Thailand also appear influenced by the behavior of their rivals.

Finally, instead of country dummies, we explored how perception of specific country characteristics—market size, labor costs, and foreign direct investment (FDI) policy—influenced the likelihood of investment.[9] Perceptions of large market potential and low labor costs tend to increase the attractiveness of countries. FDI policy was explained to respondents to include elements such as the ability to repatriate earnings, restrictions on foreign ownership, and the requirements to export and source inputs locally. Perceptions of FDI policy are strongly influential in conditioning future plans to invest in a country. The coefficient on FDI policy is positive and significant at the 5 percent level. However, since the coefficients on PAST and RIVAL also remain positive and significant at the 1 percent level, the evidence seems to suggest that FDI policy is information additional to that obtained by from past investment experience and actions of competitors. Perceptions of FDI policy interact in interesting with ways with PAST and RIVAL. The coefficient on the interaction term, FDIplcy*past, is negative. When PAST is equal to 1—that is, when the firm has a past presence in that country—the effect of FDI policy is more than wiped out. In other words, perceptions of FDI policy matter little when the firm has first-hand operational experience in the country. The corollary is that perceptions of good FDI policy are especially important in attracting new investors.

Conclusions and discussion

Using a firm-level data set, we explored the empirical importance of privately held information in foreign investment location decisions. Though the limitations of a one-time survey did not permit us follow an information "cascade" over successive generations, the value of private information, which is central to the cascade phenomenon was consistently evident.

The data permitted us, moreover, to distinguish between information obtained through direct experience in the host country and information inferred from observing competitors. Direct experience is seen to provide the more credible information, as may be expected. However, in the early phases of investing in a new country when few firms have experience in the country, the actions of competitors are likely to dominate, leading to an apparent herd behavior. Such was apparently the case for China and Vietnam, which attracted new investors in the early 1990s. In contrast, countries, such as India and the Philippines, that did not draw the attention of a critical mass of investors are in danger of being bypassed for significant periods of time.

We also found privately held information was complementary to publicly available information. Thus, while firms from "average" perceptions about countries, leading all of them to view particular locations favorably, considerable variation in investment plans exists around these averages; an important element of such variation is explained by privately held information. Industry agglomeration effects were not found to be significant, though, as noted, they could not be eliminated conclusively.

For policy makers, these findings represent a challenge. A generally favorable view of the country based on its fundamentals as well as perceptions of good policy and low labor costs lead to increased foreign investment. However, creating the right conditions for investors to directly experience the rigors of operating in a country is empirically important, as is the opportunity to observe competitors. This raises the controversial issue of special zones for foreign investors. While successful in many instances, especially in East Asia, they have also been a waste of scarce investment resources where not appropriately planned. An emerging approach is for the government to take the lead in creating the policy conditions for the creation of such zones but allow private investors to undertake the necessary investments, thus ensuring greater efficiency. Mexico offers an example. Under the *maquiladora* program, the policy environment has been created to attract foreign investors. Several private initiatives have resulted in so-called shelters that provide early hand-holding services to new foreign investors.

Notes

1 Bikhchandani and Sharma (2000) note that "informational cascades" and "reputational herding" are especially likely to occur in emerging markets where the environment is relatively "opaque" and "information is costly" on account of weak reporting requirements, lower accounting standards and/or lax enforcement of regulations. Calvo and Mendoza (1998) propose a model in which fixed costs of acquiring information lead to investors specializing in a few emerging markets while relying on other investors with respect to investment decisions in other emerging markets.

2 A perceived "first mover" advantage has contributed to the rush of motorcycle investors to Vietnam. Referring to the interest in Vietnam, a German investor thus summarized his firm's interests: "We simply cannot sit back and let the Japanese take over another market unchallenged" (*Financial Times*, 28 March 1995).

3 Introduction of the firm dummies strengthens the result both in the size of the coefficients and statistical significance. The increased coefficient sizes on the PAST and RIVAL variables suggests that the composite error term is negatively correlated with these variables: in other words, those who have past presence or perceive active rivals are generally more conservative in reporting their investment likelihood.

4 After the crisis in July 1997, foreign investment in Thailand experienced a surge following a sharp decline in land prices and depreciation of the exchange rate.

5   We are not able to control for industry *and* firm characteristics at the same time, since firms within an industrial sector tend to have similar investment plans, such that when firm dummies are included, the standard errors on the industry dummies tend to be very large. This also implies that firm-level dummies are proxying for the same information as industry-level dummies. As such, when we drop the firm-level dummies and include instead the industry-level dummies, we can expect the basic results to remain the same.

6   Inclusion of industry dummies does not change the relative rankings of the country dummies. However, the extent of country differentials changes since, for example, firms in industrial sectors with a high propensity to invest are especially likely to invest in China.

7   As noted above, stocks of foreign investment by industrial sector are not available. However, the United Nations Conference for Trade and Development (UNCTAD) does provide estimates of a country's entire stock of foreign investment. We interacted the country's average stock of foreign direct investment in the years 1990–92 with the industry dummies. If foreign investment into a country is attracted by specific industry characteristics, then past and new investments may primarily reflect those attractions, in which case the past and rival variables should have no independent effects. However, as is the case with the industry and country interactions, the introduction of the stock of foreign direct investment and industry interactions does not change the key results.

8   The industry dummies are not reported here, since the relative rankings do not change.

9   These country characteristics were coded on a 1–10 scale by firms, with 10 representing the most favorable.

References

Arthur, Brian (1995) "Complexity in economic and financial markets," in *Complexity* (New York: John Wiley).

Bardacke, Ted (1996) "General Motors" Thai hub will boost drive into Asia," *Financial Times*, 31 May.

Bikhchandani, S., and S. Sharma (2000) "Herd behavior in financial markets: a review," International Monetary Fund Working Paper 2000–56, 1–39.

Bikhchandani, S., D. Hirshleifer, and I. Welch (1992) "A theory of fads, fashion, custom, and cultural change as informational cascades," *Journal of Political Economy* 100, 922–1026.

Calvo, Guillermo, and Enrique Mendoza (1998) "Rational herd behavior and globalization of securities markets," mimeo, University of Maryland.

Greene, William (1993) *Econometric Analysis*, 2nd ed. (Englewood Cliffs, NJ: Prentice-Hall.

Head, Keith, John Ries, and Deborah Swenson (1995) "Agglomeration benefits and location choice: evidence from Japanese manufacturing investments in the United States," *Journal of International Economics* 38, 223–47.

Kinoshita, Yuko, and Ashoka Mody (1997) "The usefulness of private and public information in foreign investment decisions," Policy Research Paper 1733, World Bank, Washington D.C. Also (2001) "Private information for foreign investment in emerging economies," *Canadian Journal of Economics* 34(2), 448–464.

Knickerbocker, Fredrick T. (1973) *Oligopolistic Reaction and Multinational Enterprise* (Boston: Harvard University, Graduate School of Business Administration).

Kogut, Bruce, and Sea Jin Chang (1996) 'Platform investments and volatile exchange rates: direct investment in the U.S. by Japanese electronic companies," *Review of Economics and Statistics* 78, 221–31.

Kuran, Timur (1995) *Private Truths, Public Lies: The Social Consequences of Preference Falsification* (Cambridge, MA: Harvard University Press).

Lee, I. H. (1993) "On the convergence of informational cascades," *Journal of Economic Theory* (December) 395–411.

Mody, Ashoka, and Krishna Srinivasan (1998) "Japanese and United States firms as foreign investors: do they march to the same tune?" *Canadian Journal of Economics* 31, 778–99.

Mody, Ashoka, Susmita Dasgupta, and Sarbajit Sinha (1999) "Japanese multinationals in Asia: drivers and attractors," *Oxford Development Studies* 27, 149–64.

Scharfstein, D., and Jeremy Stein (1990) "Herd behaviour and investment," *American Economic Review* 80, 465–79.

United Nations Conference on Trade and Development (Various years) *World Investment Report* (Geneva).

Wheeler, David, and Ashoka Mody (1992) "International investment location decisions: the case of US firms," *Journal of International Economics* 33, 57–76.

5 The global disconnect

The role of transactional distance and scale economies in gravity equations

With Prakash Loungani and Assaf Razin

1. Introduction

The nations of the world remain stubbornly apart. Physical separation acts as natural barrier, restricting trade and asset flow linkages across nations. Despite apparent globalization, the constraints due to distance have remained significant. Thus, at a time when globalization is taken for granted—and policy makers and others debate the pros and cons of the associated changes—it is not obvious that the nations of the world are truly coming closer together.

In this chapter, we estimate gravity models for trade and foreign direct investment (FDI) flows to explore if comparisons of the two sets of estimates can clarify the role of distance and, hence, the nature of global linkages. Gravity models postulate that bilateral international transactions are positively related to the size of two economies and negatively to the distance between them. A selective literature review suggests that, though they are widely used as empirical benchmarks, coefficients in the gravity equation vary widely and, moreover, do not have straightforward interpretations. In particular, the large fall off observed in trade and investment flows with increasing physical distance remains a puzzle.

Evidence of the global disconnect comes in two forms. First, nations trade in goods and assets to a smaller extent than would be warranted by the gains from increased specialization and possibilities of risk diversification. In a recent contribution Obstfeld and Rogoff (2000) discuss the various disconnections, more commonly referred to as "puzzles." The puzzles are especially troubling in relation to asset flows since national borders should have little or no bearing on investments in financial assets. Thus, the continued persistence of the "home bias" in equity investment (disproportionately high investment by residents in domestic assets) and of the Feldstein-Horioka puzzle (the high correlation between domestic savings and domestic investment) are among the important stylized facts that reflect the limits to international transactions in financial assets. The second set of evidence shows that the international transactions that do occur, both in goods and financial assets, are strongly conditioned by the physical distance between countries. It is this latter evidence—based on so-called "gravity" models—that is the focus of this chapter.

But why exactly does distance matter? Most obviously, greater distance can be thought of as a proxy for higher transportation costs. If distance is truly a good proxy for transport costs, then it has a special attraction. Obstfeld and Rogoff (2000) have proposed that transportation costs may, in fact, be relevant not only for trade but also for the constraints in international asset transactions. This line of reasoning could explain the finding that distance appears with a negative and highly significant sign in gravity equations for FDI and for financial assets.

However, there are at least two problems in identifying distance with transport costs. First, Grossman (1998) has argued that for plausible values of transport costs, the distance coefficient in trade equations should be much smaller in magnitude than the typically estimated coefficient. Second, various theoretical models predict that distance should actually appear with a positive sign in asset flow equations. Thus, FDI from a source country may increase with distance if high transport costs make it expensive to export to the host country destination (Brainard 1997). For financial assets, greater distance between source and host country should be associated with reduced correlation of business cycles and hence, through greater possibilities for diversification, to more equity flows (Portes and Rey 2000).

Thus, some authors have pursued the notion that distance captures more than transport costs. More specifically, Rauch (1999) suggests larger distance may be associated with greater information and search costs. Similarly, Eichengreen and Irwin (1998) suggest that trading partners build long-term relationships that embody significant informational capital. When they proxy for such information capital through the addition of the lagged dependent variable as an additional regressor, the distance coefficient—and hence the short-run distance elasticity of trade—drops sharply. However, as we discuss, some have argued that this resolution of the distance elasticity is far from satisfactory. Finally, Portes and Rey (2000) and Portes, Rey, and Oh (2001) deal with the possibility of information ease by adding bilateral telephone traffic as a regressor in the gravity equation for financial asset transactions. They find that ease of information flows is important for those categories of financial assets that are the least standardized or where private information has high value. Once again, the coefficient for physical distance falls when explicit account is taken of ease of communication.

In this chapter, we pursue two sources of the global disconnect: "transactional distance" and "scale economies." Obstfeld and Rogoff (2000) suggest the concept of "transactional distance," which could be thought of as a hedonic measure of physical and informational distance, a more inclusive measure of the costs of undertaking transactions. From a theoretical viewpoint it is this multifaceted transactional distance that creates frictions in goods and asset markets. The possibility that "distance" may be lowered through reducing the barriers to informational flows creates optimism for countries that are located at large distances from the main trading and financial centers.

However, the possibility also exists that information networks are associated with significant scale economies on account of network externalities. Transactional scale economies could thus reinforce agglomeration economies due to proximity or due to paucity of private information (as discussed in Kinoshita and Mody 2001; also Ch. 4 this book) and thus enhance trade and investment flows between select (typically the richer) locations by reducing the costs of intra-industry trade generated through such forces as preference for variety in consumption, specialization in the production of intermediate inputs, and monopolistic competition.

This chapter has two additional sections. We begin with selective review of the "distance puzzle": how does the literature interpret the distance measure and the estimated distance elasticities; how have past efforts incorporated informational distance in gravity models; and what insights do we gain from comparisons across trade and asset gravity models? We then present some new results for trade and FDI gravity equations to assess the importance of information links, consider the endogeneity of such links, and finally discuss the interactions between physical distance and informational infrastructure in driving trade and investment flows.

2. The "distance puzzle"

The gravity equation postulates a positive relationship between trade (or investment flows) and the sizes of the host country and source countries and a negative relationship with physical distance between the host and source countries. Size proxies, or scale variables, typically include two of the following three: GDP, population, and per capita GDP. While GDP measures the economic size, there is a theoretical basis for also including per capita income since whether a country is rich or poor may make a difference to its trading and international investment patterns.

As noted above, both trade in goods and services and trade in assets have been found in earlier studies to be strongly negatively correlated with distance, more so than is predicted merely by a consideration of transport costs. This suggests that distance is likely proxying for both transportation and transactions/information costs associated with trade and that further tests are needed to sort out the relative importance of each. This section describes some attempts that have been made in the literature to analyze the implications of distance barriers. Our bottom-line conclusion is that while a number of interesting hypotheses have been advanced and tested in the literature, we are still far away from a convincing explanation for why distance matters.

2.1 Trade in goods and services

Gravity models have described bilateral trade flows empirically for four decades now. Until fairly recently, distance was taken as a proxy for transportation costs. In all studies, distance enters the bilateral trade equation with a negative sign and with a magnitude in the range of −1.5 to −0.8. It is almost always statistically significant despite the inclusion of a multitude of other independent variables. Grossman (1998, p. 31) notes that while the sign on the distance coefficient is plausible, the magnitude is not. He presents an illustrative calculation suggesting that if shipping costs are of the order of 5 percent of the value of traded goods, then the distance elasticity should be around −0.03 rather than the much higher values reported in the empirical work.

Eichengreen and Irwin (1998) argue that historical factors are an important omitted variable in many gravity models and that including a lagged dependent variable is a way of capturing such factors. When a lagged dependent variable is included, the estimated (short run) distance elasticity drops in magnitude, and is in some instances close to about −0.10. However, this resolution of the "distance puzzle" appears far from satisfactory. First, as noted by Lawrence (1988, p. 58), "the appearance of lagged dependent variables with large coefficients can be rationalized as lagged adjustment, but it may also indicate serious mis-specification." For example, it could be that what is really missing from the gravity model is lagged values of the independent variables. While inclusion of a lagged dependent variable may be thought of as a parsimonious way of including the other lagged independent variables, it imposes the timing of adjustment to all independent variables to be the same; this may be implausible. Second, while inclusion of a lagged dependent variable lowers the estimate of the short run distance elasticity, the estimate of the long-run elasticity still remains quite large.

Anderson and Wincoop (2001) propose that estimating a more theoretically grounded gravity equation can account for the large effect of national borders on the volume of trade observed by McCallum (1995). However, while Anderson-Wincoop's estimation shrinks the size of the border, it does not have much of an impact on the distance elasticity, which remains on the order of −0.80.

Rauch (1999) presents some evidence that proximity and common language/colonial ties are more important for trade in differentiated products than for trade in products traded on organized exchanges. Surprisingly, distance effects are smaller for organized exchange commodities than for differentiated commodities. However, the differences across markets are fairly small and the estimate of the distance elasticity remains in the range of −0.8 to −0.6.

2.2 Multinational sales and FDI

The literature on multinational sales and FDI typically emphasizes the distinction between horizontal and vertical FDI. As noted by Lim (2001, p. 12), horizontal FDI will tend to replace exports if the cost of market access through exports is high. If transport costs are higher the greater is the distance between host and source countries, then horizontal FDI should increase with distance. However, vertical FDI—where the production process is geographically fragmented—may be discouraged by distance because of the need to ship intermediate inputs and semi-finished products. Since the data on FDI are a mix of horizontal and vertical FDI, the impact of distance is uncertain.

Empirically, Carr, Markusen and Maskus (2001) find that production by foreign affiliates of multinationals decreases with distance between the host and source countries. Other studies that use data on bilateral FDI also tend to find that it decreases with distance. For instance Wei (2000) finds that a "1% percent increase in distance is associated with a 0.6% reduction in the FDI." When he uses a modified Tobit estimation technique to account for the zero observations on FDI, the distance elasticity drops to −0.30, but remains highly significant. Similarly, Evenett (2001) finds the distance elasticity in the same range as Wei (2000).

In contrast, Brainard (1997) uses a more direct measure of transport costs, namely, the freight and insurance charges reported by importers. She finds that the higher are such transport costs, the higher is the share of overseas production by multinationals relative to their exports. Hence there is support for the hypothesis that horizontal FDI should increase with transport costs. While this is an appealing direct test of the role of transport costs, Brainard does not include distance as a separate regressor. Hence, she does not provide evidence on whether her transport cost measure accounts fully for the impact of distance on FDI.

2.3 Portfolio flows

Portes and Rey (2000) estimate a gravity equation for trade in financial assets. They note that transportation costs or transactions costs should not play a big role in trade of assets because these assets "are pretty weightless." They add: "And as far as transactions costs are concerned, they seem very small, a few basis points, and not clearly connected with geographical features. Therefore, distance seems a highly improbable variable to encounter in a regression explaining asset trade." If portfolio diversification is an important motive for trade in assets, it might even be argued that distance should increase asset trade if business cycle correlations between countries decrease with distance. Their empirical finding, however, is that distance comes up remarkably strongly with a negative sign in a gravity model estimated using data on cross-border transactions in portfolio equities.

This finding suggests that informational costs have to be at least partly behind the impact of distance on trade. Countries that are near each other probably know more about each other because of greater interaction between their citizens, more media coverage, or greater knowledge of each other languages. Portes and Rey (2000) introduce a measure of bilateral telephone traffic to proxy for transactional distance between countries. Portes, Rey and Oh (2001) further test the relevance of informational barriers by estimating gravity models for trade in different financial assets. Trading in homogenous products such as treasury bonds should pose fewer informational barriers than trade in equities or corporate bonds. Empirically, they find that distance does not matter for trade in treasury bonds (once they control for ease of information flows through their measure of the telephone traffic between countries).

3. Informational infrastructure in gravity equations

In this section, we pursue one avenue for a deeper understanding of the significance of distance between nations: the role of informational infrastructure. Cheaper communications bring the promise of reducing the global disconnect. What is the evidence? We ask three questions:

- To what extent are physical and informational distance correlated?
- Is informational distance between countries endogenous? And, if so, how does accounting for the endogeneity influence the results?
- Do physical and informational distance substitute for or complement each other? And, does the degree of substitution or complementarity vary for developing and developed countries?

3.1 Data and methodology

The data for the analysis of FDI flows is drawn from the International Direct Investment Database of OECD (www.oecdsource.org).[1] For 12 source countries, FDI flows to 45 host countries are available on an annual basis from 1981–1998.[2] The FDI flows are *inflows* from the host country's perspective. To facilitate comparison, we created a matching data set for exports from the same source countries to the same host countries, using data from the IMF's *Direction of Trade Statistics*. From the host country's perspective, these are *imports* and we refer to them as such in the rest of the paper. To reduce the noise in the data, we took three-year averages of all variables. This gives us 6 time periods and allows us to control for unobserved host country characteristics through panel data techniques. In principle we have a maximum possibility of 3240 observations (12×45×6); however, on account of missing data we lose some observations.

To obtain "real" flows over time, we deflated the nominal flows by an index of the unit value of manufactured exports obtained from the IMF's *World Economic Outlook*. For our independent variables, we obtained data from a variety of sources: host and source country populations (the World Bank's *World Development Indicators*), real host and source country GDPs (the IMF's *World Economic Outlook*), physical distance between countries (Shang Jin Wei's website: www.nber.org/~wei), bilateral telephone traffic

(*Direction of Traffic: Trends in International Telephone Tariffs*, International Telecommunications Union) and telephone densities (the World Bank's *World Development Indicators*).

An important substantive issue, with econometric implications, is that over one-third of the FDI flows are zero.[3] In contrast, though trade flows are sometimes modest in size, they are virtually always positive for the pairs in our data set. We would expect, therefore, that the elasticities are greater for FDI; however, to correctly estimate these elasticities we need to consider the bias due to FDI values being censored at zero. Thus, for the FDI flows, we use the so-called "Tobit" model that estimates the coefficients through a maximum likelihood procedure. This is not necessary for the trade equations. For both trade and investment flows, we control for host country effects.[4]

3.2 Correlation between physical and informational distance

If an important variable was omitted in the equations being estimated and that variable was correlated with distance, then the influence of the omitted variable would be incorrectly attributed to distance. Figure 5.1 illustrates the problem. Bilateral information capability (I) and trade/FDI are shown in the figure to be characterized by a positive relationship. The influence of physical distance is shown by assuming that for any value of I, a larger distance ($D_2 > D_1$) results in lower volume of trade or FDI, i.e., by shifting the trade/FDI-information relationship down. Thus, the "true" impact of distance would be the vertical difference between the two parallel lines. Now, if it were the case that greater distance was correlated with low information capability, then we would observe two points (T_2,D_2) and (T_1,D_1). Failure to explicitly

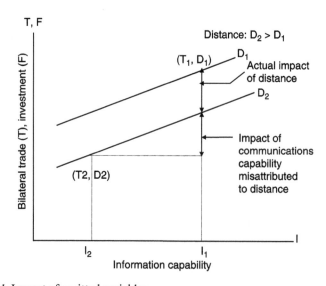

Figure 5.1 Impact of omitted variables.

account for informational distance would then result in inferring a much greater impact of distance measured as the vertical distance between T_1 and T_2 rather than the vertical distance between the two lines. The steeper the slope of the trade/FDI-information curve, the more serious would be the omitted variable bias.

Table 5.1 considers the consequences of including bilateral telephone traffic as an additional regressor (but not yet controlling for the endogeneity of the bilateral traffic). The main findings are easily summarized. First, both

Table 5.1 Gravity models for imports and inward foreign direct investment

	Dependent variable				
	Log imports		*Log FDI*		*Log FDI–Log imports*
	(1)	(2)	(3)	(4)	(5)
Log host population	0.636 (8.50)	0.478 (6.44)	1.361 (30.65)	1.821 (16.73)	0.418 (3.63)
Log source population	0.981 (93.17)	1.023 (98.27)	1.358 (34.66)	1.535 (36.36)	−0.006 (−0.21)
Log host per capita income	0.764 (13.74)	0.597 (10.87)	2.471 (36.28)	1.404 (17.35)	0.599 (5.60)
Log source per capita income	0.665 (12.58)	0.767 (15.03)	2.773 (14.88)	3.218 (17.35)	1.390 (10.49)
Log distance	−0.923 (−57.2)	−0.775 (−43.2)	−1.199 (−25.12)	−0.639 (−10.70)	0.084 (1.79)
Common language	0.416 (9.75)	0.179 (4.13)	1.303 (9.66)	0.749 (4.70)	0.738 (6.43)
Telephone traffic		0.952 (16.12)		3.218 (14.10)	0.182 (1.19)
Number of host country groups	44	44	44	44	44
Number of observations	2,870	2,870	2,934	2934	2870
R-squared: within*	0.804	0.821	–	–	0.067
R-squared: between*	0.703	0.663	–	–	0.112
R-squared: overall*	0.751	0.739	–	–	0.078
Log of Likelihood*	–	–	−4697.57	−4650.89	–

Note: All estimates are based on the assumptions of random country effects for host countries. Z-statistics are presented in the parentheses.
* Columns (4) and (5) were estimated using the Tobit method to allow for the substantial number of observations with a zero value for foreign direct investment. For these regressions, an R-squared is not reported but the log of likelihood is.

trade and FDI increase with host and source country populations and with country per capita incomes. The size of these coefficients is significantly less than one for trade (with one exception, when it is almost exactly one) but is always higher than one and generally substantially so for FDI flows. Thus, there is evidence of scale economies in FDI, reflecting in part the fact that many country pairs have no FDI transactions and thus FDI is much more concentrated than are trade flows. The size of the coefficients on per capita income also implies that intra-industry activity is much more pronounced for FDI (for similar results, see Eaton and Tamura 1994).

Second, the distance coefficient is negative and highly significant in both sets of equations. Compare column (1) for trade with the corresponding column (3) for FDI. The distance coefficient is somewhat larger in size for FDI. Similarly, the language coefficients are positive—with the relative sizes implying that common language helps FDI more than trade. Thus, both distance and language are consistent with an inference that information costs are higher for FDI, an inference that is reinforced when we consider the influence of bilateral telephone traffic.

Third, when we add bilateral telephone traffic (normalized by the square root of the product of the source and host country GDPs) as an additional regressor (in columns (2) and (4)), we find that this variable is positive and highly significant, with the FDI coefficient again being much larger. At the same time, the coefficients for distance and language fall significantly. The decline in these coefficients, moreover, is greater for FDI than for trade.

In combination, these results suggest that greater physical distance between two countries is associated with lower telephone traffic. In part, therefore, distance proxies for the inability to communicate. That this effect is present even for trade suggests that information and search costs are also important in creating disconnections in trade. That the effect, however, is greater for FDI is not surprising because informational distance has greater relevance for investment decisions that tend to be more irreversible than trade flows. The economic size of these effects is significant. The index of telephone traffic (traffic normalized by the square root of the product of the source and host country GDPs) was about 2.5 in the first three-year period, 1981–1983 and rose steadily to 2.7 in the final three-year period, 1996–1998, an increase of 0.2 units. The coefficient on telephone traffic for FDI is 3.2, implying that an increase in the telephone traffic intensity of 0.2 is associated with roughly a 65 percent increase in FDI. Real FDI flows over the same period increased by about 700 percent.

Finally, in column (5), we present results with the log FDI minus the log of imports as the dependent variable. Though the R-squared for this regression is rather low, it is consistent with the results presented above for the individual flows. FDI is more sensitive to size of host country population and to both host and source country per capita incomes, reflecting the greater scale economies and intra-industry activity associated with FDI. Note that FDI travels greater distances than does trade, consistent with horizontal FDI undertaken to overcome transportation barriers to trade (the distance variable, however, is significant only at the 10 percent level). Common language has a more positive effect on FDI than on trade, reflecting its more intense informational requirements. Also, heavier bilateral telephone traffic leads to more FDI, though this variable is surprisingly not significant (considering the large difference in the individual equations); when we control below for endogeneity of telephone traffic, the sign remains positive and the coefficient then is statistically significant.

3.3 Endogeneity of telephone traffic

Bilateral telephone traffic may be endogenous: more trade and FDI may result in greater communication. Also, measured telephone traffic between countries may not accurately reflect their capacity to communicate. Thus, it is important to distinguish between telephone "traffic," the actual volume of calls between nations, and informational infrastructure, or the physical capacity to make calls. While traffic is potentially endogenous and, therefore, may respond to international trade and investment flows rather than "causing" them, the infrastructure (proxied here by telephones per capita in the source and host countries) is slower moving and, over short time spans, can be thought of as exogenous to international flows. Moreover, additional information infrastructure is characterized by strong scale economies due to network externalities—the benefits increase as users are added to the network. Thus, better-developed information infrastructures in two trading economies can reduce transactions costs between those economies at an increasing rate.

Figure 5.2 illustrates the possibility of endogeneity in telephone traffic,

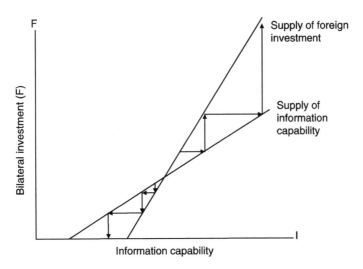

Figure 5.2 Role of endogeneity.

combined with scale economies in information infrastructure. FDI is used as the example, though the same line of thinking can apply to trade also. The steeper curve, marked as the "supply of FDI," reflects the willingness of foreign investors to increase their FDI flows as infrastructure availability improves the ease of communication. The endogeneity arises when foreign investment, in turn, spurs greater bilateral communication—reflected by the line with the smaller slope. Notice, if the curves have the relative slopes as drawn, then the tendency beyond a threshold (the point at which the two lines intersect) would be for more foreign investment to induce greater communications capability, which in turn would spur more investment and so on. In contrast, below the threshold, bilateral investment and communications could both unravel and go to zero. In practice, we do observe that many countries receive no investment from several source countries and that FDI is highly concentrated. We do not see the extreme concentration suggested by Figure 5.2 presumably because there are adjustment costs and other countervailing factors.

To test these propositions, we attempted to control for the reverse causation using instrumental variables for bilateral telephone traffic. The main instruments we used were the telephone densities in the host and source countries. These variables have a statistically significant effect on telephone traffic.[5] We also used year dummies to allow for the possibility of secular increase in telephone traffic. Finally, for the trade equation, we report a result using lagged imports as an additional instrument; though this result is interesting, further work would be necessary to justify the use of the lagged dependent variable as a valid instrument.

Again, a few salient features of the results may be noted (Table 5.2). First, for trade, it makes a difference whether lagged imports are included or not as an instrument. When, and only when, that variable is included, the coefficient on distance falls sharply, to −0.29. Otherwise, the endogeneity correction does not have much of an effect for the trade equation.

Second, for FDI, the effects observed are robust to the inclusion or otherwise of the lagged dependent variable—the results shown do not include it. The instrumented telephone traffic variable is statistically more significant and quantitatively more important than before. This could either imply that bilateral telephone traffic mismeasures "communications capability" between countries and failure to take the mismeasurement into account biases the coefficient downwards. Alternatively, endogeneity is a serious concern: more investment does increase bilateral traffic, but the stimulus from communications capacity to investment is the stronger relationship, which is camouflaged when endogeneity is not considered. Note that superior communications capability is now seen to more clearly favor FDI than trade (column (4)). Third, the distance coefficient is now *positive* for FDI, strengthening the case that horizontal FDI lies behind the results. The insignificant sign of this coefficient reflects differences across country groups, as discussed below in section 3.4. The clear implication, however, is that properly measured

Table 5.2 Gravity models for imports and inward foreign direct investment: instrumental variable estimates

	Estimation method and dependent variable						
	Random-effects				Country pair fixed-effects		
	Log imports	Log imports	Log FDI	Log FDI–Log imports	Log imports	Log FDI	Log FDI–Log imports
	(1A)	(1B)	(2)	(3)	(4)	(5)	(6)
Log host population	0.775 (14.56)	0.547 (7.03)	1.765 (26.79)	0.475 (4.16)	0.881 (34.28)	1.971 (19.90)	0.576 (7.41)
Log source population	1.132 (114.01)	1.010 (84.81)	1.676 (38.96)	0.101 (3.43)	0.793 (21.62))	1.309 (9.61)	0.250 (2.26)
Log host per capita income	0.716 (15.89)	0.710 (12.49)	1.586 (24.13)	0.570 (5.42)	0.813 (33.12)	2.132 (22.34)	0.867 (11.68)
Log source per capita income	1.425 (28.81)	0.778 (13.63)	4.026 (21.17)	1.751 (12.77)	−0.012 (−0.13)	3.881 (10.57)	2.083 (7.29)
Log distance	−0.292 (−13.11)	−0.803 (−28.30)	0.088 (1.01)	0.536 (7.95)			
Common language	−0.480 (−10.97)	0.249 (4.64)	−0.401 (−2.43)	0.098 (0.74)			
Telephone traffic**	3.580 (36.14)	0.651 (5.11)	6.982 (17.25)	2.624 (8.84)	1.167 (10.99)	4.712 (10.90)	1.268 (3.95)
Number of host country groups	43	44	44	44	44	44	44
Number of observations	2407	2,870	2934	2870	2870	2934	2870
R-squared: within*	0.882	0.806	–	0.090	–	–	–
R-squared: between*	0.778	0.667	–	0.146	–	–	–
R-squared: overall*	0.802	0.735	–	0.110	0.951		0.558
Log of likelihood*	–	–	−4614.76	–	–	−4105.81	–

Note: All estimates are based on the assumption of random country effects for host countries. Z-statistics are presented in the parentheses.
* Column (2) was estimated using the Tobit method to allow for the substantial number of observations with a zero value for foreign direct investment. For this regression, an R-squared is not reported but the log of likelihood is.
** Predicted value of telephone traffic using all the right hand side variables in this table (other than telephone traffic, of course) the logs of telephone densities in the host and source countries, and time dummies, plus the log of lagged imports in column (1A).

telecommunications capacity is highly correlated with physical distance and direct consideration of "transactional distance" reduces the apparent influence of geography on FDI. The implication is also that strong network economies operate to strengthen ties between countries with sound communications. Fourth, the language coefficients turn negative, as if they primarily proxied better telecommunications, and once we control directly for such capacity, then common language countries are not necessarily favored.

To test the robustness of the informational distance variable, we estimated also a fixed-effects model that controlled for host- and source-country pair dummies. Thus, all unchanging relationships between host and source countries, including distance, linguistic ties, and other possible variables that are omitted by us, are accounted for in this procedure.

This procedure allows us to test if informational distance was merely proxying for some unobserved variables or is still relevant when the observed and unobserved country pair characteristics are controlled for. Columns 5 through 7 of Table 5.2 show the results. The results are robust. Informational distance is clearly important and is more important for FDI than for trade, as the earlier results also showed.[6]

3.4 Are physical and informational distance substitutes or complements

Thus far, we have been concerned with explaining the distance puzzle and so have focused on whether the influence of physical distance is exaggerated on account of omitting bilateral information capacity. In this section, we presume that both physical distance and informational distance are relevant in determining trade and FDI flows and ask if these two forms of distance are substitutes or complements.

Three possibilities exist. First, if better information can substitute for physical distance, then we would find (as in Figure 5.3(a)) that greater physical distance is a disadvantage but less so as information capacity between the countries increases. In this case, we would expect to find a positive sign on the interaction between physical distance and our information variable. Second, the opposite is possible (Figure 5.3(b)) if the effect of physical distance gets magnified when there is greater information capability, leading to a negative sign on the interaction term. This may occur when, for example, trade in differentiated products dominates: such trade is information intensive and benefits from lower freight costs (shorter physical distances). Finally, FDI adds a special consideration since horizontal FDI increases with greater distance while vertical FDI (like trade) is discouraged by greater distance. Figure 5.3(c) suggests that horizontal FDI is likely to dominate when bilateral information capability is below the threshold I* and physical distance generates more FDI as information capability becomes less effective. In contrast, when information capacity is above I*, then (as with trade) more vertical FDI (a): Information substitutes for distance

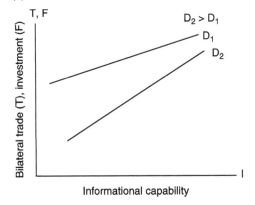

(b): Information reinforces the distance advantage

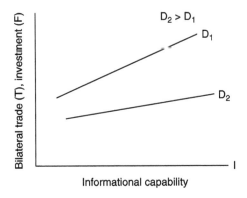

(c): Horizontal and vertical FDI

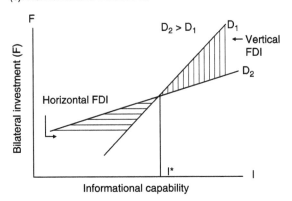

Figure 5.3 Interaction between physical and informational distance.

occurs, encouraged by shorter distances and greater information transactions capability.

Table 5.3 presents the results with the interaction term, separately for all countries, developed countries, and developing countries.[7] Consider first the relationships for trade. For all countries, and for the range of values on our information variable, the distance elasticity is always negative; but (as in Figure 5.3(b)) the elasticity is increasingly negative for higher values of the information index since the interaction term is negative. The implication is that differentiated products' trade has a dominant effect on these regressions and that physical proximity and high information intensity reinforce each other in fostering such trade.

Note, however, from column (2) that this pattern reflects trade within the group of developed countries. Considering the exports from the same host countries to developing countries, we find the interaction term to be positive.[8] This is more akin to Figure 5.3(a) where information capability can substitute for distance disadvantage.

For FDI, developed and developing country patterns are, once again, quite different. For developed countries, for the range of the information index, the distance elasticity values are now almost always *positive*, implying in terms of Figure 5.3(c) that the bulk of the observations lie to the left of I* where horizontal FDI predominates. Thus, within developed countries, FDI appears to mainly substitute for trade, though the extent of vertical FDI, which is complementary to trade, increases with the capability for information exchange.

For developing countries, as observed above for trade, physical distance acts as a disadvantage for FDI for almost the entire range of telecommunications capacity. Thus, the same forces that limit trade to distant developing countries appear also to restrict FDI. However, once again, as communications improve, they compensate for physical distance and the distance elasticity becomes less negative.

4. Conclusions

In this paper, we demonstrate that a comparison of trade and FDI flows can prove useful in achieving a deeper understanding of global linkages. The good news is that the geographical tyranny of distance is less potent than has been thought. This creates a more optimistic basis for bringing nations together. However, though geography is less powerful than implied by many studies, economic forces can act to maintain distance among nations. We find, in particular, that informational infrastructure matters in fashioning global linkages.

Comparing trade and FDI flows, we find that, in keeping with its greater geographical concentration, FDI is more sensitive to scale variables such as population and per capita income. Similarly, FDI is more sensitive to bilateral informational capability.

Table 5.3 Interactions between physical and informational distance: instrumental variable estimates

	Dependent variable					
	Log imports			Log FDI		
	All	Developed	Developing	All	Developed	Developing
	(1)	(2)	(3)	(4)	(5)	(6)
Log host population	0.580 (7.89)	0.917 (6.99)	0.506 (6.17)	1.429 (20.49)	1.500 (14.17)	1.895 (17.65)
Log source population	1.008 (85.19)	0.916 (57.24)	1.110 (63.53)	1.664 (38.41)	1.554 (27.29)	1.830 (26.83)
Log host per capita income	0.710 (12.81)	0.347 (2.18)	0.790 (11.16)	1.617 (25.50)	0.811 (4.37)	1.750 (14.57)
Log source per capita income	0.749 (13.20)	1.059 (12.92)	0.550 (6.54)	4.061 (21.52)	3.955 (15.61)	3.935 (13.65)
Log distance	0.069 (0.43)	0.518 (3.27)	−0.999 (19.87)	0.658 (1.33)	1.902 (3.36)	−2.217 (13.55)
Common language	0.224 (4.18)	0.157 (2.22)	0.186 (2.27)	−0.265 (−1.53)	−0.210 (−0.89)	−0.900 (−3.45)
Telephone traffic**	3.311 (6.61)	4.746 (9.42)		8.637 (5.58)	12.151 (6.84)	
Log Distance X Telephone traffic**	−0.304 (−5.51)	−0.417 (−7.83)	0.060 (3.27)	−0.187 (−1.11)	−0.630 (−3.29)	0.789 (12.95)
Number of host countries	44	22	22	44	22	22
Number of observations	2870	1416	1454	2934	1416	1518
R-squared: within*	0.808	0.844	0.799			
R-squared: between*	0.667	0.704	0.582			
R-squared: overall*	0.736	0.751	0.736			
Log of likelihood*				−4619.45	−2642.05	−1965.72

Note: All estimates are based on the assumption of random country effects for host countries. Z-statistics are presented in the parentheses.
* Columns (4) (5) and (6) were estimated using the Tobit method to allow for the substantial number of observations with a zero value for foreign direct investment. For these regressions, an R-squared is not reported but the log of likelihood is.
** Predicted value of telephone traffic using all the right hand side variables in this table (other than telephone traffic, of course) plus the logs of telephone densities in the host and source countries, and time dummies.

Key to the reduction of the distance puzzle is the concept of transactional distance, a measure that encompasses the ability to communicate and undertake transactions. Empirically, this can be implemented by adding telephone traffic as an additional regressor in gravity equations, as suggested by Portes and Rey (2000). We find that trade and investment flows increase as "transactional distance" falls. However, since telephone traffic is likely to be influenced by the trade and investment dependent variables, consideration of the potential endogeneity of bilateral telephone traffic is necessary and turns out to have quantitatively important effects for FDI. Once endogeneity is considered, the implausibly large effects of physical distance decline sharply in FDI equations and the distance coefficient actually turns positive, suggesting the prevalence of so-called "horizontal" FDI undertaken to overcome costs of transporting goods. For trade equations, the decline in the distance coefficient depends on the addition of lagged imports as an instrument; further work would be needed to justify this approach.

Our results further suggest that for FDI scale economies can be misconstrued as distance effects. If FDI benefits from scale economies, then firms will concentrate in a limited number of locations. Thus, countries far away from major investment centers may receive relatively small amounts of investment, but this would be the outcome of agglomeration benefits in closely located nations rather than because transportation costs create disincentives to investment in distant locations. In turn, agglomeration may arise due to several reasons: traditional benefits of proximity (Wheeler and Mody 1992; also Ch. 2 this book), private information costs that cause firms to follow each others' lead (Kinoshita and Mody 2001; also Ch. 4 this book), or because, as the results in this paper suggest, international information networks are associated with scale economies. Of course, each of these sources of agglomeration is likely to reinforce the other.

Finally, we find that developing countries can invest in superior information infrastructure to overcome the disadvantage of distance, i.e., information flows can substitute for distance. In contrast, within developed countries, physical proximity of nations and greater information capacity reinforce each other, in keeping with the differentiated products nature of the trade and investment flows that benefit from the ability to move goods rapidly and from the greater ease of communication. The evidence is also consistent with the generally held view that the bulk of the FDI within developed countries is "horizontal" in nature.

Notes

1   We used the series on outflows from a source to a host country but also relied on the outward position (stock of FDI) for crosschecking.
2   The *source countries* are: Australia, Austria, Canada, France, Germany, Italy, Japan, the Netherlands, Norway, Sweden, the United Kingdom and the United States. The *developed host countries* are: Australia, Austria, Belgium, Canada, Denmark, Finland, France, Germany, Greece, Ireland, Israel, Italy, Japan, the Netherlands,

New Zealand, Norway, Portugal, Spain, Sweden, Switzerland, the United Kingdom and the United States. The *developing host countries* are: Argentina, Brazil, Chile, China, Colombia, Ecuador, Egypt, Hong Kong, India, Korea, Kuwait, Malaysia, Mexico, Nigeria, Peru, the Philippines, Saudi Arabia, Singapore, South Africa, Taiwan, Thailand, Turkey and Venezuela.

3   In the actual dataset, a clear distinction was not always made between a zero flow and a missing value. Based on other corroborating evidence, we imputed several "zero" values.

4   We use random effects models, estimated by STATA using the procedures xtreg and xttobit. We do not use time dummies since these correlate with other variables on the right-hand side and we also do not use source country dummies since source countries seem well-characterized by their populations that are slowly moving.

5   The correlation between the actual and predicted telephone traffic is about 0.76. See footnotes to Table 5.2 for a complete description of the "first-stage" regression.

6   Also, instead of estimating the relationship in a panel data setting, we estimated the relationships for each of the six periods that our data permits. These results are very extensive and so are not reported here. The main finding is confirmed: the distance elasticity falls in absolute magnitude with the introduction of bilateral telephone traffic and reduces further, especially for FDI, when endogeneity of telephone traffic is accounted for.

7   F-tests showed that it is appropriate to distinguish between developed and developing countries. The list of developed and developing countries is in footnote 2.

8   In both the trade and FDI regressions for developing countries, we had to drop the communications variable by itself since its inclusion generated significant multicollinearity and the coefficients were not significant, though they were signed as in the regressions presented.

References

Anderson, James and Eric van Wincoop (2001) Gravity with Gravitas: A Solution to the Border Puzzle. National Bureau of Economic Research Working Paper 8079, January.

Brainard, Lael S. (1997) An Empirical Assessment of the Proximity-Concentration Trade-Off between Multinational Sales and Trade. *American Economic Review* 87: 520–44.

Carr, D.L., J.R. Markusen, and K.E. Maskus (2001) Estimating the Knowledge-Capital Model of the Multinational Enterprise. *American Economic Review*, 91 (June): 693–708.

Eaton, Jonathan and Akiko Tamura (1994) Bilateralism and Regionalism in Japanese and U.S. Trade and Direct Foreign Investment. *Journal of the Japanese and International Economies*, 8: 478–510.

Eichengreen, Barry and Doug Irwin (1998) The Role of History in Bilateral Trade Flows. In J.A. Frankel (ed.), *The Regionalization of the World Economy*. Chicago and London: The University of Chicago Press.

Evenett, Simon (2001) Do All Networks Facilitate International Commerce? The Case of US Law Firms and the Mergers and Acquisitions Wave of the Late 1990s. http://papers.ssrn.com/sol3/papers.cfm?abstract_id=293804

Grossman, Gene (1998) Comment. In J.A. Frankel (ed.), *The Regionalization of the World Economy*. Chicago and London: The University of Chicago Press.

International Monetary Fund, *Direction of Trade Statistics*, Washington D.C., various issues.

International Monetary Fund, *World Economic Outlook*, Washington D.C., various issues.

International Telecommunication Union, *Direction of Traffic: Trading Telecom Minutes*, Geneva.

Kinoshita, Yuko and Ashoka Mody (2001) Private Information for Foreign Investment in Emerging Economies. *Canadian Journal of Economics*, 34 (May, 2): 448–464.

Lawrence, Robert (1998) Comment. In J.A. Frankel (ed.), *The Regionalization of the World Economy*. Chicago and London: The University of Chicago Press.

Lim, Ewe-Gee (2001) Determinants of, and the Relation between, FDI and Growth: A Summary of the Recent Literature. IMF Working Paper 01/175, November.

McCallum, John (1995). National Borders Matter: Canada–U.S. Regional Trade Patterns, *American Economic Review*, 85: 615–23.

Obstfeld, Maurice and Kenneth Rogoff (2000) The Six Major Puzzles in International Macroeconomics: Is There a Common Cause? *NBER Macroeconomics Annual*, 15 (1): 339–390. Cambridge and London: MIT Press.

Portes, Richard and Helene Rey (2000) The Determinants of Cross-Border Equity Flows: The Geography of Information. Revised version of CEPR Discussion Paper 2225, January.

Portes, Richard, Helene Rey and Yonghyup Oh (2001) Information and Capital Flows: The Determinants of Transactions in Financial Assets. *European Economic Review* 45: 783–96.

Rauch, James (1999) Networks versus Markets in International Trade. *Journal of International Economics* 48: 7–35.

Wei, Shang-Jin (2000) How Taxing is Corruption on International Investors? *Review of Economics and Statistics* 82: 1–11. www.nber.org/~wei/

Wheeler, David, and Ashoka Mody (1992) International Investment Location Decisions: The Case of U.S. Firms. *Journal of International Economics* 33 (August, 1/2): 57–76.

World Bank, *World Development Indicators*, Washington D.C., various issues.

6 Japanese multinationals in Asia
Capabilities and motivations

With Susmita Dasgupta and
Sarbajit Sinha

Introduction

Using a specially designed survey, this chapter identifies: (a) the character-istics of Japanese firms likely to undertake foreign investments—worldwide and in key Asian countries; and (b) country characteristics associated with Japanese investments in Asia. The survey-based, firm-level analysis here con-trasts with the macro approach that correlates country characteristics with *aggregate* flows into that country (see Wheeler and Mody 1992; also Ch. 2 in this book). It contrasts also with the industry-level analysis where industry characteristics such as the degree of competition, the level of entry barriers, and the degree of technological sophistication are examined as determinants of foreign investment (e.g., Kogut and Chang 1991). The firm-level perspec-tive is important because much of the theorizing on decision to invest abroad derive from the interplay of firm capacity and motives to invest abroad (see Caves 1982 for a literature review). This chapter confirms certain findings obtained from the more aggregative studies, but highlights the significant importance of firm characteristics (or capabilities) in the decision to undertake foreign investment.

The data permits us to distinguish between the *capabilities* of firms—proxied by their size, export propensity, and research and development (R&D) expenditures—and their *motives* for investing abroad. The motives, in turn, arise from operating cost conditions in Japan (due for example to increasing wage costs or an appreciating yen) and from the pursuit of lower production costs and investment incentives offered by host countries. The procedure followed is to examine the various motivating factors after control-ling for firm characteristics; in certain instances, where interesting results were obtained, we also present the interactions between capabilities and motivations.

In studying motives, survey-based analyses are typically limited to deter-mining the subjective preferences of investors ("do you value low wages?" or "does country X have a favorable foreign investment policy?"). Such analyses are intended to elicit the priority accorded by investors to the cost and policy characteristics of alternative investment locations. While the subjective perceptions are valuable, it is also necessary to determine if firms in fact act according to the priorities they state in such surveys, i.e., do they put their money where they say they would?

In this project, we did ask firms to rank the factors they considered important in their decisions to invest outside Japan and in specific Asian countries. However, we also asked them for their: (1) share of foreign investment in total investment; (2) share of foreign investment undertaken in Asia; and (3) their likelihood of investing in specific Asian countries in the following three years. Thus the information available allows us both to rank their stated preferences and to conduct an econometric analysis that identifies partial correlations between investments undertaken and firm and (perceived) country characteristics.

Analysis of the actual investments undertaken help not merely in validating the stated preferences but also in drawing more complete explanations of investment behavior. High costs of Japanese labor exert a general push towards investing abroad. However, we find that the variation in the investment undertaken depends much more on differences in firm attributes. Also, our respondents do state a strong preference for low wage locations. But perception of low wages in specific Asian countries do not seem to have been a determining factor thus far in determining investment levels in those countries—in fact, low wages have actually been a disincentive where they were associated with low labor quality. The new Japanese investment that is expected to flow into Asian economies *is* being guided more by low wages, though considerations of labor quality continue to be very important, confirming the importance of developing country domestic human capital in attracting foreign investment (Lucas 1990).

Another important finding of the paper is the importance accorded by investors to actions they perceive are being taken by other investors. Strategic rivalry, or the importance of staking out early positions in growing markets, clearly is a key influence in the foreign investment decision-making process, creating the possibility of cascading effects (Vernon 1993).

We begin in the next section by describing the firms in this survey. Then, we examine the firm characteristics and Japanese cost conditions leading to investment out of Japan, irrespective of the country of destination. This is followed by an analysis of the past investment decisions in Asia. Finally, we describe the expected flow of Japanese investment and its distribution within Asia, where we focus on China, Malaysia, Thailand, Indonesia, the Philippines, India, and Vietnam.

The investors: some descriptive statistics

The survey questionnaire, designed by the authors, was mailed by the Japanese Ministry of Trade and Industry (MITI) to several hundred Japanese firms of which 173 returned usable responses in March 1993. The sample thus obtained cannot be treated as representative of all Japanese firms—we do not know the characteristics of firms who did not respond. There is, however, sufficient heterogeneity amongst the respondents to permit a statistical analysis of their foreign investment behavior; also, as described below, the foreign investment pattern of this sample mirrors that of all Japanese manufacturing firms.

The firms in our sample are relatively large (Table 6.1). The average annual sales are 330 billion yen (over $3 billion). For the purpose of this analysis, we have found it useful to sort the firms by size and then divide them up into five equal groups. The average size of the largest fifth is 1.4 trillion yen (about $14 billion)—the largest firm is truly large, with sales of $70 billion. The smallest fifth of the firms in our sample has average annual sales of around $40 million—the smallest firm has sales of about $2 million.

This is also a set of firms that is prone to making significant foreign investments (Table 6.1).[1] In the three years prior to the survey, over a fifth of their investment was undertaken outside Japan. The very interesting feature, though, of the sample is the strong tendency of the smallest firms to investment abroad: in the three years prior to the survey, about 28 percent of their investment was undertaken abroad. The next three larger groups of firms have a lower propensity to invest abroad. Only the largest fifth of the firms invest a higher proportion—35 percent—outside Japan. Thus, the smallest and the largest firms are amongst the trailblazers of Japanese foreign investment.

Small and large firms are being driven to invest by different concerns. As may be expected, small firms have low research and development (R&D)

Table 6.1 Characteristics of the sample firms (mean values)

	Worldwide sales (billion yen)	Share of foreign investment in all investment (%)	R&D expenditure to worldwide sales (%)	Exports to worldwide sales (%)	Investment share in Asia (%)
0.2–8.6 (33)	4.1 (33)	28.1 (17)	1–3 (24)	8 (31)	56.4 (8)
8.7–37.8 (32)	20.5 (32)	15.8 (20)	1–3 (31)	12 (32)	65.0 (4)
37.9–94.6 (32)	63.9 (32)	17.3 (18)	1–3 (30)	13 (32)	57.0 (10)
94.7–300.0 (33)	190.0 (33)	20.0 (22)	3–5 (30)	13 (32)	26.9 (16)
300.1–7450.0 (31)	1414.7 (31)	35.1 (10)	3–5 (30)	17 (31)	20.4 (21)
ALL FIRMS (161)	329.0 (161)	21.9 (94)	1–3 (155)	13 (158)	35.2 (62)

Notes
Numbers of Respondents in parentheses.
Respondents were asked to give the range of their R&D investment rather than an exact number.

ratios (expenditures divided by total sales), with this ratio rising steadily as the size of the firm increases (Table 6.1).[2] Thus, we infer that smaller firms are technologically less sophisticated than larger firms. Two possibilities exist: smaller firms are principally in low technology sectors or, within particular sectors, small firms perform tasks that are technologically less demanding than those of larger firms. From our survey, we find that there is a slightly greater tendency for larger firms to be in the continuous process sectors, such as food and chemicals. However, all sizes of firms are represented in electrical machinery, general machinery, and transport equipment sectors, where much of the sample is concentrated. The implication is that the smaller firms are generally at the lower end of the product quality range in each sector.

As with R&D, the ratio of exports (from Japan) to worldwide sales rises with size of investor. However, the smaller firms are clearly not shy of exports: indeed, our data shows that from their foreign investment locations smaller firms have a higher export propensity than larger firms. As such, it appears, *prima facie*, that smaller firms have invested abroad in response to high and rising costs of production in Japan, making it increasingly difficult for them to competitively sell Japanese-made products and inducing a shift to lower cost locations. Thus, given the lower technological sophistication of small firms, they can be expected to focus on low wage locations; however, their export requirements from the foreign locations also suggest that high labor quality is also likely to be of value to them to ensure quality standards in export markets.

Which Japanese firms invest abroad and why?

To explore further the characteristics of Japanese foreign investors and why they invest abroad, we investigated the determinants of the share of all foreign investment in the firm's total investment (in the three years prior to the survey). The share of foreign investment was regressed on firm characteristics (size, R&D, export propensity) and the firm's perceptions of cost conditions in Japan. We also controlled for sectoral characteristics through the use of sector dummy variables.

Three features of the econometric estimation methodology are worth highlighting. First, a number of firms report zero foreign investment. These firms could "desire" a "negative" foreign investment; however, all observed values are censored at zero. Thus the data contain a potential non-linearity at the point where zero foreign investment becomes the preferred objective. Forcing a linear regression through the data would bias the results since it would require that the slopes with respect to the explanatory variables be the same for foreign investment less than and greater than zero, even though they are clearly observed to be different. This requires us to use the so-called "Tobit" regression to prevent bias in estimates (see Maddala 1983).

Second, not all firms reported the share of foreign investment in their overall investment. A natural question that arises, therefore, is whether the responses are missing in a random or a systematic manner. If firms that did not respond vary systematically from firms that did, the estimates obtained will be biased when the regression analysis is performed with the reduced number of observations. To guard against such a selection bias, we followed a two-step procedure. We estimated a "reporting" equation to predict the probability that an enterprise reports its foreign investment share, as requested in the questionnaire. A binary choice (choosing to report or not to report) probit model was estimated for all 173 observations as a function of firm characteristics. From this estimation, a "correction" term was obtained. The correction term, which reflects the firm's features that lead it to report or not to report, was then added to the Tobit regression. The coefficient on this correction term provides a measure of the selection bias. In our estimates, the coefficient on the correction term was always statistically insignificant and hence we cannot reject the null hypothesis that the non-reporting is indeed random and hence there is no selection bias (see Maddala 1983, Ch. 9 and Heckman 1979).

Finally, no attempt is made to establish or claim causality from the chosen firm characteristics to the share of foreign investment. It is possible that export shares and R&D are influenced by the extent of foreign investment. Any credible attempt at establishing causality would require time-series data on the firm characteristics. As such, the results here should be viewed as partial correlations (i.e., correlations between the share of foreign investment and the individual firm characteristics, controlling for other variables included in the regression). This same limitation and interpretation applies to industry level analyses where, for example, an industry's foreign investment and level of R&D may be jointly determined (example, Kogut and Chang 1991).

Firm characteristics Controlling for other factors, larger Japanese firms have a greater foreign presence (Table 6.2). Note here the difference between the ordinary least squares estimates (OLS) and the Tobit estimates. The size variable is positive but not significant at conventional levels in the OLS estimates, whereas the significance is strong in the Tobit estimates. The relevance of the Tobit analysis here is clear: forcing a linear relationship through observations where foreign investment is zero leads to biased results. (For other variables too, the statistical significance of the results improves when the Tobit method is used.) The size effect, though statistically significant for the Tobit regressions, is not large in terms of magnitude. An increase in firm size (worldwide sales) of 1 trillion yen (or $10 billion) leads to an increase in the foreign investment share by 0.7 percentage points.[3]

In contrast to firm size, more R&D is associated with a lower foreign investment propensity. Recall that larger the size of firm, the more R&D it undertakes. These results, therefore, imply that while larger firms are more prone to invest abroad, within groups of similar-sized firms the propensity is dampened if firms are engaged in greater R&D (and hence in sophisticated

Table 6.2 The decision to invest abroad (dependent variable: share of foreign investment in total investment, 1990–92)

Variable	Model 1 (OLS)	Model 1 (Tobit)	Model 2 (OLS)	Model 2 (Tobit)
Worldwide sales	0.0006 (1.36)	0.0007* (2.22)	0.0007 (1.53)	0.0008 (2.70)
R&D ratio	−6.41** (−1.96)	−6.77* (3.68)	−6.59** (−1.93)	−7.02** (3.82)
Export ratio	0.73* (3.40)	0.72* (9.68)	0.70* (3.16)	0.70* (8.88)
Appreciation of yen			1.91 (.84)	2.24 (.88)
High labor cost in Japan			−0.021 (0.0087)	−0.06 (−0.001)
High capital cost in Japan			1.12 (.56)	.41 (.04)
Error correction term	−15.97 (−0.93)	−13.64 (0.54)	−11.98 (−0.65)	−11.56 (0.36)
Constant	44.62* (2.18)	41.64** (3.59)	28.88 (1.16)	28.54 (1.21)
R-squared	0.25		0.27	
Log likelihood		−260.75		−259.66
No. of observations	62	62	62	62

Notes
T-statistics in parentheses for OLS estimates and chi-square statistics for Tobit estimates.
* significant at 5%, ** significant at 10%.

product or process technologies). The result also reflects the relatively high propensity of small firms with little R&D to invest abroad. This effect is stronger than is apparent from the regressions. We asked firms only to provide the range of their R&D ratio. Hence, the R&D variable in the regression is measured with error, biasing its coefficient towards zero. The fact that it is still significantly different from zero, implies a strong effect.

This finding—that a firm's foreign investment is inversely related to its R&D to sales ratio—may appear at odds with the result that an *industry's* foreign investment is typically positively related to the extent of R&D undertaken in the home country (Caves 1982; Cantwell 1989; Kogut and Chang 1991). Such a relationship is thought to reflect advantages from home technological capability. Three comments are in order. First, consistent with our result, the finding also exists that R&D capability *abroad* causes investment to flow abroad in search of new technologies and rising home technological capability limits foreign investment (Kogut and Chang 1991). Second, comparing foreign investment and home R&D *across* industries must be distinguished from an analysis that focuses more heavily on a *within-industry* analysis. Since we use firm-level data, we capture within-industry variation, suggesting that even where high home R&D and foreign investment are positively related at the industry level, more investment abroad is undertaken by firms that do a smaller amount of research either to search new technologies or to seek lower cost production sites for less sophisticated products. This is a reminder also of the substantial variation in technological sophistication that remains even within narrowly defined industrial sectors. Finally, R&D generates only one element of technological capability (see discussion in Swedenborg 1979, where high R&D Swedish firms are found to prefer exports while those undertaking less R&D invest abroad). Production efficiency based on factory-floor learning may often be a more substantial element of a firm's technology capital. A firm's export share may better reflect its more inclusive technology capacity.

Greater export orientation is strongly conducive to foreign investment. A one percentage point increase in the export ratio (exports as a percent of total sales) leads to a 0.7 percentage point increase in the share of foreign investment. As noted in the descriptive statistics (Table 6.1) large firm size is associated with greater export intensity (as it is with more R&D); as such, the result here indicates that within groups of similar-sized firms a greater interest in export markets is associated with greater foreign investment from Japan. The direction of causality is difficult to determine from a single survey: it could be that firms with traditionally high export propensities (and significant technological capabilities) are being forced to invest abroad (due to increased trade barriers) or it could also be that firms undertaking investment abroad export (especially intermediate goods) to their foreign subsidiaries.

What conclusions follow on Japanese investor capabilities? A variety of intangible assets are thought to create the advantage for the potential foreign investor—these assets include product or process knowledge, brand names, and marketing or distribution channels. The interesting result from our survey is that R&D does not seem to be the source of asset driving Japanese foreign investment—on the contrary, firms doing greater R&D tend to stay at home. It could be that brand names are the source of Japanese advantage; certainly, the big electronics firms derive much of their market power from their established market positions. However, that does not explain what competitive advantage allows the smaller firms to successfully invest abroad.

A likely explanation, supported indirectly by our survey, is that small firms have access to Japanese marketing channels—these channels are used not just to export from the subsidiaries to Japan but also to other parts of the world. Exports constitute about a third of the output from the foreign subsidiary and so create a need for strong export channels. Moreover, these same distribution channels are perhaps of equal (or greater) importance in importing high quality and competitively priced inputs. In addition, while the R&D

ratios of the investing firms may be low, the production capabilities of the firms are likely to be quite high. Japanese production and management techniques are widely believed to give them a competitive edge over producers in other parts of the world. These techniques are widely diffused among Japanese firms, even ones that do little R&D of their own.[4]

Sectoral distribution   As noted above, the distribution of firms across industrial sector shows a heavy concentration in the areas of electrical and heavy machinery and automobiles. In doing these regression, we added dummy variables for the different sectors to examine if firms in particular sectors have particularly strong tendency to invest abroad. These dummy variables are not reported in the regressions. However, the results are of some interest. The dummy variables show no statistical significance. In other words, once the variables described above are accounted for, sectoral differences do not seem important in driving foreign investment. Specifically, the size, R&D ratio, and export propensity of the firm are more important predictors of its propensity to invest abroad than is its sectoral identity. This, once again, suggests the importance of firm-specific advantages in determining the flow of Japanese foreign investment.

Japanese cost conditions   Is Japanese foreign investment sensitive to cost conditions at home? Here we consider both the stated weight placed on specific cost factors when operating in Japan as well as the influence of these perceptions on the amount of investment undertaken.

The question asked was: "How important have the factors listed below been in influencing your decision to invest abroad?" Respondents were asked to place a check mark (√) in any one of the boxes on the scale provided.

	Not important		Very important
Appreciation of the Yen	:_:_:_:_:_:_:_:_:_:_:_:_:_:_:		
High labor costs in Japan	:_:_:_:_:_:_:_:_:_:_:_:_:_:_:		
High capital costs in Japan	:_:_:_:_:_:_:_:_:_:_:_:_:_:_:		

Note first from Table 6.2 that the relative importance of these Japanese cost factors does not explain the differences in the share of foreign investment. Firms that consider a high yen and high Japanese capital costs as important factors leading to foreign investment do invest more abroad, but the standard errors of the coefficients are high and the statistical significance of the coefficients is therefore low. For labor costs, the standard errors are even higher.

Are these results a reflection of low importance accorded by respondents to Japanese cost conditions? A look at the stated perceptions is helpful (Table 6.3). All firms report labor costs to be of considerable importance in creating an incentive to invest abroad: the average importance (on a scale of 1 to 7) is 5.40, with a high of 5.85 for small firms and about 5.2 for firms in

Table 6.3 Perception of disadvantage due to high Japanese costs (mean responses on a 1–7 scale, from favorable to very unfavorable)

Firm size (billion yen)	Appreciation of yen	High labor cost in Japan	High capital cost in Japan
0.2–8.6 (33)	4.52 (25)	5.85 (27)	4.26 (23)
8.7–37.8 (32)	4.82 (28)	5.55 (29)	4.44 (27)
37.9–94.6 (32)	4.43 (30)	5.10 (30)	4.10 (30)
94.7–300.0 (33)	4.90 (31)	5.28 (32)	4.19 (32)
300.1–7450.0 (31)	4.73 (30)	5.19 (31)	4.57 (30)
All firms (161)	4.70 (153)	5.40 (159)	4.29 (151)

Note: Number of respondents in parentheses.

the larger groups. Thus, most Japanese investors think that Japanese labor costs are high and view foreign investment favorably as means of lowering production costs. However, the amount of foreign investment actually undertaken does not correlate with the perceived severity of the labor costs faced in Japan. Similarly, yen appreciation and high capital costs do not appear to seriously influence the extent of foreign investment undertaken. Thus, in the absence of other identifying factors, the conclusion is that while these cost factors act to push investment abroad, the extent of a specific firm's international investment depends more on its capabilities to exploit opportunities in foreign locations.

Investment in Asia

Our focus now shifts from the extent of foreign investment to the *allocation* of that investment across alternative regions. Thus the variable we examine is the *share* of Japanese foreign investment in Asia. Indirect inferences are also possible regarding firm characteristics that lead to investment in other major locations—the United States and Europe.

Asia's share of foreign investment by the sample firms is 35 percent. However, there is a strong inverse relationship between the size of a firm and its share of investment in Asia (Table 6.1). The smallest firms, on average, undertake 60 percent of their foreign investment in Asia; the share falls to about 20 percent for the largest firms. Presumably, smaller firms have fewer opportunities for diversification. To examine this relationship more closely, we regress the share of investment in Asia against firm characteristics and the strength of various preferences stated by firms.[5]

Firm and industry characteristics   The regression results confirm that, all else equal, smaller firms place a larger proportion of their foreign investment in Asia (Table 6.4). Unlike for aggregate investment flows, we do not now see any impact of firm's R&D on its location decision in Asia. It could have been expected that a greater share of investment in Asia is associated with lower R&D intensity and that technologically sophisticated firms invest to a greater degree in the United States and Europe. However, any effect of techno-logical sophistication appears subsumed by size of investor, since small firms also tend to do less R&D. This speculation draws support from our later discussion on future plans of the surveyed firms where we find that in coming years large firms are more likely to make investment in Asia than small firms, and where R&D does show up as a negative influence on Asian investment.[6]

A feature of some interest (and robustness) is the negative relationship between the export propensity of the investing firm and the share of its foreign investment in Asia. This, it will be noted, is the opposite of the

Table 6.4 Determinants of allocation of investment to Asia (dependent variable: Asian share of past foreign investment)

Variable	OLS	OLS with selectivity correction
Worldwide sales	−0.0009* (−2.14)	−0.0009* (−2.19)
Export/worldwide sales	−54.39** (−1.98)	−51.54** (−1.87)
High capital cost in Japan	7.25* (2.85)	8.04* (3.06)
Low labor cost in host country	−5.53 (−1.67)	−6.21** (−1.85)
Good labor quality in host country	13.14* (3.70)	12.45* (3.47)
Restriction on repatriation of earnings	−11.24* (−3.31)	−11.08* (−3.27)
Correction term		3.30 (1.14)
Constant	37.38 (1.33)	37.11 (1.32)
R-squared	0.49	0.50
No. of observations	50	50

Note: * significant at 5%, ** significant at 10%—t-values in parentheses.

relationship between export propensity and the flow of all foreign investment (measured as a share of the firm's aggregate investment). The implication also is that investment outside Asia (mainly in Europe and the United States) is undertaken by firms with high export intensity. A possible interpretation of this finding is that the Japanese firms investing in Europe and the United States have long exported to those destinations and undertook major investments in these countries during the second half of the 1980s and the early 1990s to produce locally under the threat that their exports would be restricted; the survey captures a snapshot of the tendency of these highly export-oriented firms to increase their production facilities in Western industrialized nations.

In contrast, firms investing in Asia are not doing so under the threat of barriers to exports in that region. Rather, in seeking to participate in the rapid growth elsewhere in Asia, they are also choosing production locations that offer the possibility of efficient production and low costs of inputs. Thus, while perceptions of high Japanese costs do not differentiate foreign investors, the high negative perception of domestic production costs creates the basis for seeking low cost sites, provided (as we shall see) no sacrifice is entailed in production quality. We next explore these production cost and quality features in some detail.

Labor costs   While there is a general presumption from the discussion above that high costs of labor in Japan are a major reason for driving Japanese investment abroad and there are reasons to believe that investment in Asia specifically seeks low wage labor, the survey points to a more nuanced analyses of investment flows to Asia. For example, perceptions of Japanese labor costs was not a significant explanatory variable for investment into Asia. Thus, as before, while Japanese firms consider labor costs in Japan to be onerous, there is little variation in this perception and so it has limited ability to explain the variation in foreign investment undertaken.

To approach the matter from a different perspective, we also asked how important (on a scale from 1 to 7) were low Asian wages in their decision to invest in Asia. Firms did report that low wages were important, the average response being 5.6. However, though low Asian wages are attractive to all investors, regression results presented in Table 6.4 indicate that the perceptions of Asian wages by Japanese investors also do not differentiate the investment decisions. If anything, it appears that firms potentially attracted by low Asian wages tend actually to place a smaller share of their investment in Asia.[7]

Rather, firms require high quality labor—not merely cheap labor. Our results show that it is the variations in the demand for high quality labor that influence the investment decision. Firms that think highly of the labor quality in the Asian region are the ones who undertake substantial investment in that region—greater the perception of labor quality in Asia, greater is the share of investment in Asia. The important message from these findings is that while low wages may be desirable, perceptions of labor quality are key to attracting foreign investment.

These results support the hypothesis proposed by Robert Lucas (1990) that the lack of complementary human capital inputs lowers the productivity of physical capital in developing countries and hence limits the flow of foreign investment to these countries. However, the measure of human capital is not necessarily the levels of educational attainment in that country. For example, our respondents find Thai labor quality to be higher than in the Philippines although the secondary enrolment rates in the Philippines are much higher. Thus the labor quality of interest to foreign investors is related more to industrial experience rather than to formal educational achievements. This does create the possibility of a self-reinforcing condition where an industrially literate labor force attracts foreign investment and such investment further enhances the quality of the labor force. Those not in this loop are in danger of being excluded from the benefits of international capital flows.

Our data does identify differences between firms with regard to their attitude towards low wages. Small firms place a significant premium on low wages. This is seen by the interaction of labor cost perception variable with a dummy for the small 20 percent of the firms. Here the coefficient is positive and significant. Importantly, though, small firms also place a premium on labor quality.

Capital costs   The regression result shows that the severity of perceived Japanese capital costs correlates strongly with the share of investment undertaken in Asia. The surveyed investors, on average, do not consider the capital cost disadvantage in Japan to be high. However, the perceptions of the firm in this regard very much more and this variation is, in turn, reflected in the variation in foreign investment undertaken.

We find further that perceptions of high capital costs in Japan are positively and significantly (at the 5 percent level) correlated with the goal to raise capital from the country in which the investment is being made. The question asked was: How important (on a scale of 1 to 7) is availability of local financing in your decision to invest in Asia? The correlation between this variable and the severity of perceived capital costs in Japan (also measured on a scale of 1 to 7) was 0.29, which is significant at the 5 percent level. Thus, capital costs (and/or the easy availability of finance) appears to be an important factor determining the choice of investment location.

To conclude: we found in the previous section that costs in Japan relative to those prevailing abroad (particularly high Japanese labor costs) play virtually no role in the decision to invest abroad—rather the extent of investment undertaken depends much more on firm-specific attributes. In this section, we have found that relative costs are a much more significant factor in determining the allocation of investment across competing locations. However, costs need to be interpreted here in the broader sense of costs of doing business. Thus, low wage costs do not by themselves constitute low production costs—the quality of labor is critical. Capital costs and availability of local financing are also important considerations in the location decision. These findings closely match the findings from the aggregate data (Mody and Srinivasan 1998; also Ch. 3 this book).

Country policy characteristics In choosing their production locations, what country policies do Japanese investors look for? Limitations on repatriation of earnings is considered a serious disincentive by Japanese investors planning investments in Asia (on a scale of 1 to 7, with 7 being the most severe disincentive ranking, limits on repatriation rank 5.62). Moreover, this perception of disincentive is strongly correlated with a low share of foreign investment going to Asia.

Note, however, the absence of any other country policy measure as correlate of the share of Asian investment in aggregate foreign investment. Of particular interest is the absence of ownership restrictions as influencing Asian investments. Once again we find that the raw perceptions and regression results give seemingly different results. However, it is more appropriate to view these as reflecting different perspectives on investor preferences. We do find that government restrictions on foreign ownership are strongly resented by Japanese investors. Requirements to export are similarly considered a major disincentive: on a scale of 1 (low disincentive) to 7 (high disincentive), restriction of ownership to less than 50 percent of firm equity is rated at 5.7. The requirement to export more than 50 percent of output is rated at 4.9.

However, most countries in which the Japanese firms invest have limited or no ownership restrictions on foreign investors. This results in foreign investors owning a large share of the equity of their venture abroad. For example, investors responding to our survey note that, on average, they owned about 45 percent of the venture in the Philippines and 60 percent of the venture in China. For Thailand, Indonesia, and Malaysia, the average share of equity lay between 50 and 60 percent. Only in Vietnam and India was the share of equity owned on the low side—below 25 percent.

One can interpret these findings in the following manner. Japanese firms screen out those countries with the most onerous ownership restrictions and export obligations. In countries where they do invest, they do view ownership restrictions (and local content requirements) as a disincentive if those restrictions are in place; however, for the most part, these are countries with low restrictions or countries in the process of dismantling restrictions. The results also point to a warning. If, for some reason, the restrictions were reintroduced, then firms with the greatest investment in the country would be the most seriously affected, creating the possibility of large investment outflows.

The implication also is that concerns about repatriation of earnings are both strong and current—unlike ownership restrictions which are in practice being phased out, repatriation of earnings is not thought to be a concern that can be dismissed as practically unimportant. Thus, firms that view repatriation of earnings as a serious problem in Asia do, in fact, lower their Asian investments.

Future plans of Japanese investors in Asia

Currently, Malaysia and Thailand are the most favored locations, followed closely by China. Indonesia is next, but the Philippines, India, and Vietnam have attracted very little Japanese investment (see Table 6.5, which gives the number of firms that have investments in each of the countries). However, as these Japanese firms plan substantial new investments in East Asia, a shift in direction is discernible.[8]

In this section, we describe the determinants of expected Japanese investments in Asia. A question was asked to determine the likelihood of the firm's investment in each of the seven Asian countries in the three years following the survey. For each country, the firm was asked to rank the likelihood from 1 (very unlikely) to 7 (very likely). Table 6.5 compares this likelihood with current presence in the countries considered. There is clearly increasing interest in China, Indonesia, and Vietnam. From an already strong position, China emerges as a strikingly popular likely destination and Japanese investors maintain a solid interest in Thailand and Malaysia. India and the Philippines are currently positioned relatively poorly and there are no indications that they will gain significant Japanese investment in the near future.

As in previous sections, we present now a more detailed analysis of future investment preferences. Our dependent variable is the likelihood of investing in a specific country in the next three years. This set of investigations also permits us to examine the effect of country specific attributes on the plans of investors.[9]

The regression presented in the first column in Table 6.6 assumes that planned investment bears the same relationship to investor characteristics and country features for all host countries. Since this is unlikely to be the case, we also repeat the regression for three country groups: (1) China, Vietnam, and Indonesia; (2) India and the Philippines; and (3) Malaysia and Thailand.

Table 6.5 Characteristics of likely future investors by country

Variable	China	India	Indonesia	Malaysia	The Philippines	Thailand	Vietnam
Number of firms likely to invest in next 3 years	162	155	155	155	155	156	158
Likelihood of future investment (1–7 scale)	4.10	1.74	2.86	2.87	2.03	3.18	2.55
Of those likely to invest, the number who are already present	33	5	28	40	11	47	2
Total number currently present	34	5	31	43	11	52	2

Table 6.6 Determinants of expected investment in Asia (dependent variable: likelihood of future investment)

Variable	All countries	China, Indonesia and Vietnam	India and the Philippines	Malaysia and Thailand
Worldwide sales	0.00003* (4.574)	0.00003* (3.131)	0.00005* (4.246)	0.00002** (1.714)
R&D ratio	−.185** (−1.926)	−0.229 (−1.563)	−0.162 (−1.031)	−0.083 (−0.453)
Export/sales	−2.108* (−3.063)	−2.008** (−1.909)	−0.096 (−.088)	−3.911* (−2.864)
Investment by competitors	0.285* (6.847)	0.317* (5.078)	0.161* (2.092)	0.308* (3.987)
Domestic market	0.179* (5.048)	0.121* (2.436)	0.134** (1.924)	0.157* (1.988)
Labor cost	0.195* (4.670)	0.155* (2.212)	0.059 (0.915)	0.282* (3.071)
Labor quality	0.079** (1.703)	0.046 (0.681)	0.056 (0.711)	0.079 (0.791)
Equipment and parts	0.007 (0.13)	−0.072 (−0.931)	0.126 (1.228)	0.135 (1.373)
FDI policy	0.121* (2.132)	0.280* (3.511)	0.077 (0.704)	−0.144 (−1.271)
Constant	−0.463 (−0.997)	0.171 (0.225)	0.057 (0.081)	−0.191 (−0.204)
Adjusted R-squared	0.38	0.38	0.36	0.29

Note: * significant at 5%, ** at 10%, t-values in parentheses.

Any grouping runs the risk of being arbitrary. Our reason for this particular division was that the first group is experiencing the most growth in investors; the second group has had low investment and is not attracting much investor attention either; the third group, Malaysia and Thailand, has had significant investment in the past and is continuing to retain strong investor interest.

Firm characteristics The likelihood of investment in the countries under consideration increases as the size of the firm increases, this being true for all countries and for each of the three groups. This suggests that unlike in the past when small firms were more focused on Asia, the larger firms are displaying strong interest with the possibility of increased share of their investment in that region. Consistent with previous results, once size is controlled for, then firm R&D has a negative influence on planned investment. Finally, the export ratio of the firm is also negatively correlated with its planned investment in the Asian countries under consideration. This implies a continuation of the past investment pattern: those serving the Japanese market are more actively seeking Asian investment locations than those who have a significant export presence.

Role of competitors   A most interesting finding is that foreign investment decisions are very closely related to those that competitors are expected to take. We asked our respondents how likely it was that their competitors would invest in each of the seven countries. The regression results show a strong partial correlation between the firm's plans and its expectations regarding the behavior of its competitors: if a firm expects that its competitors are very likely to invest in China, the firm itself considers it very likely that it would invest in China.

Of interest here is the difference between the three country groups. The influence of competitors is most powerful for the China/Indonesia/Vietnam group. The coefficient of 0.33 could crudely be interpreted as indicating that a one percent increase in the likelihood of competitors investing in these countries will have the effect of raising the respondent firm's likelihood of investing in those countries by 0.33 percent. (This elasticity interpretation assumes that the scales represent logarithmic preferences.) At the other extreme, the coefficient for India and the Philippines has a value of 0.16, suggesting that while investors are influenced by the behavior of other investors in these countries, the rush to India and the Philippines is much less. Finally, the coefficient for Malaysia and Thailand is 0.28, which is a strong indication that these countries are not close to saturation in terms of the flow of new investment, as some observers are inclined to believe. Our findings here support Raymond Vernon's observations on the importance of strategic considerations in driving foreign investment.[10]

Host country characteristics   Respondents to our survey reported that their most important market was the domestic market of the country they were investing in, with importance measured on a scale from 1 (not important) to 7 (very important). Here both the stated perceptions and the regression results point in the same direction. The raw score for importance of the domestic market was 5.5 (for all other markets, the score was less than 5.0). Moreover, the pooled regression results, as well as the results for different groups, show that perception of the size of the host country's domestic market exerts a positive influence on planned investment in that country.

Availability of parts and equipment is an important factor in guiding future investment, though the results are not significant at conventional levels. The effect appears most pronounced for Malaysia and Thailand, and for the pooled regression. The implication is that investors are sensitive to perceptions of availability of parts and equipment when making investment decisions within Malaysia and Thailand, and when choosing between the three groups.

Low labor cost and high labor quality are also important factors. Notice that while labor quality continues to be important, low wages emerges as a strong factor here, in contrast to the case where we explained the share of Asian investment in all foreign investment. The finding could reflect a change from the past when Japanese investment was only in its early stages; with major new investment planned, wages may play a more key role in determining investment locations. However, one difference between the results here and in the previous section is that here we are considering investments in specific countries whereas earlier we were investigating determinants of investments in all these countries. The implication could be that when taken as a group, low wages in these countries are not the main feature attracting Japanese investment, but choice within the group of countries is influenced by perceived wage levels.

Finally, favorable FDI policy is a desirable country characteristic. Here we are unable to distinguish between different aspects of FDI policy. Our earlier discussion (in the previous section) was based on generally desirable properties of FDI policy. In this section, our explanatory variables refer to specific countries and attempting to elicit views on specific aspects of FDI policy for every country was determined to be unworkable. However, we did try one variation on the basic regression to further examine the role of FDI policy. We interacted the country perception of FDI policy with the presence or absence of the firm in that country. The result shows that policy has less influence on likelihood of investment if the firm is already present in the country under consideration. The implication is that perception of FDI policy is more relevant as a potential barrier to entry rather than as an impediment to expansion of existing firms that, presumably, have learnt to work within the system.

Conclusions and discussion of findings

The payoff from this micro-level analysis of Japanese investment has been two-fold. First, we have been able to identify key firm characteristics that influence decisions to invest abroad. Second, we were able to relate stated preferences to actual investments undertaken and to likely future investments.

Firm characteristics We find that firm characteristics have a very significant influence in determining both aggregate foreign investment flows and their allocation across competing locations. In particular, firm characteristics are the dominant discernible influence on the decision to invest abroad. Perceptions of cost conditions in Japan—generally negative, especially with regard to labor costs—may well influence the extent of foreign investment but since the perceptions are held with some uniformity across firms, the ability to distinguish their influence is limited. Thus while there may be a general push based on rising domestic costs, the differential response to this push indicates that those with favorable inherent capabilities are best able to exploit opportunities for establishing production facilities abroad.

The precise nature of foreign investment capabilities can only be indirectly inferred from the data. Firm size is important in determining investment abroad—large firms, all else equal, invest more abroad. An important finding was the dampening effect of high R&D on foreign investment. Technologically sophisticated Japanese firms are under less competitive threat than other Japanese firms and hence have less need to move production closer to customers or seek cheaper locations. If not R&D, then what are the firm-specific advantages that enable Japanese firms to be successful foreign investors? An important clue may lie in the strong positive relationship between foreign investment and export propensity. Large size, low R&D, and high export intensity combine to suggest that Japanese foreign investors exploit their access to marketing channels (for international trade) and their superior factory-level production techniques.

In considering the allocation of foreign investment to Asia, the results show that in the past smaller firms have had a greater share of their investment in Asia; but looking ahead, large firms have stronger expectations about investments in Asia, implying that they could increase the share of their foreign investment in that region. The share of investment in Asia is inversely related to export propensity, suggesting that investments undertaken by Japanese firms outside Asia (especially in Europe and the United States) to leap over trade barriers while, in contrast, Asian investments are being driven more by perceptions of market growth in that region. It is possible that the growing Asian markets could equally be served from production locations in Japan. However, the attraction of Asia is augmented by favorable production conditions in some countries in the region. The race with competitors is indicative of the pressure to establish early presence in the markets to be served.

Market orientation   According to this survey, foreign subsidiaries of Japanese firms export about one-third of their output from their operations in Asia. However, our analysis of the expected trends in the coming few years suggests that the domestic market will continue to be a major attraction for foreign investors in all countries. Indeed, except for exports to Japan from the China–Indonesia–Vietnam group, expectations of exports play no part in explaining the likelihood of a firm making an investment in a particular country.

What are the factors that can increase Japanese investor interest in exports from their host locations? The survey shows that firms that export a larger share of their output from their subsidiary in the host country, tend to import a larger share of their inputs. Where imports are being restricted by trade barriers and local content rules, the implication of our survey would be removal of such barriers would permit greater exports. The survey also indicates that exports from host countries depend upon the availability of a pool of trained manpower, specially technicians and supervisors.

Human capital development   The survey results highlight the strong Japanese investor preference for operating in conditions where the human capital is well developed. We saw this in different ways: the share of investment in Asia was higher for firms looking for high labor quality and the likelihood of investing in a country in the coming years was also influenced by its labor quality. In addition, the size of operation of the subsidiary (measured by the number of employees) is correlated with the labor quality in that country and, as noted, the share of exports in sales is related to easy availability of technicians and supervisors.

This is strong confirmation of the Lucas (1990) hypothesis on the need for complementary human assets for the flow of financial capital. However, it also raises questions about the developmental role of foreign investment. It is widely presumed that foreign investment can be an effective means for bringing "best practice" to a country and for widely disseminating these practices through labor turnover from the foreign enterprises or through training to local suppliers. We were unable to verify the extent to which such diffusion occurs through on-the-job training, Japanese practices such as job rotation that leads to multiple-skilling, or the imposition of quality standards on suppliers leading to an indirect transmission of knowledge.

What we do see, however, is that Japanese investors demand a minimum labor quality—which includes availability of technicians and supervisors and, hence, is a pretty stiff minimum. Where such a high quality environment exists, Japanese production techniques are effective, and lead to further enhancement of skills. Where the relevant skills are not available, the probability of attracting Japanese investors, and the ensuing further development of human skills, is less likely. This, of course, raises the difficult question of how such minimum skills are to be identified and developed. Since perceptions of labor quality are only loosely related (and sometimes quite contrary) to conventional educational measures, measures undertaken to encourage firm-level training would have a higher pay-off than secondary school enrolment. An implication could be to explicitly require foreign investors to undertake significant training programs, as apparently was the case in Singapore.

FDI policy   The findings strongly support investor preferences for favorable FDI policies. For the three groups of countries considered, perception of favorable FDI policy leads to greater investment in the country. There is, of course, a difficult question of causality here. Firms that invest a lot in a particular country are likely to be more familiar with the workings of policy and could view it as less intimidating than firms that have no (or limited presence) and hence limited experience in the country. If this is indeed the case, then the FDI policy would have more of an influence on entry than on continued expansion in the country. The evidence presented suggests there is in fact some basis for thinking so. The implication is that better information and dissemination of information on FDI policy may have dividends, such as through using existing investors more actively to convey their experiences to potential investors at carefully organized symposia.

Alternatively, specialized and proactive agencies that "hold the hands" of potential investors could also be a useful instrument in attracting foreign investment. These agencies do not have to be a part of the government—non-governmental organizations and even private enterprises could play an important role. The example of "shelter operations" in northern Mexico is instructive. Despite the favorable maquiladora policies that allowed foreign investors easy imports of equipment and materials, foreign firms still find themselves hesitant to make the first investment. About two decades ago, a largely private initiative led to the formation of shelters, which provide the foreign firm with all local services (including dealing with the government, hiring workers, and renting space). This has proved to be a lucrative business and has fostered foreign investment in the region. The role of the government was in financing some of the early industrial estates that became the homes for some of the shelters; much industrial estate development since has also been privately financed.

FDI policy covers a diverse range of initiatives and it is necessary to peel open its components. Where it was possible to do so, we found that repatriation of earnings was a very serious concern to investors, not just in terms of their perceptions but also in terms of how it influenced their investment decisions. That this should be the case is easily understandable. A clear implication is that greater freedom to transmit earned profits has to be a high policy priority. Other dimensions of FDI policy, although perceived by investors as important, seemed to have less influence on actual investment decisions. Ownership restrictions and export requirements for example were perceived as serious disincentives but had no clear effect on investments undertaken. One explanation we offered is that ownership restrictions are, in practice, not very strong in most East Asian economies. Thus, while investors would view them as disincentives if they were in place, their practical lack of restrictiveness makes them not very relevant in explaining investment decisions.

Export requirements and local content rules seem to go together. If export requirements are present, it is important, as discussed above, that local content rules be relaxed—firms that need to export require international quality inputs at international prices. Thus, a policy that imposes export targets without allowing virtually free imports is going to be a serious deterrent to investors. Alternatively, if local content rules are in place, foreign entrepreneurs will have to be allowed to sell a substantial proportion of their output in the domestic market.

Notes

1 According to a survey conducted by the Japan External Trade Organization (Jetro), one-fifth of production by Japanese firms is located overseas and this share

is expected to grow to a third. The shift abroad is often described as the "hollowing" out of Japanese manufacturing. U.S. firms produce 25 percent of their output abroad while German firms are the least international with less than 20 percent of their output produced at foreign locations (Dawkins 1996).

2 To reduce the burden on survey respondents, we did not ask them to specify their exact R&D ratio. Instead, we asked them to state the range of their R&D expenditure to total sales ratio: zero, less than 1 percent, 1–3 percent, 3–5 percent, and greater than 5 percent.

3 For the United States, Horst (1972) also finds increased size to be a predictor of the likelihood that a firm will invest abroad; however, he finds a much stronger positive effect than we do here. As the descriptive statistics show, small Japanese firms do undertake significant foreign investment.

4 For a recent survey of the literature relating Japanese foreign investment to its "organizational prowess", including factory-level practices and long-term inter-firm networks, see Caves (1993).

5 Once again, as above, we control for bias due to non-reporting by some firms. However, here a Tobit regression was not required since all reported shares of investment in Asia were greater than zero.

6 This result is consistent with the Kogut and Chang (1991) finding that a Japanese industrial sector is more likely to undertake investment in the United States the higher the level of R&D in the industry. Thus, although high R&D firms are in general not likely to undertake foreign investment, if they do so, the investment is more likely to be in the more industrialized nations.

7 Once again, there is a similarity between Japanese and Swedish foreign investors. Swedenborg (1979) reports that Swedish firms are found to invest in high wage locations and interprets this to indicate a preference for high skill labor required for the relatively sophisticated production operations undertaken by Swedish multinationals.

8 A similar shift is evident in the aggregate as investments in Europe and the U.S. have grown at a slower pace in recent years while Asia and Latin America have become increasingly favored locations (Dawkins 1996).

9 In this set of regressions, there is no 'correction' term for missing observations since almost all firms reported their likelihood of investing in different countries.

10 Such rivalry evidently extends beyond Japanese investors. A German investor recently summarized well the phenomenon: 'We simply cannot sit back and let the Japanese take over another market unchallenged' (*Financial Times*, March 28, 1993). It is very likely that Japanese and other investors feel similarly.

References

Cantwell, John (1989) *Technical Innovations in Multinational Corporations*. London: Basil Blackwell.

Caves, Richard (1982) *Multinational Enterprise and Economic Analysis*. New York: Cambridge University Press.

Caves, Richard (1993) "Japanese investment in the United States: Lessons for the Economic analysis of foreign investment." *World Economy* 16(3): 279–300.

Dawkins, William (1996) "Japan shifts foreign investment focus." *Financial Times* February 13: 8.

Heckman, James (1979) "Sample selection bias as a specification error." *Econometrica* 47: 153–161.

Horst, Thomas (1972) "Firm and industry determinants of the decision to invest abroad: an empirical study." *Review of Economics and Statistics* 54 (August): 258–266.

Kogut, Bruce and Sea Jin Chang (1991) "Technological capabilities and Japanese foreign direct investment in the United States." *Review of Economics and Statistics* 73(3): 401–413.

Lucas, Robert E. (1990) "Why capital doesn't flow from rich to poor countries?" *American Economic Review* 80(2): 92–96.

Maddala, G.S. (1983) *Limited Dependent and Qualitative Variables in Econometrics*. New York: Cambridge University Press.

Mody, Ashoka and Krishna Srinivasan (1998) "U.S. and Japanese investors: do they march to the same tune?" *Canadian Journal of Economics* 31(4): 778–799.

Swedenborg, Birgitta (1979) "*The Multinational Operations of Swedish Firms: An Analysis of Determinants and Effects*." Stockholm: The Industrial Institute for Economic and Social Research.

Vernon, Raymond (1993) "Where are multinationals headed?" In Kenneth A. Froot (ed.) *Foreign Direct Investment*. Chicago: The University of Chicago Press.

Wheeler, David and Ashoka Mody (1992) "International investment location decisions: the case of US firms." *Journal of International Economics* 33: 57–76.

Part II

FDI benefits

Growth, investment, and efficiency

7 Explaining industrial growth in coastal China

Economic reforms . . . and what else?

With Fang-Yi Wang

In the 1980s China experienced an explosion of pent-up entrepreneurship facilitated by wide-ranging, although often unorthodox, economic reforms. Walker's (1993) apt metaphor rightly focuses the spotlight on China's entrepreneurs who include not just factory managers but also local government officials, especially mayors of cities and counties. Growth in gross domestic product (GDP) jumped from 6.4 percent a year between 1965 and 1980 to 10.1 percent between 1980 and 1989. From 1985 to 1989, the years on which we focus, the pace of economic reforms was stepped up and performance was especially outstanding: GDP grew at 11.5 percent a year, and industrial output, the principal engine of growth, grew at a yearly rate of 14.4 percent. Moreover, factor productivity—which made virtually no contribution to growth in the three decades before 1980—grew at an annual rate of 2.4 percent for state-owned enterprises and 4.6 percent for collectively owned enterprises and accounted for 27 percent of growth between 1980 and 1988 (Chow 1993; Jefferson, Rawski, and Zheng 1990). At the same time China's share of world markets jumped dramatically between 1985 and 1989, particularly (but not exclusively) in light manufactured goods, such as shoes, clothing, toys, and small electrical appliances.

Gains in industrial output were especially marked in the coastal region, where growth during 1985–89 was significantly higher than that in other regions and was also substantially above its own growth rate in the previous five years (see Table 7.1). Five coastal provinces (Fujian, Guangdong, Jiangsu, Shandong, and Zhejiang) were at the center of the "miracle," registering growth rates of about 20 percent a year between 1985 and 1989. The performance of the three coastal counties (Beijing, Shanghai, and Tianjin) was less impressive. Throughout China, but especially in the coastal provinces, enterprises in the nonstate sector were the star performers. In the Chinese context, the nonstate sector includes collective enterprises, which are typically owned by local governments—that is, by governments below the provincial or county level—whose officials have been a key source of domestic entrepreneurship (see Bateman and Mody 1991 and Oi 1992). Table 7.2 provides the share of industry by ownership for the eight coastal provinces and counties.

Table 7.1 Growth in industrial output by ownership in Coastal China, 1980–89 (average annual percent)

Region	Total		State-owned		Collectively owned		Others[a]	
	1980–85	1985–89	1980–85	1985–89	1980–85	1985–89	1980–85	1985–89
Coastal counties								
Beijing	8.7	12.9	6.2	8.3	12.0	12.1	37.9	36.2
Tianjin	9.1	11.4	7.2	4.9	11.6	12.0	24.5	35.8
Shanghai	7.3	6.6	5.1	2.2	15.7	8.8	23.3	30.8
Coastal provinces								
Jiangsu	15.1	17.3	8.6	9.9	19.3	18.4	27.5	26.6
Zhejiang	18.7	17.8	10.4	8.2	23.4	18.0	33.0	28.6
Fujian	13.5	20.5	9.2	11.4	13.8	16.6	33.7	37.5
Shandong	11.2	21.5	6.8	10.2	15.6	21.9	26.8	55.3
Guangdong	14.4	23.5	11.2	15.1	16.6	22.2	23.4	40.7
Total	12.0	16.5	7.4	8.0	17.6	18.0	27.7	34.6
China	11.3	14.4	7.9	8.7	17.9	19.0	—	—

— Not available.
a. Includes mainly collectively owned enterprises below the township level, private enterprises, partnerships, individuals, and joint ventures with foreigners.

Source: China, State Statistical Bureau (1990).

Table 7.2. The share of industry by ownership in Coastal China, 1980, 1985, and 1989 (percent)

Region	State-owned			Collectively owned			Others[a]		
	1980	1985	1989	1980	1985	1989	1980	1985	1989
Coastal counties									
Beijing	80.6	71.1	59.6	17.4	20.5	19.6	2.1	8.4	20.8
Tianjin	80.1	72.1	55.8	15.6	17.7	18.4	4.4	10.2	25.8
Shanghai	87.5	77.5	65.8	9.6	15.4	16.3	2.9	7.1	18.0
Coastal provinces									
Jiangsu	57.2	40.5	30.6	33.4	40.6	42.4	9.4	18.9	27.1
Zhejiang	56.1	35.5	24.6	34.5	44.4	44.6	9.4	20.1	30.9
Fujian	71.2	56.8	40.1	21.1	21.8	18.7	7.7	21.4	41.2
Shandong	67.6	54.6	38.5	26.6	32.4	32.6	5.9	13.0	28.9
Guangdong	63.0	52.5	37.6	27.1	30.6	28.6	9.9	17.0	33.9
Total	71.4	55.7	40.8	22.5	29.9	31.4	6.1	14.3	27.8

a. Includes mainly collectively owned enterprises below the township level, private enterprises, partnerships, individuals, and joint ventures with foreigners.

Source: China, State Statistical Bureau (1990).

To examine China's exceptional growth experience, this article attempts to explain the variation in the growth of 23 industrial sectors in each of seven provinces and counties along the east coast of China during the period 1985 to 1989. The unit of analysis is the growth rate of an industrial sector in a specific region in a specific year. Three sets of influences on the growth rate are examined:

- *Industry-specific features:* the degree of specialization and competition.
- *Regional growth factors:* the availability of infrastructure, educational levels, and direct foreign investment; also, the initial per capita income of the province or county measures the extent of backwardness and hence the catch-up potential.
- *Regional spillover effects:* the relationship between growth in a region and growth in other regions.

Certain distinguishing features of this analysis, as well as its limitations, are worth noting. First, by comparing growth rates within a relatively homogeneous region (the Chinese east coast), the study overcomes some concerns in interpreting cross-country growth regressions, where it is difficult to control for widely different economic, social, and political regimes.[1] Second, studies of developing-country growth focus principally on a country's GDP (Mankiw 1995 surveys that literature); our focus on individual industrial sectors is likely to yield more reliable estimates. In this respect, we follow Glaeser *et al.* (1992) and Henderson, Kuncoro, and Turner (1995) who study industrial growth within the United States. Third, we build on the analysis of Glaeser *et al.* (1992) by including the possibility of regional spillovers along with regional influences. Fourth, although covering only a short time span of four years, we are able to exploit the panel features of the data to examine factors influencing growth within and across the provinces and counties. Finally, we also study whether heavy and light industries have been subject to different growth impulses.

The main limitation of the study arises from the concern that the industrial output data used may have built-in biases. We are reassured, however, by the significant variation in growth rates across sectors, regions, and time, suggesting that measured growth rates are not merely a reflection of some bureaucratic data-recording process. Moreover, we conduct a number of sensitivity analyses running regressions for different samples, checking for the presence of influential observations, and testing the robustness of important explanatory variables. However, we have attempted to interpret the results conservatively, highlighting the most quantitatively and statistically significant findings.

Section I decomposes output growth into time-dependent, regionwide, and industry-specific components, as well as their interactions, to identify the proximate sources of growth. Section II describes the approach to studying the correlates of growth used and our explanatory variables. Section III presents and interprets our findings. Section IV summarizes our major findings and also draws some lessons for other countries.

I. A decomposition of growth of output

Did growth occur across the board or only in certain regions or industries? Within regions or industries, did growth vary substantially from year to year? Variance analysis allows us to quantitatively decompose output growth into time, region, and industry-specific effects and their interactions. Identifying the main sources of variance in the data through decomposition analysis helps in a preliminary quantitative assessment of the different sources of growth. The finding of significant time and regional differences in growth rates after controlling for sectoral growth patterns also provides some reassurance that the industrial output data are not being generated in a bureaucratically mechanical manner.

Growth in time period t, region r, and industry i, G_{tri}, is assumed to be the additive result of main and interaction effects.

$$G_{tri} = m + a_t + \beta_r + \tau_i + a_{tr} + b_{ti} + c_{ri} + \varepsilon_{tri} \tag{1}$$

where m is a constant, a_t, β_r, and τ_i are the main time, region, and industry effects, respectively, a_{tr}, b_{ti}, and c_{ri} are the second-order interaction terms between two main effects, and ε_{tri} is the interaction term for the three main effects.

Following Schankerman (1991), the variance of output growth can therefore be expressed as:

$$\text{Var}(G_{tri}) = \text{Var}(a_t) + \text{Var}(\beta_r) + \text{Var}(\tau_i) + \text{Var}(a_{tr}) + \text{Var}(b_{ti}) + \text{Var}(c_{ri}) + \text{Var}(\varepsilon_{tri}). \tag{2}$$

4.98	5.72	2.88	1.33	48.14	2.18	34.78

The numbers below the variables in equation 2 are the results derived by equating the expected values of the variance components with their observed values (see Appendix for the derivation). Because this is a decomposition, the values add up to 100 percent. The small variance of a_t—4.98 percent—implies that during 1985 to 1989, time-varying factors had only a minor effect on growth. Thus, although the overall pace of reforms accelerated, the effect was not felt uniformly in all regions and industries.

Purely regional effects, β_r, were also small—5.72 percent—implying that across years and industrial sectors, there was no consistent ranking of regional growth. Together with their interaction, time, and region effects, a_t, β_r, and a_{tr} explain 12 percent of the variation in growth. Thus reforms did not manifest themselves primarily through general coastal expansion or through growth in specific coastal provinces or counties.

Industry-specific factors, τ_j, were small as well, accounting for 2.88 percent of the variation in growth. Hence, no industrial group grew uniformly rapidly or slowly throughout the period. For example, the electronics and telecommunications sector grew only 5.6 percent in 1985–86, whereas in 1987–88, it rose a remarkable 19.3 percent.

The dominant source of variation in the data comes from the interaction of time and industry (b_{ti}), which explains 48.14 percent of the total variance in growth. Thus output growth rates for specific sectors varied from year to year, but within a year they were strongly correlated across regions. This effect captures an industry-specific wave phenomenon evident from a visual examination of the time pattern of sectoral growth rates for miscellaneous light industries in Table 7.3. The term wave is used here not to suggest any predictable sequence of industries experiencing successive surges in growth, but only to indicate that specific industries achieved high rates of growth across regions at the same time. Different industries led in different years; some of the most labor-intensive sectors, such as garments, achieved their biggest spurt only very late. The wave phenomenon was not restricted to light industries. In 1985–86 rapid growth was evident in leather products, pharmaceutical products, chemical fibers, and metallic products in most of the coastal region. In 1986–87 electronics and chemicals replaced leather and metallic products. In 1987–88 paper products, transportation equipment, electronics, and pharmaceutical products expanded rapidly, only to lose their position to the apparel industry in 1988–89.

Such synchronization could be accounted for by shifts in buyers' preferences for goods, industry-specific technological improvements rapidly transmitted along the coast, or coordinated strategies among decision makers to promote growth of specific industries at specific times. Also formal and informal interactions among firms and labor turnover, particularly of highly skilled managers and engineers, may have extended technology and skills learned in the open areas to the rest of the coastal region (Ho and Huenemann 1984, p. 55). Another intriguing possibility is that decision makers (whether in the communist party or industrial administration) maintained close ties that led to the rapid diffusion of development strategies along the coast (see Yusuf 1993 and the literature he cites). This network of decision makers could provide a grid for information flows leading to replication of sectoral targeting strategies, among other things. In a field study of major decision makers, Oi (1995) found considerable support for this hypothesis.

But the synchronization could also reflect data limitations. If price deflators for particular industrial groups are biased in different directions in different years, then high synchronization would be built into the data, making it *appear* that certain sectors grew more rapidly than others in a given year when, in fact, they did not. Such biases in industrial price deflators would exaggerate the extent of synchronization. Here, in this variance decomposition, the limited objective is to describe the variance in the data, whether it arises from data artifacts or from interesting economic forces. In the

Table 7.3 Growth in output of light industries in Coastal China, 1985–89 (average annual percent)

Years and industries	Guangdong	Fujian	Jiangsu	Zhejiang	Shandong	Beijing	Tianjin	Shanghai
1985–86								
Apparel	27.0	20.6	11.8	1.1	12.7	−5.6	6.7	−14.7
Leather products	31.2	28.8	22.7	15.0	26.3	5.7	9.8	8.3
Wood products	3.1	9.3	13.1	17.5	5.0	−0.7	−7.4	0.5
Furniture	4.4	−1.9	11.2	11.0	18.6	3.3	−4.3	2.1
Paper products	15.8	11.8	18.8	15.8	18.0	8.8	5.4	2.4
Art products	14.9	39.5	−7.6	11.8	25.6	−36.7	−3.0	−16.6
Plastic	17.3	17.5	8.4	11.3	19.7	3.6	6.7	5.1
1986–87								
Apparel	36.1	19.1	14.5	17.6	13.8	4.3	−0.1	11.3
Leather products	54.5	13.5	24.1	13.0	18.7	−2.3	−2.8	3.9
Wood products	15.3	16.2	24.1	1.1	16.3	−3.0	−15.7	−0.7
Furniture	26.1	12.6	19.8	14.6	21.0	13.1	0.4	5.8
Paper products	28.1	16.8	27.8	20.2	20.8	10.2	6.2	15.5
Art products	20.8	12.1	21.1	20.4	41.1	14.4	8.6	2.1
Plastic	27.3	13.4	18.7	17.6	21.6	−8.7	6.5	4.0
1987–88								
Apparel	15.4	21.0	12.7	17.4	20.1	13.2	−8.9	7.1
Leather products	17.2	17.0	9.1	9.1	9.7	−22.2	−3.4	−2.2
Wood products	25.1	20.0	−7.1	8.8	16.3	−7.6	−27.2	−16.0
Furniture	10.5	6.0	6.6	14.2	17.5	1.9	−2.7	0.5
Paper products	95.7	56.0	79.5	64.3	60.7	155.6	66.4	103.2
Art products	0.8	21.2	13.2	18.5	28.7	18.0	11.9	6.2
Plastic	14.8	18.4	6.8	16.7	26.5	−1.4	−3.2	−4.6
1988–89								
Apparel	28.2	49.8	13.1	16.9	15.2	12.4	14.5	7.3
Leather products	26.6	5.0	−1.8	10.7	10.4	−3.0	−4.0	−3.5
Wood products	5.1	13.4	−5.5	5.0	23.6	−10.0	−12.0	−3.7
Furniture	6.9	1.7	−11.1	−7.0	10.3	3.8	−6.6	−1.3
Paper products	5.7	11.1	−0.4	4.7	10.4	2.5	−5.2	−2.3
Art products	10.7	8.7	11.5	20.8	27.0	−3.6	8.9	18.4
Plastic	15.5	14.2	2.6	4.0	17.5	0.8	−8.9	0.9

Note: The underlined values indicate an industry-specific wave phenomenon evident from a visual examination of the time pattern of sectoral growth rates for miscellaneous light industries. Although output growth rates for specific sectors varied from year to year, certain sectors achieved high rates of growth across regions.

Source: China, State Statistical Bureau, *China Statistical Yearbook* (various years).

regression results reported below, however, interpretation is more critical. A conditioning term—growth of the same industry outside the region—could be viewed as a control variable for this deficiency in the quality of data. But in this case, we would have to downplay its interpretation as a measure of regional spillovers. The continued plausibility of the regional spillover hypothesis arises from the differences in degree of the cross-regional synchronization for heavy and light industries and the findings of a field study (Oi 1995). Such synchronization is also evident in the study by Glaeser *et al.* (1992).

The remaining 34.78 percent of the variance in output growth is attributable to the third-order interaction between time, region, and industry (ε_{tri}). We interpret this as a regional effect conditional on time-varying industry-specific factors. Although the changing identity of high-growth sectors is a major source of variation in growth, this third-order interaction indicates that growth in an industrial sector during a particular year is not uniform in every region. Regional differences in initial conditions, human capital endowment, and infrastructure availability, among others, may cause industries in some regions to grow faster than those in others. Thus even though the own effect of regional differences (β_r), and its interactions with time (a_{tr}) or industry (c_{ri}), do not explain much of the variation in growth, after adjusting for time-varying *and* industry-specific factors, significant regional effects remain.

Unconditional time, industry, and regional factors do not carry significant explanatory power for variation in growth. Instead, about half the variation in growth during 1985–89 is associated with time-varying sectoral growth differences (b_{tr}). Regional effects, by contrast, emerge only after controlling for the time *and* industry effects.

II. Investigating the correlates of growth

The annual growth rate of output in an industrial sector in a given region is our dependent variable. Various industry-specific, regionwide, and cross-regional factors are the independent variables whose correlation with growth we seek to examine. The goal here is not to test any specific model of growth but to describe its most robust partial correlates.

Following Glaeser *et al.* (1992), we focus on growth itself rather than on increases in productivity. (Their dependent variable was employment growth; we use output growth.) Although it may be more appropriate to use increases in labor or total factor productivity as the dependent variable, this is not possible in our case because consistent labor force data by industrial sector are not consistently available. We find, however, that the data on growth of industrial output are so rich that considerable insights can be obtained even in the absence of information on labor and capital inputs. Indeed, if we believe that enterprise-level decisions to acquire or invest in labor or capital inputs are influenced by available knowledge, infrastructure, human capital, and industrial organization, then not only productivity but also a considerable amount of output growth can be attributed to these factors.

The basic framework of analysis is described in Figure 7.1 for two regions (A and B) and three industrial sectors (1, 2, and 3). The most proximate influences on an industry's growth rate are industry-specific variables that condition the extent of knowledge flows within an industry and the incentives to invest in the development and appropriation of knowledge. The variables we use—the degree of industry specialization and entrepreneurship—are the same as those used by Glaeser *et al.* (1992). We add a set of regional variables

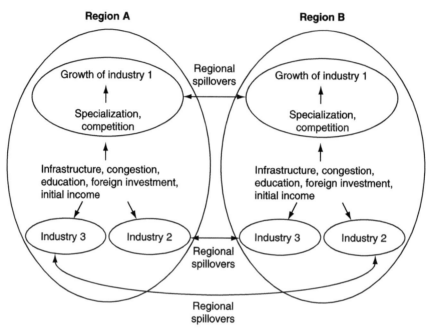

Figure 7.1 A framework for industrial growth in Coastal China.

to the regressions. The assumption is that having controlled for industry-specific characteristics, the effect of region-specific variables (such as infrastructure) will be similarly felt by all industries (for a similar assumption, see Waldmann and De Long 1990, who analyze growth across industries in different countries, and Stockman 1988). Finally, if there are regional spillovers, an industry in a particular region will be influenced by growth in other regions.

Table 7.4 provides descriptive statistics for the seven provinces and counties used in the regression analysis below for 1986–89. The regression analysis, unlike the variance decomposition, is based on data only for seven regions (the five coastal provinces and two counties—Shanghai and Tianjin); foreign investment data for Beijing are not available.

Industry-specific variables

An important structural feature of an industry is its degree of regional specialization. Presumably greater specialization is good if the relevant knowledge is best acquired within the industry, but deleterious when diverse skills and information from other industries are important. Another important industry characteristic is the degree of entrepreneurship and competition that can spur investment, although too much competition can lead to diminished investible surpluses. With the data at hand, the existence of entrepreneurship

Table 7.4 Descriptive statistics for the data on industry in Coastal China, 1986–89

Variable	Mean	Standard deviation	Minimum value	Maximum value
Industry specific				
Specialization index,[a] S	1.028	0.466	0.000	4.347
Entrepreneurship index,[b] E	1.203	0.839	0.018	5.292
Region specific				
Secondary school enrolment rate	0.444	0.125	0.300	0.731
Accumulated foreign direct investment per person (thousands of dollars)	0.015	0.019	0.000	0.067
Roads[c] (kilometers)	0.434	0.174	0.262	0.882
Interaction between roads and congestion (population per square kilometer)	389.543	532.696	75.648	1,797.400
Telephones per 1,000 persons	13.462	9.473	4.712	36.194
GDP per capita (current yuans)	1,845.360	1,188.910	708.000	5,161.000
Regional spillover				
Growth in industry in region, G (percent)	0.112	0.151	−0.423	1.032
Growth in industry outside region (percent)	0.104	0.119	−0.195	0.886

Note: Statistics are for beginning-of-period values, based on annual data for 1985–86 to 1988–89 for seven provinces and counties: Fujian, Guangdong, Jiangsu, Shandong, Shanghai, Tianjin, and Zhejiang.

a. The specialization index for industry i in region r, at time t is S_{irt} = (output in industry i / total output) for region r / (output in industry i / total output) for all regions.

b. The entrepreneurship index for industry i, in region r, at time t is E_{irt} = [(number of firms/total output) for industry i in region r] / [(number of firms / total output) for industry i in all regions].

c. Length of road routes (kilometers) is normalized by area (square kilometers).

Source: Authors' calculations based on data from China, State Statistical Bureau (1990); *China Statistical Yearbook* (various years); Hayase and Kawamata (1990); *Statistical Yearbook of Fujian* (various years); *Statistical Yearbook of Guangdong* (various years).

or competition is inferred only indirectly from the size of firms in industry i in region r relative to its average in all seven regions.

As in Glaeser *et al.* (1992), we calculate the following measures of specialization, S_{irt}, and entrepreneurship, E_{irt}:

S_{irt} = [(output in industry i / total output) for region r] / [(output in industry i / total output) for all regions]

E_{irt} = [(number of firms / total output) for industry i in region r] / [(number of firms / total output) for industry i in all regions].

The time subscript indicates that these measures are different for each year.

S_{irt} is the ratio of the share of industry i in region r to its average share across the seven regions. S greater than 1 implies that the industry commands a larger share of the region's output than the average share that industry enjoys in the seven regions. We interpret a rising S_{irt} for a region-industry as an indication of increasing specialization of that industry in that region. As S increases, knowledge flows will be increasingly restricted to sources within that industry. Learning from other industrial sectors is likely to be greater when S is low. Jacobs (1969), who contends that exchanges of information between different sectors are more productive than exchanges within a sector, predicts that high-S industries will grow more slowly than low-S industries. Porter (1990) makes the opposite prediction. Interpretations other than knowledge flows can also be used to explain the link between S and growth. For example, suitability of regional factor endowments to the sector may contribute to a positive relationship between S and growth.

We interpret E_{irt} as a possible measure of entrepreneurial strength, but it could also measure the degree of competition. If small firms are synonymous with more competition, and more firms imply the existence of entrepreneurship, then the interpretations of the variable will be indistinguishable. A high E for a region-industry implies more firms for a given output in that region relative to the average number of firms divided by output in the industry across all seven regions. A high E could, therefore, be interpreted as more entrepreneurship or greater competition. In any case a high E indicates smaller average firm size. In terms of effects on growth, an unresolved debate centers around whether competition or monopoly is more effective in encouraging innovation. Similarly, the effect of size on growth remains controversial.

Region-specific variables

The region-specific variables are the beginning-of-year values for GDP per capita, secondary school enrolment rate, foreign direct investment per person, road network (the length of roads in the region divided by the region's area), telecommunications availability (telephone lines per capita), and congestion (population density).

These regional growth-related factors not only are important in their own right but also can have important spillover effects. Lucas (1988) notes that human capital is twice blessed: first because it is inherently productive and second because interactions among well-educated people further increase efficiency. Shleifer (1990) suggests that good infrastructure provides the focal point for the development of agglomerations, which in turn create the environment for knowledge spillovers. Foreign investors bring knowledge on international best practices in production technologies but also provide links to international markets.

Regional spillovers

A control variable, growth of the industry outside the province or county (that is, growth of the industry in the other six counties and provinces), is also included in the regressions. By construction, it is a time-varying region- and industry-specific variable. However, as a practical matter, because it captures across-the-board industrial growth, it is close to being a time-varying industry-specific factor with little regional variation in a given time period. In view of the discussion above that cross-regional correlation may be built into the data on account of biases in price indexes, the interpretation of the coefficients on this variable requires some care.

Before reporting our growth regression results, it is important to note the difficulty of identifying causality in these regressions (Mankiw 1995 has an extended discussion). Our goal, as a first step, is to identify the bundle of influences that coexist through a growth process. However, certain techniques are used that bear on the issue of endogeneity. The potential endogeneity of the industry-specific variables, competition and specialization, is addressed by using their lagged (beginning-of-period) values. The endogeneity of regional variables poses a less serious problem. First, beginning-of-period values are used in the regression, and second, our dependent variable is not growth in a region, but rather growth of a specific industry within the region. Infrastructure, education, and flows of foreign investment are likely to be influenced by overall regional growth rather than by the expansion of a particular industry.

III. Correlates of growth

The regressions are run for 23 industrial sectors: food processing, textiles, apparel, leather products, wood products, furniture, paper products, art products, plastic products, electronics, petroleum, chemicals, pharmaceutical products, chemical fibers, electricity, rubber products, nonmetal products, ferrous products, nonferrous products, metallic products, transportation equipment, electrical machinery, and other machinery. The eight regions for which industrial output data are available include the three coastal counties—Beijing, Shanghai, and Tianjin—and five coastal provinces—Fujian, Guangdong, Jiangsu, Shandong, and Zhejiang. However, Beijing, although considered in our output decomposition analysis, cannot be included in the regression analysis because of incomplete availability of explanatory variables.

Limited degrees of freedom prevent running separate regressions for each industrial sector. This poses a problem because growth has not been uniform across sectors, raising the possibility that independent variables have very different influences on the different sectors. Because a significant feature of China's recent growth has been the rapidly growing share of light industrial sectors, our intermediate solution to this problem is to group sectors into light and heavy industries and to reestimate the basic regression. Although the coefficients show interesting differences in magnitudes, we find the basic results unchanged and hence focus on the pooled results, noting the differences that do arise when light and heavy industries are considered separately.

Pooling time series and cross-sectional data

Because we are pooling time series and cross-sectional data, we first test for serial correlation in growth rates. If observations in growth rates in four adjoining years in a specific industry in a particular region are not independent of one another, the standard errors will be biased and the inferences drawn will be stronger than warranted. Recall that we have three dimensions in our data: industry, region, and year. Our interest is in the correlation over time. We can, therefore, sort the data by region, then by industry, and finally by year; alternatively, we can sort by industry, followed by region and year. Both procedures ensure that the adjoining observations are for four successive years. In either case, the Durbin-Watson statistic for the base regression is 1.87, implying that the autocorrelation problem is not serious.

The base regression is estimated with time and industry dummies, but without regional dummies. When dummy variables for regions are added to the regression, we, in effect, remove from the data the variation due to differences in the levels of variables across regions. The coefficients thus obtained are weighted averages of within-region relationships, which are sometimes described as short-run effects. When region dummies are not included, we are able to compare across regions. Because interregional differences occur over a longer period of time than do variations within a region, dropping regional dummies, as we do in our principal regressions, captures the long-run effects. We also report the more interesting short-run estimates.

The time, region, and industry dummies are not reported in the tables that present our regression results. But the main patterns of the results for the time and regional dummy variables are worth noting. Table 7.5 presents the results for the time dummies. The size of the coefficients for the time dummies in the first column in Table 7.5 shows an upward trend through the period under consideration, and the coefficients are significantly different from the constant term for the base year. However, excluding the time dummies only reduces the R^2 marginally, indicating their limited explanatory power. The statistical significance of the time dummies is sensitive to whether the observations are weighted by the population of the region; when observations are not weighted by population, the influence of the two counties, Shanghai and Tianjin, increases and the time dummies are not significantly different from 0, suggesting that the time effects were felt primarily in the five coastal provinces.

The inference we draw from the increasing coefficients on the time dummies, consistent with the variance decomposition analysis, is that there were independent, though limited, time effects during this period. In other words,

Table 7.5 Time dummy coefficients, 1986–88

Year	Base regression[a]	Regression without regional explanatory variables[b]
1986	−0.08	0.02
	(−3.2)	(1.80)
1987	−0.05	0.05
	(−1.89)	(4.15)
1988	−0.04	0.03
	(−1.97)	(2.41)

Note: Results are relative to the base year 1989. The *t*-staristics are in parentheses.
a. Overall regression results for the base case are given in column 4 in Table 7.7.
b. Overall regression results are not reported for the regression without regional explanatory variables.
It is the model reported in column 4 in Table 7.7 excluding the following variables: secondary school enrolment, foreign direct investment, roads, population density, telephones, and GDP per capita.

Source: Authors' calculations.

the gradual move toward a more market-oriented economy appears to have had some secular effects independent of the region and industrial sector. The second column in Table 7.5 gives the results for the time dummies after dropping the region-specific variables (secondary school enrolment, foreign direct investment, roads, population density, telephones, and GDP per capita). Again, the estimated coefficients on the time dummies are statistically different from the base year.

Table 7.6 presents the coefficients for the regional dummy variables, using Shanghai as the base for comparison. The coefficients in the first column are positive but not significantly different from 0 (even at the 10 percent level of confidence). The second column gives the results when we drop the region-specific variables from the regression. The pattern of regional dummies in the second column mirrors more closely the statistics of regional growth presented in Table 7.1, with the regional coefficient higher for Guangdong than for Fujian, followed by Jiangsu, Zhejiang, and Tianjin. The exception in the regional order of growth is Shandong, whose coefficient indicates a higher growth rate than Guangdong's, although the *F*-test shows that the two coefficients are not significantly different from each other. These results give some confidence that the regional variables, such as foreign investment (and accompanying know-how), domestic investment (especially in infrastructure), human capital, and initial per capita income levels are good explanatory variables for differences in regional growth. Industry dummies show no interesting pattern, and including or excluding them makes little difference to the results.

Table 7.6 Regional dummy coefficients, 1986–89

Region	Base regression[a]	Regression without regional explanatory variables[b]
Guangdong	1.8	0.11
	(1.1)	(6.4)
Fujian	1.8	0.08
	(1.0)	(3.8)
Jiangsu	1.6	0.07
	(1.1)	(3.7)
Zhejiang	2.0	0.05
	(1.2)	(2.2)
Shandong	1.7	0.12
	(1.1)	(7.4)
Tianjin	2.4	−0.02
	(1.8)	(−0.6)

Note: Results are relative to the base region Shanghai. The (*t*-statistics are in parentheses.
a. Overall regression results for the base case are given in column 1 in Table 7.7.
b. Overall regression results are not reported for the regression without regional explanatory variables.
It is the model reported in column 1 in Table 7.7 excluding the following variables: secondary school enrolment, foreign direct investment, roads, population density, telephones, and GDP per capita.

Source: Authors' calculations.

The principal results

Because results in this type of analysis are sensitive to the variables included (Levine and Renelt 1992), Table 7.7 reports those results that appear robust to various specifications based on sensitivity tests (described at the end of this section).

Industry-specific variables   After controlling for other variables, industrial specialization has a largely negative effect on growth. This result suggests that the flow of knowledge across industries is more conducive to growth than is the flow within an industrial sector (Jacobs 1969). Less-specialized industrial sectors gain from knowledge spillovers from other sectors. The short- and long-run effects are not very different (Table 7.7). Recall that at *S* equal to 1, the output share of industry *i* in region *r* equals the average output share of industry *i* in the seven regions. A decline in *S* to 0.9 increases the growth rate 0.5 percentage points (for example, from 6 to 6.5 percent). However, the relationship between industrial specialization and growth does not appear to be linear. Beyond *S* equal to about 2, specialization enhances growth.[2] The evidence, therefore, is also consistent with Porter's (1990) hypothesis on the benefits of knowledge flows within the same industry, although the degree of specialization must be large enough. We report below that specialization promotes growth in the heavy industrial sectors.

Table 7.7 Determinants of industrial growth in Coastal China, 1986–89

Variable	Short run			Long run		
	1	2	3	4	5	6
Industry specific						
Specialization index, S	−0.061	−0.060	−0.060	−0.061	−0.061	−0.057
	(−2.477)	(−2.462)	(−2.416)	(−2.470)	(−2.501)	(−2.326)
Specialization index squared, S^2	0.014	0.014	0.014	0.014	0.015	0.013
	(1.899)	(1.864)	(1.855)	(1.902)	(2.015)	(1.788)
Entrepreneurship index, E	0.035	0.038	0.034	0.033	0.031	0.042
	(1.683)	(1.863)	(1.638)	(1.714)	(1.646)	(2.199)
Entrepreneurship index squared, E^2	−0.006	−0.007	−0.005	−0.006	−0.005	−0.007
	(−1.267)	(−1.432)	(−1.188)	(−1.244)	(−1.117)	(−1.507)
Region specific						
Secondary school enrolment rate	−3.617		−1.449	0.779	1.373	1.121
	(−3.496)		(−1.366)	(2.962)	(2.371)	(2.219)
Secondary school enrolment rate squared					−0.663	−0.281
					(−1.151)	(−0.552)
Foreign direct investment	7.815	4.130	6.060	1.628	1.655	1.946
	(4.360)	(2.822)	(3.502)	(4.747)	(4.816)	(6.199)
Roads	6.647	5.089		−0.489	−0.587	
	(3.087)	(2.393)		(−2.657)	(−2.896)	
Roads squared	−13.569	−10.532		0.688	0.832	
	(−3.335)	(−2.625)		(3.530)	(3.593)	
Interaction between roads and congestion	0.006	0.005				
	(3.302)	(2.803)				
Telephones			−0.015			−0.017
			(−1.513)			(−4.248)
Telephones squared			0.0005			0.0003
			(2.169)			(3.078)
GDP per capita	−0.0006	−0.0003	−0.0006	−0.0002	−0.0002	−0.0001
	(−5.003)	(−3.548)	(−3.897)	(−5.005)	(−4.969)	(−2.136)
Regional spillover						
Growth in industry outside region	0.785	0.782	0.783	0.777	0.778	0.780
	(20.033)	(19.776)	(19.923)	(19.492)	(19.519)	(19.675)
Regional dummy variables included?	Yes	Yes	Yes	No	No	No
Adjusted R^2	0.617	0.610	0.615	0.604	0.604	0.609
Number of observations	640	640	640	640	640	640

Note: The dependent variable is growth of industry i in region r at time t (G_{irt}). All regressions include time and industry dummy variables and observations are weighted by regional population. Short-run regressions report within-region relationships; long-run regressions drop regional dummies and report interregional relationships. The t-statistics are in parentheses. See Table 7.4 for more complete definitions of variables and descriptive statistics.

Source: Authors' calculations.

The statistical significance of the coefficients for E and E^2 is weak. The general thrust of the results is similar across various specifications and hence worth noting: increasing relative firm size has a deleterious effect on growth. The values of the coefficients, however, also suggest that when the average size of firms in an industrial sector in a particular region is smaller than a third of the average firm size in all regions, growth in that region-industry suffers (possibly through excessive competition and/or diminished investible surpluses).

Foreign direct investment   We begin the discussion of the regional influences with the role of foreign investment. A key element of economic reform in China has been the open door to foreign investment. Although triggered by government policy, growth in foreign investment has taken on a life of its own, reaching close to $20 billion in 1993. Many overseas Chinese have invested large amounts of capital and know-how, despite what, by Western standards, would be considered a great deal of uncertainty regarding property rights and enforcement of contractual obligations (see Yusuf 1993).

Our results show that foreign direct investment has a strong impact on growth, particularly in the short run (column 1 in Table 7.7). The short-run elasticity of growth with respect to foreign direct investment, calculated at the mean value of the foreign direct investment variable, is 0.10, indicating that a 10 percent increase in foreign investment can raise the growth rate 1 percent. However, the apparent effect of foreign investment is influenced by trends in secondary school enrolment rates, which, as noted below, fell during this period of rapid growth. Hence human capital is seen to have a perverse effect on growth in the short run (see column 1, Table 7.7). Because a change in school enrolment rates is not a good measure of change in the stock of human capital, the perverse effect is overstated, and to that extent, the positive effect of foreign investment is probably exaggerated in the short-run estimates.

When the secondary school enrolment rate is dropped, the coefficient for foreign investment falls by about half (see column 2, Table 7.7). If we assume that there was little change in human capital within any region during the period under consideration, then the new estimate for foreign investment is closer to being right, and hence the elasticity of the growth rate with respect to foreign investment is closer to 0.06. When the secondary enrolment rates are dropped from the equation, the coefficient on foreign investment declines, but other coefficients remain essentially unchanged (see column 2, Table 7.7). The effect of foreign investment declines in the long run (and hence is a less potent source of differences in growth between regions), but still remains statistically significant and quantitatively important. The foreign investment coefficient decreases from about 4 to about 2, and the growth elasticity falls from 0.06 to 0.03.

One interpretation of these results is that in the short run, foreign investment is the most mobile factor and hence is a dominant driver of growth. In the longer run, such variables as education and infrastructure respond to increased demand for complementary assets, and the contribution of foreign investment declines. There is also a complementary relationship between domestic human capital formation and foreign investment flows, as discussed below.

Human capital: education and foreign knowledge Measurement of the stock of knowledge available for productive use is a complex task even under normal conditions and is especially difficult in a dynamic situation when knowledge from many different sources is being utilized. Traditionally, secondary school enrolment rates have been used as proxies for the domestic stock of knowledge, or domestic human capital, and serve well as long-run approximations. Using data for the only year available—1987—we compare enrolment rates with the more appropriate proxy, average years of schooling in the labor force, and find a very high correlation coefficient (0.965, significant at 99 percent) between the two indicators.[3] If this finding applies to the whole period between 1985 and 1989, then secondary school enrolment is a good surrogate for at least the part of human capital endowment due to years of formal education, and our long-run estimates can be considered reasonably reliable.

However, short-run changes in human capital are more difficult to measure. The extensive reforms that began in 1984 were accompanied by an actual fall in school enrolment rates in most of the coastal provinces and counties. This is not altogether surprising during a period of rapid growth accompanied by increases in the demand for labor. Many of the new entrants to the labor force were young women who probably dropped out of school to take up newly available jobs. Over the short period under consideration, the stock of domestic human capital is unlikely to have changed as a consequence of such labor force responses, although unless the trend is reversed, human capital will deplete over time.

The short-run, or within, estimate shows a negative coefficient for secondary education (first column in Table 7.7), reflecting the cyclical shift out of education described above. The finding tells us little about the relationship between domestic human capital and growth in the short run, because, as noted, changes in secondary enrolment rates greatly overstate the depletion of human capital. In the long run, that is, when the comparison is across regions, education has the expected positive effect on growth. However, returns to secondary education diminish beyond a point.[4] Similar results have been obtained for cross-country regressions; see Pritchett (1996) for a recent review. The coefficients for the education variables in column 5 show that when enrolment increases from 30 to 35 percent (that is, approximately from the Fujian enrolment rate to the Guangdong enrolment rate), growth rises 5 percentage points. However, when enrolment increases from 55 to 60 percent, the increase in growth is only 3 percentage points. Thus Tianjin gets a smaller effect from raising its enrolment rate than does Fujian; Shanghai, with an enrolment rate in the mid-60 percent range, gains even less.

Education becomes even more effective when it is associated with foreign knowledge. Column 1 in Table 7.8 shows that the interaction between school enrolment rates and foreign investment is significantly positive, suggesting mutual reinforcement between domestic human capital and foreign

Table 7.8 The interaction of foreign investment with infrastructure and education in explaining growth in Coastal China, 1986–89

Variable	1	2	3
Industry specific			
Specialization index, S	−0.061	−0.061	−0.056
	(−2.480)	(−2.517)	(−2.309)
Specialization index squared, S^2	0.015	0.016	0.013
	(1.976)	(1.999)	(1.764)
Entrepreneurship index, E	0.033	0.033	0.042
	(1.757)	(1.737)	(2.162)
Entrepreneurship index squared, E^2	−0.005	−0.005	−0.007
	(−1.209)	(−1.199)	(−1.508)
Region specific			
Secondary school enrolment rate	1.021	1.076	0.879
	(3.546)	(3.619)	(4.229)
Interaction between secondary school enrolment rate and foreign direct investment	8.631 (2.041)		
Foreign direct investment	−1.373	0.241	1.660
	(−0.910)	(0.328)	(2.688)
Roads	−0.152	−0.118	
	(−0.617)	(−0.465)	
Roads squared	0.325	0.249	
	(1.233)	(0.878)	
Interaction between roads and foreign direct investment		4.608 (2.121)	
Telephones			−0.016
			(−3.961)
Telephones squared			0.0003
			(1.798)
Interaction between telephones and foreign direct investment			0.023 (0.494)
GDP per capita	−0.0002	−0.0002	−0.0001
	(−5.374)	(−5.448)	(−2.413)
Regional spillover			
Growth in industry outside region	0.779	0.779	0.779
	(19.591)	(19.594)	(19.671)
Adjusted R^2	0.606	0.606	0.609
Number of observations	640	640	640

Note: The dependent variable is growth of industry i in region r at time t (G_{irt}). All regressions include time and industry dummy variables but no regional dummy variables and observations are weighted by regional population. t-statistics are in parentheses. See Table 7.4 for more complete definitions of variables and descriptive statistics.

Source: Authors' calculations.

knowledge that accompanies the investment. Also, the coefficient on foreign investment becomes negative when the interaction term is introduced, implying that much of the power of foreign knowledge may come through the local base of human capital. Perhaps exposure to foreign knowledge breaks the isolation of the local economy and brings experience-based practices that are rarely available in textbooks and are best communicated in a hands-on manner in a production setting (Romer 1993).

Infrastructure   Good infrastructure not only facilitates the flow of information but also provides the focal point for the development of agglomerations (Shleifer 1990). We consider two types of infrastructure: roads and telecommunications. Roads represent the traditional infrastructure, and their stock has grown only slowly to date. Phone lines, in contrast, have grown rapidly to meet the needs of the international trading community—much, possibly all, of the new telecommunications investment uses modern digital technology.

The results show that a network of roads has a positive effect on growth but is subject to diminishing returns in the short run (column 1, Table 7.7), possibly reflecting indivisibilities in infrastructure investment (Weitzman 1970). Roads are more productive in high-density areas (as reflected in the positive coefficient on the interaction term between roads and population density). The long-run increasing returns are possibly related to network effects: gains from an increase in the length of a route rise as the route interconnects new areas and multiplies the connections possible. The effectiveness of foreign investment flows also appears to depend on the availability of infrastructure, as is shown in the strong positive interaction between foreign investment and the roads network (column 2, Table 7.8).

Telecommunications growth has an even stronger effect; telephones per 1,000 residents show increasing returns both in the short run and in the long run (columns 3 and 6, Table 7.7). The short- and long-run elasticities are both approximately 0.10.

Initial conditions   The initial per capita income of a region turns out to be an important variable in explaining subsequent growth. When initial per capita income is not included in the regressions, the partial correlations between growth and the other variables change significantly; as noted below in our discussion of sensitivity tests, variables other than per capita income do not have a similar influence when added or dropped from the analysis.

The strongly negative relationship between industrial growth rates in a region and the initial per capita income of the region suggests that growth is being influenced not just by steady-state factors but also by transitory influences. If steady-state growth had been achieved in the different industrial sectors and regions, both neoclassical and endogenous growth models predict that the initial levels of backwardness will have no influence on subsequent growth (Mankiw, Romer, and Weil 1992). Only when an economy is moving to a new steady state will initial levels of backwardness provide an additional impetus to growth. This seems particularly appropriate for coastal China, which has indeed been shaken up and put on a new growth trajectory.

Figure 7.2 shows a strong inverse relationship between the rate of growth of industrial output during 1985–89 and the log of per capita GDP in 1985. In the terminology suggested by Mankiw, Romer, and Weil (1992) and by Barro and Sala-i-Martin (1992), there is evidence of absolute convergence. In other words, even without controlling for other variables that may affect steady-state growth, the relatively backward provinces grew faster than the more advanced regions. For example, initial backwardness partly explains why Fujian grew so fast despite low educational attainment and limited infrastructure.

Absolute convergence applies not only to industrial growth (as described in Figure 7.2) but also to per capita GDP. Over the 1980s the per capita GDP of the five, relatively poor, coastal provinces increased relative to that of the three richer counties (the ratio of GDP per capita in the five provinces to that in the three counties rose from 0.23 in 1980 to 0.38 in 1988, see China, State

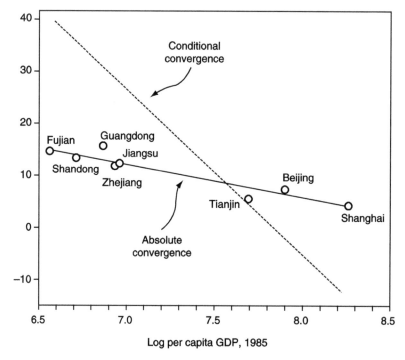

Figure 7.2 Absolute convergence versus conditional convergence.

Note: Absolute convergence is plotted by fitting the observed values of the five provinces and three counties Conditional convergence is plotted according to Table 7.6, equation 4. Its slope is based on the coefficient of per capita GDP, *Y/N*. Its intercept is the sum of the products of the mean values of the independent variables (except *Y/N*) and their respective coefficients.

Source: Authors' calculations.

Statistical Bureau, 1990). But while there was convergence *within* the coastal region, there was divergence between the coast and the rest of China. The per capita income was higher in the coastal region than in the rest of China when the reforms were launched, and the gap has increased over time. The region's GDP per capita was 50 percent higher than the average in the rest of the nation in 1980; it was 74 percent higher in 1988.

These observations point to an interesting international parallel. In cross-country comparisons, absolute convergence is observed among advanced industrial countries but not among poor economies. Poor economies converge conditionally, that is, after controlling for education and investment rates. Within the group of industrial nations, the rate of conditional convergence is higher than the rate of absolute convergence, because the richer ones typically also have higher education and investment rates (see Mankiw, Romer, and Weil 1992).

We have not investigated the possibility of conditional convergence outside the coastal region. However, not surprisingly, conditional convergence within the coastal region, as within the industrial economies, is more rapid than absolute convergence. The richer coastal regions also tend to have better education and infrastructure, and thus it may be supposed that they have higher steady-state growth rates. The fact that the poorer regions are growing faster despite their lack of endowment indicates that they are benefiting from their backwardness.

The common interpretation of this catching-up phenomenon is that regions with low per capita income also have low capital per worker and so have a higher marginal product of capital than regions that are well endowed with capital. Thus the poorer regions potentially attract new capital (along with new ideas). Our evidence certainly supports this view: the poorer regions have attracted huge amounts of foreign capital and knowledge. But in addition, as discussed above, the more advanced regions have been burdened by an institutional setup that has been a drag on growth. But the Chinese are also fortunate in this regard that the backward regions are in proximity to Hong Kong and Taiwan (China), both major centers of knowledge and capital.

Growth of the industry outside the region   Results show that the growth of an industrial sector in any region is powerfully influenced by the growth of the same industry in other regions during the same year. On average, a 1 percent increase in the growth rate of an industrial sector outside the region is associated with a 0.78 percent increase in the growth rate of that industry within the region. Unlike other variables, this variable not only passes the test of significance but also accounts for 49 percent of the total sum of squares. This is another way of capturing the wave phenomenon noted in the variance decomposition exercise. The high *t*-statistics for the coefficient for growth outside the region are also obtained by Glaeser et al. (1992), who interpret the result as a demand effect—exogenous growth in demand, in this view, conditions the growth of specific sectors irrespective of the region. As noted above in the discussion on variance decomposition, synchronization across regions can also occur as a result of technology diffusion or networking among decision makers. A concern arises, however, because there may be biases in the data-gathering process, which build in cross-regional correlations. To that extent, this variable conditions for these correlations.[5]

We try two extensions of the basic regression to gain further insight into the cross-regional influences at work. First, we interact growth outside the region with the specialization variable. The results indicate that growth outside the region has a stronger effect in conditions lacking industrial specialization (Table 7.9, column 1). In other words, the more a sector is specialized within a region, the less it is affected by growth of that same industry outside the region. This is not surprising. With scale economies, certain industries will be concentrated in particular regions. At the same time, they will also develop certain technical specializations or market niches that limit the usefulness of the experience of firms in the same industrial sector but located in other regions. Also, intellectual property is likely to be more protected in such specialized sectors. In general, light industrial sectors, with lower capital intensity and less specialization than the heavier sectors, are likely to be more able to absorb external influences rapidly, as discussed below.

Second, in view of the policy attention accorded to Guangdong (and more recently to Fujian), and also given their physical proximity to Hong Kong and Taiwan (China), a question of interest is whether these regions are conduits of growth impulses. For the time span studied, no evidence to this effect is found. When growth outside the region is interacted with region dummies, the coefficients show that Guangdong benefited most from growth outside the province and Fujian was third on the list, with Jiangsu in between (Table 7.9, column 2). This indicates that Guangdong, Jiangsu, and Fujian are most responsive to macro influences, such as changes in buyer perceptions and changes in government policies. We then replace growth outside the region (which is growth in *all* outside regions) with growth in Guangdong as an independent variable to isolate the effects that Guangdong may have had on growth in other regions (Guangdong itself is not included in this regression). Guangdong's growth does have a statistically significant impact on other regions, but the magnitude of the effect is much smaller than when growth in all other regions is considered (Table 7.9, column 3). Similar conclusions apply to Fujian.

It is, however, likely that spillovers from Guangdong and Fujian to the other provinces will be significant in the long run. Within the coastal region, these provinces have the greatest flexibility to respond to external stimuli. As other regions become more receptive to change, Guangdong and Fujian can be expected to have greater spillover effects. Field surveys in Guangdong and Fujian show unambiguously that modern production techniques, including sophisticated methods of quality control, are being rapidly adopted in these

Table 7.9 Cross-regional influences on industrial growth in Coastal China, 1986–89

Variable	1	2	3
Industry specific			
Specialization index, S	−0.028	−0.069	−0.042
	(−1.092)	(−2.834)	(−1.622)
Specialization index squared, S^2	0.010	0.016	0.010
	(1.328)	(2.152)	(1.303)
Entrepreneurship index, E	0.030	0.032	0.032
	(1.634)	(1.694)	(1.571)
Entrepreneurship index squared, E^2	−0.005	−0.005	−0.003
	(−1.214)	(−1.172)	(−0.724)
Region specific			
Secondary school enrolment rate	0.728	0.638	1.311
	(2.785)	(2.206)	(3.464)
Foreign direct investment	1.616	0.994	4.053
	(4.750)	(2.478)	(3.020)
Roads	−0.475	−0.919	−0.132
	(−2.605)	(−4.121)	(−0.546)
Roads squared	0.678	0.982	0.355
	(3.510)	(4.106)	(1.493)
GDP per capita	−0.0001	−0.0001	−0.0002
	(4.914)	(−3.619)	(−4.674)
Growth in Guangdong			0.458
			(13.302)
Regional spillover			
Growth in industry outside region	1.009		
	(12.136)		
Interaction between growth in industry outside region and specialization index	−0.211		
	(−3.179)		
Interaction between growth in industry outside region and regional dummy variable			
Guangdong		0.969	
		(13.714)	
Fujian		0.797	
		(8.751)	
Zhejiang		0.700	
		(9.297)	
Jiangsu		0.902	
		(13.271)	
Shandong		0.607	
		(9.908)	
Tianjin		0.750	
		(4.471)	
Shanghai		0.714	
		(4.840)	
Adjusted R^2	0.610	0.613	0.550
Number of observations	640	640	548

Note: The dependent variable is growth of industry i in region r at time t (G_{irt}). All regressions include time and industry dummy variables but no regional dummy variables, and observations are weighted by regional population. The t-statistics are in parentheses. See Table 7.4 for more complete definitions of variables and descriptive statistics.

Source: Authors' calculations.

provinces. As such experience accumulates, increasing labor mobility will complement existing administrative communication networks to diffuse the knowledge gained to other parts of China.

Light and heavy industries

Thus far we have assumed that all industrial sectors respond to the explanatory variables in the same manner. Here we note some differences between light and heavy industrial sectors (Table 7.10). Although the differences are of interest, the exercise also gives us confidence in the results reported so far—the signs of the coefficients are similar, and the key variables (barring education) continue to be statistically significant for both light and heavy industries.

The estimated equation does a better job of explaining growth in light industries ($R^2 = 0.67$) than in heavy industries ($R^2 = 0.49$). Of special interest is the finding that growth outside the region, which measures the degree of synchronization or diffusion across regions, has a higher coefficient for light industries. This is to be expected given the lower capital intensity and hence higher mobility of light industrial sectors. Guangdong, Fujian, and Jiangsu benefit especially from growth outside the region in both heavy and light industries; this difference is measured by interacting growth outside the region with regional dummies.[6] In light industries, other regions also benefit strongly from the diffusion process, whereas the effect for heavy industries falls off in other regions and is not statistically different from 0 for Shanghai and Tianjin. In both light and heavy industries, when growth in Guangdong is used as an explanatory variable, the partial correlation is positive and significant, but smaller in magnitude than the coefficient obtained for growth outside the region, implying again that Guangdong is more an imitator than a leader.

Foreign investment provides a bigger effect in light industries, although it has a significant coefficient for heavy industries. Similarly, infrastructure does more for light than for heavy industries. In contrast, education has a positive effect on growth in light industries, but the effect is not statistically different from 0. Thus, although formal education is important, its relationship with growth is imprecise, and tacit knowledge based on experience (and channeled through foreign sources) appears to be a somewhat firmer predictor of growth. For heavy industries, we observe diminishing returns to education, as was seen above for all industries; within the range of observed secondary school enrolment rates, this implies a positive, though declining, effect of education on growth of heavy industries.

The lack of specialization has a stronger association with growth among light industries, which is not surprising; skills are likely to be more mobile in such sectors. When all observations are pooled, we note that specialization is an aid to growth only beyond $S = 2$. For light industries, the positive effects of specialization are felt at even higher levels of specialization (beyond

Table 7.10 Growth in light and heavy industries in Coastal China, 1986–89

Variable	All industries		Light industries[a]		Heavy industries[b]	
	1	2	3	4	5	6
Industry specific						
Specialization index, S	−0.061	−0.061	−0.109	−0.109	−0.112	−0.117
	(−2.470)	(−2.501)	(−2.936)	(−2.939)	(−1.687)	(−1.765)
Specialization index squared, S^2	0.014	0.015	0.022	0.022	0.043	0.046
	(1.902)	(2.015)	(2.267)	(2.240)	(1.497)	(1.583)
Entrepreneurship index, E	0.033	0.031	0.142	0.143	0.017	0.015
	(1.714)	(1.646)	(1.924)	(1.933)	(0.859)	(0.761)
Entrepreneurship index squared, E^2	−0.006	−0.005	−0.034	−0.035	−0.002	−0.002
	(−1.244)	(−1.117)	(−1.483)	(−1.496)	(−0.514)	(−0.343)
Region specific						
Secondary school enrolment rate	0.779	1.373	0.813	0.611	0.778	1.654
	(2.962)	(2.371)	(1.800)	(0.622)	(2.454)	(2.368)
Secondary school enrolment rate squared		−0.663		0.223		−0.981
		(−1.151)		(0.231)		(−1.406)
Foreign direct investment	1.628	1.655	2.234	2.225	1.254	1.296
	(4.747)	(4.816)	(3.843)	(3.816)	(3.004)	(3.101)
Roads	−0.489	−0.587	−1.084	−1.053	−0.097	−0.241
	(−2.657)	(−2.896)	(−3.528)	(−3.132)	(−0.422)	(−0.961)
Roads squared	0.688	0.832	1.269	1.223	0.295	0.507
	(3.530)	(3.593)	(3.925)	(3.195)	(1.218)	(1.779)
GDP per capita	−0.0002	−0.0002	−0.0002	−0.0002	−0.0002	−0.0001
	(−5.005)	(−4.969)	(−3.184)	(−3.181)	(−3.775)	(−3.730)
Regional spillover						
Growth in industry outside region	0.777	0.778	0.827	0.827	0.583	0.590
	(19.492)	(19.519)	(16.898)	(16.864)	(6.260)	(6.339)
Adjusted R^2	0.604	0.604	0.671	0.670	0.493	0.491
Number of observations	640	640	280	280	360	360

Note: The dependent variable is growth of industry i in region r at time t (G_{irt}). All regressions include time and industry dummy variables but no regional dummy variables, and observations are weighted by regional population. The t-statistics are in parentheses. See Table 7.4 for more complete definitions of variables and descriptive statistics.
a. The light industry group includes food processing, textiles, apparel, leather products, wood products, furniture, paper products, art products, plastic products, and electronics.
b. The heavy industry group includes petroleum, chemicals, pharmaceutical products, chemical fibers, electricity, rubber products, nonmetal products, ferrous products, nonferrous products, metallic products, transportation equipment, electrical machinery, and other machinery.

Source: Authors' calculations.

$S = 2.5$); in comparison, for heavy industries, specialization is conducive to growth after $S = 1.3$. The implication is that specialized sectors, which have also grown rapidly, are principally in the heavy industry group. Although an exact correspondence cannot be easily made, our results bear some similarity to those of Henderson, Kuncoro, and Turner (1995). They find that for the mature sectors, specialization promotes growth (in the Chinese case, heavy industry has been the more traditional focus of state investment); in contrast, they find that a diverse industrial environment fosters new industrial sectors (while the light industries studied here are not new in the sense of being high-technology, they have required many new skills to meet the exacting demands of the international market).

Sensitivity and mis-specification

Our sensitivity analysis uses the methods of Belsley, Kuh, and Welsch (1980). We first drop one observation at a time and find that no single observation influences the coefficients significantly. This result could have been expected, given the large sample of 640 observations. We then drop specific sets of observations, excluding from regressions a province, a year, an industry, a region-industry, a year-industry, and a year-region. The distributions of the coefficients show a very strong concentration around the mean value. We can therefore rule out the possibility of outliers driving our regression results.

In the regressions reported, we weight the observations by the population of the region, which gives more weight to the provinces and less to the counties, reducing the influence of the counties in the regression results. To see how much the results are influenced by this weighting procedure, we also run our basic regression by treating every observation equally (column 7, Table 7.11). The results do not change qualitatively, except that diminishing returns to education are now more evident: this is as expected because the more educated counties that recorded relatively modest economic performance now have *greater* weight in the regression.

Another type of sensitivity analysis is done by adding or dropping independent variables (Table 7.11). Omitting secondary school enrolment rates has little effect on the sign and magnitude of the remaining coefficients (column 4). Similarly, the regression results are not sensitive to specifications that exclude an entire set of industry- or region-specific variables, as columns 5 and 6 demonstrate.

If there is no serious mis-specification problem, regional factors other than initial per capita income predict that the counties (Shanghai and Tianjin) should have done especially well because they had better than average access to foreign investment, education, and infrastructure. But instead, growth in these counties was slow, possibly because of the significant presence of state-owned enterprises, which is not captured in the regressions. When we include the share of state-owned enterprises as an independent variable, it does not generate significant results because the share of these enterprises is correlated with per capita income (and also with the variable E, which is the inverse of average firm size). Thus the relatively slow growth in recent years of the two richer regions reflects diminishing returns, which arise not merely from a

Table 7.11 Sensitivity analysis of growth determinants for Coastal China, 1986–89

Variable	1	2	3	4	5	6	7
Industry specific							
Specialization index, S	−0.061	−0.052	−0.066	−0.062		−0.049	−0.079
	(−2.501)	(−2.093)	(−2.688)	(−2.530)		(−1.860)	(−3.540)
Specialization index squared, S^2	0.015	0.012	0.016	0.013		0.014	0.018
	(2.015)	(1.559)	(2.096)	(1.750)		(1.723)	(2.981)
Entrepreneurship index, E	0.031	0.017	0.030	0.020		0.059	0.022
	(1.646)	(0.885)	(1.564)	(1.086)		(3.351)	(1.205)
Entrepreneurship index squared, E^2	−0.005	−0.004	−0.006	−0.004		−0.012	−0.003
	(−1.117)	(−0.820)	(−1.211)	(−0.979)		(−2.756)	(−0.662)
Region specific							
Secondary school enrolment rate	1.373		0.301		0.821		1.301
	(2.371)		(0.633)		(1.190)		(2.556)
Secondary school enrolment rate squared	−0.663		0.577		−0.407		−0.888
	(−1.151)		(1.213)		(−0.570)		(−2.081)
Foreign direct investment	1.655		1.486	0.837	1.115		1.432
	(4.816)		(5.222)	(3.866)	(2.729)		(4.004)
Roads	−0.587	−0.684		−0.741	−0.551		−0.620
	(2.896)	(4.115)		(4.521)	(−2.130)		(−3.433)
Roads squared	0.832	0.698		0.834	0.759		0.818
	(3.593)	(3.702)		(4.395)	(2.573)		(4.995)
GDP per capita	−0.0002	−0.0001	−0.0001	−0.0001	−0.0001		−0.0001
	(−4.969)	(−4.319)	(−6.275)	(−5.452)	(−3.176)		(−4.458)
Regional spillover							
Growth in industry outside region	0.778	0.771	0.775	0.774		0.754	0.818
	(19.519)	(19.022)	(19.262)	(19.297)		(17.496)	(20.161)
Adjusted R^2	0.604	0.590	0.596	0.599	0.351	0.535	0.616
Number of observations	640	640	640	640	640	640	640

Note: The dependent variable is growth of industry i in region r at time t (G_{irt}). All regressions include time and industry dummy variables but no regional dummy variables and observations are weighted by regional population. Observations are weighted by the population in the region for the regressions reported in columns 1–6. No weights are used for the regression reported in column 7. The *t*-statistics are in parentheses. See Table 7.4 for more complete definitions of variables and descriptive statistics.

Source: Authors' calculations.

technological source but also from the constraining effects of the institutional structure within which past industrialization occurred.

IV. Conclusions

We have examined three sets of influences on industrial growth along the eastern coast of China: factors specific to an industrial sector, regional influences, and regional spillovers.

Overall, industry-specific influences explain only a small portion of variance in growth. A low level of specialization, perhaps allowing for absorption of influences from other industrial sectors, seems to promote more rapid growth for light industries, whereas specialization seems to be conducive to growth in heavy industries. Our findings on the role of competition are statistically weak, possibly because of the very crude statistical proxy used for competition.

A number of regional influences are important. Higher levels of education differentiate good performers from poor performers over the long haul: gains of even a few percentage points in secondary school enrolment rates have an important effect on growth. When only light industries are considered, however, the relationship between growth and secondary school enrolment is potentially influential but imprecise. For heavy industries, education has diminishing returns, although the positive effects continue well into the range observed in the sample (as well as the range spanned by most middle-income countries).

The role of secondary school education, however, cannot be considered separately from knowledge acquired through international links. Foreign investment showed consistently as a spur to growth, especially in the short run and in light industries. Moreover, we found that foreign investment and education interact positively. It is worth noting that secondary school enrolment rates in Fujian province at 31 percent are close to the average for low-income countries (World Bank 1991). Our results suggest that China's coastal provinces were able to exploit their educational attainment better than other low-income regions because the complementary effects of foreign knowledge enhanced the educational level of the work force.

Infrastructure investment, particularly in telecommunications but also in roads, yields increasing returns. There is some question whether infrastructure is a true enabling factor; although it accelerates output growth, it also responds to growth. Large infrastructure investments are occurring along the coast in the wake of the huge growth of the past several years. Thus although good infrastructure is valuable, conditions that enable externality-generating infrastructure investments to be put in place as demand emerges are equally important.

Almost half of the variation in industrial growth along the coast is attributable to the synchronization in growth of particular industries across provincial and county boundaries. The identity of the most rapidly growing sectors changed from year to year across the entire region. Such synchronization was more pronounced in light than in heavy industries. Although many substantive possibilities exist to explain the synchronization—and a recent field study documents that the perception of synchronization exists among decision makers on the Chinese coast (Oi 1995)—we have noted that, on account of data construction and reporting, the extent of regional spillovers is likely to be less than the statistical analysis may suggest.

China has pursued a decentralized economic reform program. Particular reforms have been tried in specific regions—sometimes with and sometimes without the blessing of the central government. To complement reforms for increasing allocative efficiency, China has pursued a long-term strategy for encouraging investments by specific new entrepreneurs. The open-door policies and special economic zones have successfully attracted investments from overseas Chinese to the southeastern coast. At the same time, local governments have been given greater autonomy to invest in new business ventures (for example, the so-called collectively owned enterprises) and in infrastructure. Although many of the experiments are considered innovative, the lack of coordination and wasteful regional competition have resulted in damaging macroeconomic effects.

In any case, synchronization across regions has been quite strong. The source of this synchronization cannot be discerned from the data at hand, but it is clear that a network of communication channels exists across the country. Such a network could reflect the links between the cadres of the Communist Party or could even predate the party, reflecting much older economic and social ties (Yusuf 1993 and Oi 1995). Success has, thus, required a combination of centrally approved local experiments, local government entrepreneurship, and an effective network for diffusing success across different regions.

An interesting aspect of the decentralization has been that regions with relatively low per capita income and hence a large catch-up potential were targeted early on. These regions were relatively unencumbered by state-owned enterprises, planning bureaucracies, and other mechanisms that guided output in the pre-reform era. Indeed, some of the counties in Guangdong province that experienced the most spectacular growth rates, such as Shenzen and the neighboring areas, were essentially agricultural communities (or even wastelands) 15 or 20 years ago.

Although the successes of the strategy have been evident, questions have been raised about policy reversals and setbacks and the consequent lack of government credibility (see Sung 1991 and Chen, Jefferson, and Singh 1992). Such credibility lapses are generally viewed as expensive, inasmuch as they create investor uncertainty and reduce investment. Yet investors, especially foreign investors, have rarely been deterred. Foreign investment has been almost an exogenous force, dampened only occasionally by policy conditions. At the same time, locally financed infrastructure and human capital investments plus job training within enterprises have proceeded with vigor, fueling growth.

We suggest two related possibilities. First, the credibility of government policies as a determinant of investment is overrated; it is likely that credibility and certainty derive from overall economic performance rather than from government actions per se. Second, investors may accept contradictions and reversals as a reflection of the government's response to evolving conditions.

If this analysis of China's recent experience is in any respect correct, what lessons does it hold for other countries? Decentralized experiments are valuable, but they may well require local governments that are entrepreneurial. Human capital and infrastructure aid the process of transformation but in more complex interactive modes than usually assumed. A steady flow of foreign investment and skills provides a strong advantage. For wider impact, the lessons from decentralized experiments must flow to other regions. Mechanisms to ensure information transfers are essential, but difficult to establish. In a complex reform process, credible commitments may be desirable, but governments also need to stay flexible.

Notes

1   Islam (1995) uses country dummies to control for country-specific features but finds them correlated with the traditional explanatory variables.
2   The nonlinear specification includes the squared term. The relation is summarized with the elasticity at the mean values of the variables (see Table 7.4).
3   The labor force includes population in the age group 15 to 54. The average length of education is calculated as $(16U + 12H + 9M + 6E + 0I) / T$, where U, H, M, and E are the number of persons with university, high school, middle high, and elementary school education, respectively. I stands for illiterate. T is the total population in the working age group. The relevant data were obtained from the 1987 population census. Data are available for seven provinces and counties in the coastal region—Beijing, Fujian, Guangdong, Jiangsu, Shandong, Tianjin, and Zhejiang.
4   The coefficient of the square of secondary enrolment rate in column 5 of Table 7.7 is negative but not statistically significant; however, we find that this result is sensitive to the specification and, in certain cases, the squared term is statistically significant. Thus we believe that the nonlinearity needs to be taken seriously.
5   Coe and Helpman (1995) find large international research and development (R&D) spillovers. However, Jaffe and Trajtenberg (1996), examining patent data, find limited cross-national citations, which they interpret as evidence of limited geographical spillovers.
6   These results are not presented to conserve space but can be provided on request.

Appendix. Details of the decomposition of growth of output

The standard variance components method assumes as the first approximation a growth equation of additive main and interaction effects with zero means and covariances. Let G_{tri} denote growth in industry i in region r at time t. Variance of G_{tri} can be decomposed to the main effects of time (a_t), region (β_r), industry (τ_i), and their respective interaction effects (a_{tr}, b_{ti}, c_{ri}, and e_{tri}). Formally:

$$G_{tri} = m + a_t + \beta_r + \tau_i + a_{tr} + b_{ti} + c_{ri} + e_{tri}$$

where m is a constant, $t = 1, \ldots, n_t$, $r = 1, \ldots, n_r$, $i = 1, \ldots, n_j$.

With the assumption of zero covariance, Var_G can be expressed as follows:

$$\text{Var}(G) = \text{Var}(a) + \text{Var}(\beta) + \text{Var}(\tau) + \text{Var}(a) + \text{Var}(b) + \text{Var}(c) + \text{Var}(e)$$

or

$$s^2(G) = s^2_a + s^2_\beta + s^2_\tau + s^2_a + s^2_b + s^2_c + s^2_e.$$

Variance components are estimated by equating observed values of variances to their expected values (Searle 1971). Let $N = n_i n_r n_t$. Define:

$$T_0 = S_t S_r S_i \, G^2_{tri}$$

$$E(T_0) = n_i n_r n_t \, (m^2 + s^2_a + s^2_\beta + s^2_\tau + s^2_a + s^2_b + s^2_c + s^2_e)$$

$$= N(m^2 + s^2_a + s^2_\beta + s^2_\tau + s^2_a + s^2_b + s^2_c + s^2_e)$$

$$T_1 = G^2 / n_i n_r n_t = (S_t S_r S_i \, G)^2 / n_i n_r n_t$$

$$= (n_i n_r n_t m + S_t n_i n_r a + S_r n_i n_t \beta + S_i n_t n_r \tau + S_t S_r a + S_t S_i b + S_r S_i c + S_t S_r S_i e)^2 / n_i n_r n_t$$

$$E(T_1) = Nm^2 + n_t n_r s^2_a + n_i n_t s^2_\beta + n_t n_r s^2_\tau + n_r s^2_a + n_r s^2_b + n_t s^2_c + s^2_e$$

$$T_2 = S_t \, G_t^2 / n_i n_r = S_t (S_r S_i \, G)^2 / n_i n_r$$

$$= S_t (n_i n_r m + n_i n_r a + S_r n_i \beta + S_i n_r \tau + n_i S_r a + n_r S_i b + S_r S_i c + S_r S_i e)^2 / n_i n_r$$

$$E(T_2) = Nm^2 + Ns^2_a + n_i n_t s^2_\beta + n_t n_r s^2_\tau + n_t n_i s^2_a + n_t n_r s^2_b + n_t s^2_c + n_t s^2_e.$$

Similarly, let:

$$T_3 = S_r \, G_r^2 / n_t n_i = S_r (S_t S_i \, G)^2 / n_t n_i$$

$$E(T_3) = Nm^2 + n_r n_i s^2_a + Ns^2_\beta + n_t n_r s^2_\tau + n_r n_i s^2_a + n_r s^2_b + n_t n_r s^2_c + n_r s^2_e$$

$$T_4 = S_i \, G_i^2 / n_t n_r = S_i (S_t S_r \, G)^2 / n_t n_r$$

$$E(T_4) = Nm^2 + n_r n_i s^2_a + n_t n_i s^2_\beta + Ns^2_\tau + n_r s^2_a + n_r n_i s^2_b + n_t n_i s^2_c + n_i s^2_e$$

$$T_5 = S_r S_i \, G_{ti}^2 / n_r = S_t S_i (S_r \, G)^2 / n_r$$

$$E(T_5) = Nm^2 + Ns^2_a + n_t n_i s^2_\beta + Ns^2_\tau + n_t n_i s^2_a + Ns^2_b + n_t n_i s^2_c + n_t n_i s^2_e$$

$$T_6 = S_t S_r \, G_{tr}^2 / n_i = S_t S_r (S_i \, G)^2 / n_i$$

$$E(T_6) = Nm^2 + Ns^2_a + Ns^2_\beta + n_t n_r s^2_\tau + Ns^2_a + n_t n_r s^2_b + n_t n_r s^2_c + n_t n_r s^2_e$$

$$T_7 = S_r S_t \, G_{ri}^2 / n_t = S_r S_i (S_t \, G)^2 / n_t$$

$$E(T_7) = Nm^2 + n_r n_i s^2_a + Ns^2_\beta + Ns^2_\tau + n_r n_i s^2_a + n_r n_i s^2_b + Ns^2_c + n_r n_i s^2_e.$$

The system therefore contains eight equations with eight unknowns. The eight equations refer to the expressions of $E(T_0)$, ..., $E(T_7)$ and the eight unknowns are m^2, s^2_a, s^2_β, s^2_τ, s^2_a, s^2_b, s^2_c, and s^2_e. We can solve the system by equating sample values of T_0, ..., T_7 to their expected values, $E(T_0)$, ..., $E(T_7)$. The solutions are the following:

$$s^2_a = \{n_i[(T_1 - T_2) - (T_3 - T_6)] - [(T_0 - T_5) + (T_4 - T_7)]\} /$$
$$[n_t(n_i - 1)(n_t - 1)(n_r - 1)]$$

$$s^2_b = \{n_r[(T_1 - T_4) - (T_2 - T_5)] - [(T_0 - T_7) + (T_3 - T_6)]\} /$$
$$[n_r(n_r - 1)(n_t - 1)(n_t - 1)]$$

$$s^2_c = \{n_t[(T_1 - T_3) - (T_4 - T_7)] - [(T_0 - T_6) + (T_2 - T_5)]\} /$$
$$[n_t(n_t - 1)(n_r - 1)(n_i - 1)]$$

$$s^2_e = (T_0 - T_1 + T_2 + T_3 + T_4 - T_5 - T_6 - T_7) / [(n_t - 1)(n_r - 1)(n_t - 1)]$$

$$s^2_a = [(T_3 - T_6) - (n_r n_i - N)s^2_a - (n_r - n_t n_r)s^2_b - (n_r - n_t n_r)s^2_e] / (n_r n_t - N)$$

$$s^2_\beta = [(T_4 - T_7) - (n_i - n_r n_t)s^2_a - (n_t n_i - N)s^2_c - (n_i - n_r n_i)s^2_e] / (n_t n_i - N)$$

$$s^2_\tau = [(T_2 - T_5) - (n_t n_r - N)s^2_b - (n_t - n_t n_i)s^2_c - (n_t - n_t n_i)s^2_e] / (n_t n_r - N).$$

References

Note: The word "processed" describes informally reproduced works that may not be commonly available through library systems.

Barro, Robert, and Xavier Sala-i-Martin (1992) "Convergence." *Journal of Political Economy* 100(2, April): 223–51.

Bateman, Deborah, and Ashoka Mody (1991) "Growth in an Inefficient Economy: A Chinese Case Study." Private Sector Development Department, World Bank, Washington, D.C. Processed.

Belsley, David A., Edwin Kuh, and Roy E. Welsch (1980) *Regression Diagnostics.* New York: Wiley and Sons.

Chen, Kaug, Gary H. Jefferson, and Inderjit Singh (1992) "Lessons from China's Economic Reform." *Journal of Comparative Economics* 16(2): 201–25.

China, State Statistical Bureau. Various years. *China Statistical Yearbook*. Beijing: China Statistical Information and Consultancy Service Center.

—— Various years. *Statistical Yearbook of Fujian*. Beijing: China Statistical Information and Consultancy Service Center.

—— Various years. *Statistical Yearbook of Guangdong*. Beijing: China Statistical Information and Consultancy Service Center.

—— (1990) *Compendium of Historical Data, 1949–89*. Beijing: China Statistical Information and Consultancy Service Center.

Chow, Gregory C. (1993) "Capital Formation and Economic Growth in China." *Quarterly Journal of Economics* 108(3): 809–42.

Coe, David T., and Elhanan Helpman (1995) "International R&D Spillovers." *European Economic Review* 39(5): 859–87.

Glaeser, E. L., H. D. Kallal, J. A. Scheinkman, and Andrei Shleifer (1992) "Growth in Cities." *Journal of Political Economy* 100(6): 1126–52.

Hayase, Yasuko, and Seiko Kawamata (1990) *Population Statistics of China.* Institute of Developing Economies, Tokyo. Processed.

Henderson, Vernon, Ari Kuncoro, and Matt Turner (1995) "Industrial Development in Cities." *Journal of Political Economy* 103(5): 1067–90.

Ho, S. P. S., and Ralph Huenemann (1984) *China's Open Door Policy.* Vancouver: University of British Columbia Press.

Islam, Nazrul (1995) "Growth Empirics: A Panel Data Approach." *Quarterly Journal of Economics* 110(4): 1127–70.

Jacobs, Jane (1969) *The Economy of Cities*. New York: Vintage Books.

Jaffe, Adam, and Manuel Trajtenberg (1996) "Flows of Knowledge from Universities and Federal Labs: Modelling the Flow of Patent Citations over Time and across Institutional and Geographic Boundaries." NBER Working Paper 5712. National Bureau of Economic Research, Cambridge, Mass. Processed.

Jefferson, Gary H., Thomas G. Rawski, and Yuxin Zheng (1990) "Growth, Efficiency, and Convergence in China's State and Collective Industry." *Economic Development and Cultural Change* 40(2): 239–66.

Levine, Ross, and David Renelt (1992) "A Sensitivity Analysis of Cross-Country Growth Regressions." *American Economic Review* 82(4): 942–63.

Lucas, Robert (1988) "On the Mechanics of Economic Development." *Journal of Monetary Economics* 22(1, July): 3–42.

Mankiw, Gregory N. (1995) "The Growth of Nations." *Brookings Papers on Economic Activity* 1: 275–376.

Mankiw, Gregory N., David Romer, and David Weil (1992) "A Contribution to the Empirics of Economic Growth." *Quarterly Journal of Economics* 107(2, May): 407–38.

Oi, Jean C. (1992) "Fiscal Reform and the Economic Foundations of Local State Corporatism in China." *World Politics* 45(1): 99 126.

——(1995) "Cadre Networks, Information Diffusion, and Market Production in Coastal China." PSD Occasional Paper 20. Private Sector Development Department, World Bank, Washington, D.C. Processed.

Porter, M. E. (1990) *The Competitive Advantage of Nations*. New York: Free Press.

Pritchett, Lant (1996) "Where Has All the Education Gone?" Policy Research Working Paper 1581. Policy Research Department, World Bank, Washington, D.C. Processed.

Romer, Paul M. (1993) "Two Strategies for Economic Development: Using Ideas and Producing Ideas." In *Proceedings of the World Bank Annual Conference on Development Economics 1992*. Washington, D.C: World Bank.

Schankerman, Mark (1991) "Revisions of Investment Plans and the Stock Market Rate of Return." NBER Working Paper 3937. National Bureau of Economic Research, Cambridge, Mass. Processed.

Searle, S. R. (1971) *Linear Models*. New York: Wiley and Sons.

Shleifer, Andrei (1990) "Externalities and Economic Growth: Lessons from Recent Work." Background paper 3 to the *World Development Report 1991: The Challenge of Development*. World Bank, Washington, D.C. Processed.

Stockman, A. C. (1988) "Sectoral and National Aggregate Disturbances to Industrial Output in Seven European Countries." *Journal of Monetary Economics* 21(2/3): 387–409.

Sung, Yun-win (1991) *The China-Hong Kong Connection: The Key to China's Open-Door Policy*. Cambridge, U.K.: Cambridge University Press.

Waldmann, R. J., and J. Bradford De Long (1990) "Interpreting Procyclical Productivity: Evidence from a Cross-Nation Cross-Industry Panel." Discussion Paper 1495. Harvard Institute of Economic Research, Harvard University, Cambridge, Mass. Processed.

Walker, Tony (1993) "Hats off to the Revolution." *Financial Times*, March 30, p. 21.

Weitzman, M. L. (1970) "Optimal Growth with Scale Economies in the Creation of Overhead Capital." *Review of Economic Studies* 37(4): 555–70.

World Bank (1991) *World Development Report 1991: The Challenge of Development.* New York: Oxford University Press.

Yusuf, Shahid (1993) "The Rise of China's Nonstate Sector." China Department, World Bank, Washington, D.C. Processed.

8   Growing up with capital flows

With Antu Panini Murshid

1. Introduction

In the 1990s, foreign capital flows were stepped up to developing countries as they relaxed their capital account restrictions (Figure 8.1). Since developing countries are thought to be short of capital, the new wave of inflows held the potential for raising investment significantly. But was that potential realized?

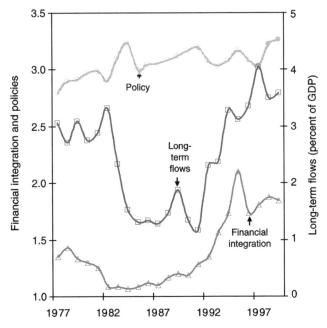

Figure 8.1 Financial integration, policies and long-term capital inflows, 1977–1999.

Note: The financial integration index was constructed using four variables proxying for restrictions on the capital and current accounts. The policy index is the World Bank's Country Policy Institutional Assesment Index and long-term flows are aggregate long-term flows to developing countries reported in the *Global Development Finance.* See text and Appendix Table A2 for details.

This apparently simple question has received surprisingly little empirical attention.

An important study by Bosworth and Collins (1999) concluded that, on average, for the period 1978–1995, a dollar of external flows raised domestic investment by more than 50 cents; moreover, the foreign direct investment (FDI) component of external flows had an even stronger influence on host country investment. Here we build on their research by extending the time period of analysis to 1999 and examining how the capital flows–investment relationship has evolved over time. In particular, we consider whether that evolution can be explained by the degree of openness to international capital and by the quality of domestic policies.

We find that even as countries liberalized to attract new flows, the impact of foreign capital on domestic investment declined. This result seems surprising. If shortage of capital is a key defining characteristic of developing economies, why, then, did investment not increase? Our results suggest that either the availability of capital was not the binding developmental problem, as in many countries of East Asia, or the ability to absorb external capital into new investments was limited. Thus, much of the new wave of capital was diverted by governments into international reserves holdings or was offset by capital outflows as domestic investors diversified their portfolios.

Foreign investors were also apparently motivated by diversification objectives rather than by significant unmet demand for investment financing. Portfolio flows, which increasingly became a more significant form of external financing for developing countries, have typically had a weak impact on domestic investment. At the same time, as FDI took on some of the characteristics of portfolio capital, its impact on investment also declined. Thus, in recent years traditional "greenfield" investments have given way to "mergers and acquisitions" as multinationals have focused on acquiring existing assets rather than making new investments.

While additional reserves, capital outflows, and shifts in the composition of long-run flows increasingly marginalized the importance of capital inflows as a source of investment-finance, our results also suggest that stronger policy environments tended to strengthen the capital flows–investment relationship. Clearly, the 1990s was a decade of transition—of growing up. Having opened their doors wider to international flows, developing countries faced the challenge of learning to handle and harness these flows.

The remainder of this chapter is organized as follows. Section 2 provides a brief theoretical overview of the foreign capital-domestic investment relationship. In section 3, we describe our empirical methodology and discuss the data. In section 4, we present our results, beginning with "base" regressions characterizing the relationship between the various components of long-term capital flows (FDI, bank lending, and portfolio flows) and domestic investment. We then briefly report the variations over time. Finally, we consider an "augmented" model that examines the extent to which the inter-temporal variation in the capital flows–investment relationship can be attributed to capital account openness and the quality of the policy environment. Section 5 concludes.

2. Theoretical overview and hypotheses

Governments often place capital controls in order to regulate capital inflows. These regulations are designed to direct capital into specific investment projects. For example, in many countries FDI is channeled into extractive industries and sovereign loans are intended to alleviate infrastructure bottlenecks. At the same time, capital controls are also designed to keep domestic savings within a country. This is not to say that residents do not find ways to take their savings abroad. However, since capital controls raise transactions costs, the scope for "capital flight" is limited. Thus capital controls may accentuate the relationship between capital inflows and domestic investment, either by funneling foreign-borrowing directly into specific investment projects or by deterring capital outflows. Moreover, in the presence of capital controls, central banks may feel less threatened by the possibility of sudden shifts in market sentiment and choose to maintain fewer reserves, so freeing up capital inflows for investment.

When an economy opens up to private capital flows, the impact on investment depends on the domestic investment environment and on the objectives of investors. Consider two different situations. First, if the marginal returns to capital are high in relation to the world rate of interest, substantial capital will enter the country and supplement domestic savings, leading to a strong relationship between foreign capital flows and domestic investment; such a relationship will persist during a transitional period while the risk-adjusted returns are relatively high. For instance, Blanchard and Giavazzi (2002) consider the opening of Greece and Portugal, in the context of their joining the European Monetary Union, and document significant capital inflows that financed increased investment and consumption.

A second case arises when an economy is open to capital inflows but domestic returns are low, or no higher than the world rate of interest. Foreign capital may still enter the country to achieve diversification (Kraay and Ventura 1999). But in this case, there can be no presumption that foreign capital inflows will boost domestic investment. Developing economies may fall in this category because the lack of complementary infrastructure lowers returns, as also advanced economies that have been open to capital flows and where risk-adjusted returns have been equalized.

It is important to distinguish across various types of foreign capital. Based on their specialized technical knowledge and market experience, FDI investors have an informational advantage over foreign portfolio investors as well as over other domestic investors. In Mody, Razin and Sadka (2003), the informational advantage ("intangible capital") allows FDI investors to "outbid" other investor-types for the most productive opportunities, leading to more domestic investment relative to that undertaken by domestic investors or foreign portfolio investors in the same context. This effect is stronger when domestic productivity is higher, since FDI investors are now able to further leverage their specialized knowledge. However, the net effect of FDI on domestic investment will depend on the consequent decisions of domestic investors. If residual domestic investment opportunities offer low returns, domestic savings may be channeled out of the country in search of higher returns or lower risk.

But foreign investment may also "crowd in" domestic investment where it generates spillovers to the domestic economy. In Borenzstein, De Gregorio and Lee (1998), such spillovers occur because foreign investments lower the costs of adopting new technologies, which in turn enhances the rate of growth. Other mechanisms may also operate, as when foreign investments generate demand for specialized inputs, thus increasing the marginal productivity of investments in those inputs. Spillovers are most likely to occur when knowledge can be rapidly transferred within the economy and domestic entrepreneurs are able to absorb that knowledge. While Borenzstein *et al.* (1998) view human capital as the main conduit for achieving spillovers, we consider the possibility that the quality of country policies is the more general stimulus for spillovers.

3. Methodology and data

We are interested in the influence of gross long-term capital inflows (measured as a fraction of GDP), K_{it}, on domestic investment, I_{it} (also measured as a fraction of GDP). Our focus is on the within-country relationships and we employ the following specification:

$$I_{it} = aK_{it} + \beta'x_{it} + \gamma I_{it-1} + \varepsilon_{it} \tag{1}$$

where i refers to each of the 60 countries in our sample (Table A1 lists the countries) and t refers to the time period from 1979 to 1999 (our data begins in 1977 (see Table 8.1) but we lose two years due to the use of lags in our estimation procedures, as discussed below). In the estimations, K_{it} represents either total capital flows or its components—FDI, loans and portfolio flows.

The controls, x_{it}, are as follows: the growth rate of real GDP, the real interest rate, the cyclical variation in the ratio of M2 to GDP, a measure of GDP uncertainty, and the change in terms of trade (see Table A2 for a description of these variables). The growth rate of real GDP captures the important accelerator effect. The cost and availability of capital are proxied, respectively, by the real interest rate and the ratio of broad money to GDP separated from its three-year trend. Our measure of uncertainty is based on one-step ahead forecast errors for an AR(2) process in real GDP growth rates (as in Servén 1998).[1] Finally the lagged value of investment, I_{it-1}, is included as an additional control to allow for persistence in the dependent variable.

Two econometric issues arise in estimating such a model. First, causality

Table 8.1 Composition and uses of private long-term flows: 1977–1999 (billions of US$)

		1977–79	1980–84	1985–89	1990–94	1995–99
Composition of flows						
	Private long-term flows	39.4	47.0	31.6	109.3	256.9
	FDI	6.6	8.7	15.3	52.7	154.6
	Loans	25.0	29.2	5.4	7.3	27.0
	Portfolio	2.4	1.8	3.6	41.8	74.8
	Other (debt flows)	5.3	7.3	7.2	7.5	0.5
Use of funds	Total resource flows	81.9	93.8	83.5	195.0	330.9
	Current account deficit	26.9	49.1	40.2	81.5	93.5
	Change in reserves	26.7	−6.0	6.0	48.6	69.3
	Capital outflows and E&O	28.4	50.7	37.2	64.9	168.1

Note: Data on the composition of flows start in 1977, while data on the use of funds start in 1978.

Source: World Bank. *Global Development Finance*, 2001.

may run from domestic investment to international capital inflows rather than the other way around. To deal with this concern, we need appropriate instruments to isolate the exogenous component of capital flows. Second, the presence of the lagged dependent variable on the right-hand side of our regressions may bias the coefficient estimates. To deal with these problems, we employ a number of different estimation strategies.

First, using annual data, we estimate a static investment equation with no lags of the dependent variable. First-differencing removes the influence of unchanging country characteristics. This is a useful benchmark, allowing comparison with the Bosworth and Collins (1999) estimates. While instrumental variable estimation reduces the reverse causality concern, the coefficients could be biased due to the presence of serial correlation in the data.

We experiment with a number of instruments, which proxy for shifts in the supply of capital flowing to developing countries. For instance, U.S. interest rates and the phase of the U.S. business cycle can be viewed as largely exogenous and at the same time important determinants of capital flows (Calvo *et al.* 1993). Our preferred instrument however is a measure of the global pool of capital (of the particular type or in the aggregate) available to developing countries. This variable, suggested by Bosworth and Collins (1999), provides a more direct measure of the supply of global financial capital and reflects a broader set of external supply-side factors.[2] We also consider an alternative instrument suggested by Tytell and Wei (2003): the weighted average of capital flows/GDP ratios to other countries in the same region; the weights are inversely related to the great circle distances between the largest two cities in any two countries.[3] This regional variable is strongly correlated with capital flows into a given country, but, as with the measure of global capital flows to developing countries, is likely to be weakly correlated with the error terms. As additional instruments we include lagged values of all the endogenous variables including capital flows.

Second, we estimate a similar model, but using data averaged over three-year windows. Since the persistence in the three-year sample is weaker, issues arising on account of serial correlation are expected to be less important. Again, we remove country fixed-effects by first-differencing the data and correct for possible endogeneity using the instruments described above.

Third, we employ the dynamic panel estimator proposed by Arellano and Bond (1991) to estimate equation (1) using annual data.[4] The Arellano–Bond estimator accounts for potential biases by employing a set of internal instruments for all endogenous and predetermined variables. These are simply an increasing sequence of lagged values of the endogenous and predetermined variables. In addition we employ the set of external instruments described above to capture the exogenous component of capital flows.

Our focus on data at higher (annual and three-year) frequencies than typically observed in the growth literature allows us to construct better instruments for two reasons. First, at higher frequencies the lagged capital flows variable should be a better predictor of current inflows. Second, if the full effect of a shock to investment occurs over an extended period of time, moving to higher frequencies should reduce feedback from investment to capital flows, thus mitigating the problem of reverse causality.

The capital flows data—all long-term capital flows and the components of long-term flows: foreign direct investment, commercial bank loans, portfolio flows—are reported in the World Bank's *Global Development Finance* (*GDF*) on a *gross* basis, though net of amortizations on account of principal repayment. The International Monetary Fund's *International Financial Statistics* (*IFS*) provides an alternative data source on aggregate international resource flows that distinguishes between foreign investment, loans, and portfolio investments. The data source does not seem to impact the key results: the relationships reported in Bosworth and Collins (1999), based on *IFS*-data are also evident in the *GDF*-data.[5]

In addition to the control variables described above, in our "augmented specification," we include interaction terms between capital flows and a financial openness variable and capital flows and a policy variable. Our measure of financial openness is based on four proxies for government restrictions that impact capital mobility. These four measures, reported in the IMF's *Exchange Arrangements and Agreements*, characterize: (a) the openness of the capital account, (b) the openness of the current account, (c) the stringency of requirements for the repatriation and/or surrender of export proceeds, and (d) the existence of multiple exchange rates for capital account transactions. For each variable, a 1 indicates a relatively open regime and a 0 otherwise.[6] We construct an index of financial integration as the sum of these four measures of government restrictions. Thus our index takes values between 0 and 4, where a 0 indicates that a country has closed capital and current accounts, places restrictions on its export receipts and further operates a system of multiple exchange rates, and a value of 4 indicates an open regime.[7] This index, which was first introduced in a systematic dataset by Grilli and Milesi-Ferretti (1995), is a graded measure of a country's financial integration with the rest of the world, consolidating the capital account restrictions dummy with other measures relating to the ability of investors to bypass controls on the capital account.[8]

Our measure of policy is the World Bank's Country Policy Institutional Assessment (CPIA) Index. This index provides an assessment of how conducive a country's current policy and institutional framework are to fostering poverty reduction and sustained growth. The overall rating is based on 20 indicators that fall into one of five categories: economic management, structural reform, social inclusion and public sector management and institutions. Each indicator receives a 5% weight in the overall rating.[9] The resulting index varies from 0–5: countries with poor polices are rated at the lower end and those with better policies take on higher values.

4. The capital flows–investment relationship

We begin by presenting the static specification of the investment equation, with the data observed annually and the instruments for endogeneity as discussed above. As with all of our regressions, unchanging country-specific heterogeneity is removed by first differencing the data. The results reported in column (1) of Table 8.2 indicate that, on average, each dollar of long-run flows raised domestic investment by 66 cents in our sample of countries. This result is similar to that obtained by Bosworth and Collins (1999), who found that an additional dollar of total inflows to developing countries raised investment by 52 cents.[10] By contrast a similar analysis conducted for a sample of industrialized countries showed no relationship between foreign capital flows and domestic investment. This is consistent with the earlier discussion that the domestic investment and financing decisions become increasingly dissociated as economic and financial integration with the rest of the world increases.[11]

In column (2) we re-estimate our investment equation using three-year averages. The results are largely unchanged. Long-run capital inflows continue to reveal a statistically significant and sizeable impact on domestic investment. These three-year data have the advantage that they are less persistent than the annual series, which is clear from the test of second order serial correlation.[12] The disadvantage is that feedback from domestic investment to capital inflows is likely to be more pronounced.

In column (3) we consider a dynamic investment equation, which is estimated using annual data. This is a more direct approach of addressing the issue serial correlation without introducing the risk of picking up stronger feedback effects. We estimate this specification using the first-difference one-step GMM-estimator developed by Arellano and Bond (1991). In column (4), we include the additional controls: GDP growth, the real interest

Table 8.2 Capital flows–investment relationship: 1979–1999

Independent variable	Annual data static specification 1 Coefficient (p-value)	3-Year data static specification 2	Annual data dynamic specification 3	Annual data dynamic specification 4
Long-term flows	0.6647 (0.00)	0.7726 (0.00)	0.4388 (0.00)	0.3161 (0.07)
Growth	0.1051 (0.14)	0.2269 (0.58)	0.5777 (0.00)	0.5955 (0.00)
Change in terms of trade				−0.02 (0.00)
Real interest rate				−0.0009 (0.31)
M2				0.1575 (0.39)
Uncertainty				−1.2563 (0.11)
Investment, lagged once			0.7069 (0.00)	0.7286 (0.00)
Test for 1st order serial correlation	(0.00)	(0.00)	(0.00)	(0.00)
Test for 2nd order serial correlation	(0.16)	(0.89)	(0.90)	(0.45)
Sargan J	(0.05)	(0.12)	(0.00)	(0.00)

Note: For each column p-values are reported in brackets. Regressions 1 and 2 were estimated using an instrumentals variables estimator. Columns 3 and 4 were estimated using the Arellano–Bond (1991) one-step first-difference GMM estimator, using DPD98 for Gauss. The coefficients and p-values are robust to heteroscedasticity.

rate, the deviation in M2 from trend, GDP uncertainty, and the change in terms of trade. Each variable except for the shock to terms of trade is treated as endogenous; hence two-period lagged-levels for each of these variables are used as instruments along with global long-run flows to developing countries.

The dynamic specification results suggest that the short-run impact of a dollar of long-term flows is to raise investment by between 32 and 44 cents. The strong persistence in investment implies that the long-run impact on investment is considerably higher, ranging from between 118 (=0.32/[1–0.729]) and 150 (=0.44/[1–0.707]) cents. Following an improvement in terms of trade, investment appears to fall. The real interest is negatively associated with investment; however this result is weak. A stronger relationship is found between the trend-deviation in M2, suggesting that this variable is perhaps better able to capture changes in the user cost of capital. Our measure of uncertainty is found to negatively impact on investment; the result is borderline significant and consistent with the results in Servén (1998).

Arellano and Bond (1991) suggest two tests to assess the validity of dynamic specifications. Crucially, second-order serial correlation should be absent and the results meet that test. They also suggest a Sargan test for over-identifying restrictions. In columns (3) and (4), the null of the validity of over-identifying restrictions is rejected. However, it is well-known that in finite samples the Sargan test statistics obtained from the one-step Arellano–Bond estimator often over-reject the null in the presence of heteroskedasticity (see Arellano and Bond 1991). While standard errors robust to heteroscedasticity can be obtained, the distribution of the Sargan test is unknown in this case. Thus the Sargan test statistic reported for the one-step estimator should be treated with caution. For this reason, researchers sometimes rely on the Sargan test statistics from the two-step estimator, which in this case does not lead to a rejection of the null hypothesis that the over-identifying restrictions are in fact valid.

Next, in Table 8.3, we repeat the same analysis as in Table 8.2, for FDI, loans, and portfolio capital. The results from the annual and three-year average static models presented in columns (1) and (2) suggest that FDI had the strongest impact on domestic investment; each dollar of new inflows raised investment by an amount between 72 and 86 cents. Bank loans have had a somewhat lower, but nevertheless sizeable impact, with each additional dollar of foreign loans raising domestic investment by a little over half the amount of the loan received. Portfolio flows also seem to have had an impact on domestic investment; however, this result is significant at only the 10 percent level. The test statistics reported for columns (1) and (2) are encouraging. The Sargan test for the validity of the over-identifying restrictions cannot be rejected in either case. While tests for second-order serial correlation reveal persistence in the annual data, it is clearly lower in the three-year data.

Column (3) reports the results using a dynamic specification. The co-efficients are broadly consistent with those reported in columns (1) and (2). FDI continues to show a strong and statistically significant impact on domestic investment. In the short-run an additional dollar of foreign investment appears to raise domestic investment by 51 cents. The persistence in investment implies that this impact is significantly amplified over the long-run. However, the influence of loans falls sharply in the dynamic specification and that of portfolio flows turns negative, though this result is only borderline statistically significant. The contrast in the results with respect to portfolio flows between static and dynamic specifications suggests that prior years of higher investment are associated with new inflows of portfolio capital. The implication is not that portfolio capital is "sucked-in" to finance new investment opportunities; rather new inflows enter only to acquire a stake in a larger stock of existing assets. The goal of such investments, which take place at arm's length, is presumably for the purpose of international diversification.

Table 8.3 Capital flows–investment relationship, by type and changes over time: 1979–1999

Independent variable	Annual data static specification 1 Coefficient (p-value)	3-Year data static specification 2	Annual data dynamic specification		
			Full sample 3	1980s 4	1990s 5
Foreign direct investment	0.7204 (0.00)	0.8626 (0.00)	0.5138 (0.05)	0.9363 (0.07)	0.2342 (0.24)
Loans	0.6114 (0.00)	0.5276 (0.04)	0.2180 (0.49)	0.4888 (0.01)	−0.0213 (0.96)
Portfolio flows	0.4644 (0.09)	0.4148 (0.10)	−0.7035 (0.10)	−0.6071 (0.61)	0.2064 (0.41)
Growth	0.0521 (0.05)	0.1089 (0.04)	1.0529 (0.00)	0.2723 (0.17)	0.2075 (0.20)
Change in terms of trade	−0.0104 (0.20)	−0.0246 (0.21)	−0.0259 (0.02)	−0.0206 (0.03)	−0.0117 (0.32)
Real interest rate	0.0005 (0.16)	−0.0004 (0.22)	−0.0009 (0.61)	−0.0010 (0.38)	0.0000 (0.97)
M2	0.0850 (0.05)	0.0006 (0.70)	0.3768 (0.01)	0.0066 (0.45)	0.0023 (0.51)
Uncertainty	0.2297 (0.60)	−0.1509 (0.63)	−1.6069 (0.18)	−0.7214 (0.09)	−0.3658 (0.47)
Investment, lagged once			0.8422 (0.00)	0.7284 (0.00)	0.2608 (0.15)
Test for 1st order serial correlation	(0.00)	(0.00)	(0.00)	(0.00)	(0.03)
Test for 2nd order serial correlation	(0.04)	(0.69)	(0.25)	(0.79)	(0.57)
Sargan J	(0.16)	(0.43)	(0.13)	(0.23)	(0.01)

Note: For each column *p*-values are reported in brackets. Columns 1 and 2 were estimated using an instrumental variables estimator. Columns 3–5 were estimated using a one-step first-difference GMM estimator attributable to Arellano and Bond (1991), using DPD98 for Gauss. The coefficients and *p*-values are robust to heteroscedasticity.

Prior to the debt crisis of the early 1980s, loans were the largest component of long-run flows to developing countries. Starting in the mid-1980s, FDI became the dominant form of foreign capital but by the 1990s portfolio investors had also become major players in emerging markets. The 1990s were also a period of policy change for many developing countries. Restrictions on financial systems were reduced and product and capital markets were opened up to foreign competition. At the same time, greater emphasis was placed on curbing domestic budgetary and monetary profligacy and on building stronger institutional foundations for growth.

In order to explore the impact of these changes, we re-estimate equation (4) of Table 8.2 using a 10-year window of data rolled forward through time. The long-run impact of aggregate inflows, calculated by normalizing the co-efficient on total flows by the coefficient on lagged investment, is plotted in Figure 8.2. It is evident that the long-run relationship between foreign capital flows and domestic investment declined sharply over time.

The changes over time in the coefficient estimates for the components of capital inflows are reported in columns (4) and (5) of Table 8.3. The results suggest striking differences in the impact of each type of financial capital across the two periods. In the 1980s, it would appear that both FDI and loans had a large impact on domestic investment. Over this period, developing countries received large quantities of both types of flows. By contrast there is no evidence of a link between portfolio capital and domestic investment. However, since the amount of portfolio capital flowing to developing countries was negligible, it would appear, overall, that external flows played an important role in financing domestic investment.

In the 1990s, the link between portfolio flows and domestic investment strengthened somewhat, while the impact of FDI and loans fell. These results are not altogether surprising. The declining impact of foreign direct investment may reflect a shift in the composition of FDI, away from the traditional

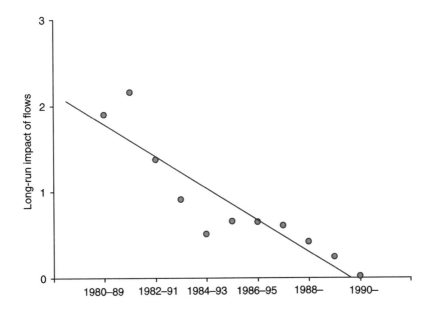

Figure 8.2 Long-run impact of private capital flows*.

Note: * The estimated relationships between long-run flows and investment are based on annual data over 10-year windows that are rolled forward through time. The specification is identical to that used in Table 10.2 column 4. The long-run impact of flows is calculated by normalizing the coefficient on long-run flows by the coefficient on lagged investment. Estimation is based on the Arellano–Bond one-step GMM estimator.

"greenfield" variety toward more mergers and acquisitions. Arguably foreign acquisitions could lead to capital formation indirectly since newly acquired firms often go through significant restructuring and also because the original shareholders may reinvest in other sectors. It does not appear, however, that either of these effects was important. It is somewhat less clear why the impact of loans declined so drastically in the 1990s. It could be the consequence of a shift from public- to private-sector borrowing. Prior to the debt crisis, the public sector was responsible for the bulk of new borrowing financed by banks. Often these loans were funneled into large scale investment projects. In the aftermath of the crisis, loans fell in importance. Lending which continued went largely to the private sector, which possibly used foreign loans as a substitute for more expensive domestic borrowing.

Thus, our results suggest that in the 1990s, as many countries experienced increased capital inflows, the marginal impact of inflows on domestic investment declined. This is consistent with the observation reported in Table 8.1 that capital inflows were also accompanied by increases in reserves and outflows following greater financial openness. However at the same time, improvements in the policy environment created new opportunities for domestic investment and reduced uncertainties regarding the macroeconomic environment. This generated additional incentives for developing country capital to stay at home, which may have offset, in part, the effects of increased financial openness.

In Table 8.4, we explicitly consider the importance of financial integration and domestic policies by allowing the coefficient on capital flows to be a function of these variables. Columns (1) and (4) of Table 8.4 report the importance of such interactions when foreign capital takes the form of FDI. Column (1) presents the results from a dynamic specification using annual data, while the regression in column (4) utilizes a static specification with the three-year averages. The results suggest that greater financial integration weakens the impact of FDI on investment. This is consistent with our earlier finding, which showed that the link between FDI and domestic investment declined in the 1990s. It is also consistent with other evidence that FDI has a strong (essentially one-to-one relationship) with investment in Sub-Saharan Africa, where most countries still have relatively closed capital accounts, but a weaker impact in Latin America and East Asia, where countries are generally more integrated (see Agosin and Mayer 2000). The interactions between portfolio flows and openness are similar, although the results are not statistically significant (columns (3) and (6)). The positive interaction between loans and financial integration in the dynamic specification (column (2)) is at variance with the results with the three-year averages, which show a negative relationship as with the other flows (column (5)).

Interactions with our policy variable suggest that the link between capital flows and investment strengthens following improvements in the policy environment. In countries with a CPIA-rating exceeding 3.5 (the top 20th percentile in our sample), additional flows have a stronger impact on investment.

Table 8.4 Nonlinearities in the capital flows–investment relationship: 1979–1999

Independent variable	Annual data dynamic specification			3-Year data static specification		
	Interactions with FDI	Interactions with loans	Interactions with portfolio flows	Interactions with FDI	Interactions with loans	Interactions with portfolio flows
	1 Coefficient (p-value)	2	5	4	5	6
Foreign direct investment	1.3640	0.5641	0.2956	0.8377	0.8452	0.7705
	(0.03)	(0.00)	(0.19)	(0.05)	(0.03)	(0.02)
Loans	0.7130	−0.3535	0.9949	0.7039	0.9212	0.6110
	(0.09)	(0.52)	(0.01)	(0.00)	(0.02)	(0.00)
Portfolio flows	0.0876	−0.2793	1.3546	0.4826	0.6635	1.1058
	(0.89)	(0.59)	(0.47)	(0.12)	(0.02)	(0.10)
Growth	0.3740	0.5192	0.3194	0.2534	0.1763	0.2308
	(0.32)	(0.02)	(0.37)	(0.34)	(0.49)	(0.35)
Change in terms of trade	−0.0164	−0.0185	−0.0168	0.0235	0.0240	0.0246
	(0.13)	(0.05)	(0.05)	(0.44)	(0.43)	(0.41)
Real interest rate	−0.0010	−0.0007	−0.0006	−0.0002	0.0004	0.0002
	(0.47)	(0.58)	(0.70)	(0.80)	(0.42)	(0.68)
M2	0.2438	0.0633	0.1513	−0.0001	0.0011	0.0014
	(0.10)	(0.68)	(0.42)	(0.92)	(0.28)	(0.16)
Uncertainty	−0.7096	−0.3272	−0.5010	−1.0740	−0.9980	−0.8502
	(0.17)	(0.18)	(0.17)	(0.05)	(0.10)	(0.11)
Financial integration	0.0189	−0.0022	0.0023	0.0109	−0.0015	0.0001
	(0.01)	(0.46)	(0.64)	(0.27)	(0.76)	(0.98)
Policy	−0.0080	−0.0098	−0.0131	−0.0666	−0.0571	−0.0545
	(0.30)	(0.20)	(0.05)	(0.00)	(0.01)	(0.00)
Flows: financial integration	−0.9041	0.5592	−0.9751	−0.5194	−0.2555	−0.4125
	(0.00)	(0.08)	(0.29)	(0.06)	(0.18)	(0.14)
Flows: high policy	1.5152	0.4936	3.4498	1.5147	0.8289	1.6018
	(0.03)	(0.55)	(0.10)	(0.00)	(0.07)	(0.06)
Investment, lagged once	0.5934	0.5862	0.4838			
	(0.00)	(0.00)	(0.00)			
Test for 1st order serial correlation	(0.00)	(0.00)	(0.00)	(0.00)	(0.02)	(0.01)
Test for 2nd order serial correlation	(0.20)	(0.80)	(0.88)	(0.53)	(0.18)	(0.23)
Sargan J	(0.06)	(0.00)	(0.01)	(0.79)	(0.97)	(0.96)

Note: For each column p-values are reported in brackets. High policy regimes are those with a CPIA-rating in excess of 3.5 (upper 20th percentile). Regressions 1–3 were estimated using the Arellano–Bond one-step first-difference GMM estimator, using DPD98 for Gauss. The coefficients and p-values are robust to heteroscedasticity. Regressions 4–6 were estimated using an instrumental variable estimator.

This is especially true of FDI, but also in the case of portfolio flows. For portfolio flows, the absolute size of the coefficient on the interaction term is approximately four times higher than the coefficient on the interaction with financial openness (for both annual and three-year estimates); and thus liberalization and policy-quality, though offsetting each other, may, in sum, have favored an increased impact of portfolio flows on domestic investment.

Sensitivity analysis (not shown here) suggested qualitatively similar findings when using different measures of financial integration and policy. The stock of external assets and liabilities of foreign direct and portfolio investment divided by GDP was used as an alternative measure of financial openness,[13] while the ICRG economic risk rating replaced the CPIA variable.

5. Conclusions

A potentially important benefit of foreign capital inflows into developing economies is the augmentation of investment resources to add to capital stock with high marginal returns. However, as the paper's theoretical discussion shows, financial integration allows agents to optimize their investment portfolios, and this may not involve increasing domestic investment. The results of this paper suggest that the surge in capital flows during the 1990s was driven largely by this diversification motive.

Countries with better policies did have greater success in absorbing foreign inflows. At least in part, this could be because improved policies raised the marginal product of new investments, while at the same time they created an environment conducive for the diffusion of new technologies and ideas intrinsic to foreign capital. Improved policies probably also reduced the risk of holding domestic assets, which in turn, by discouraging capital outflows, would have further enhanced the relationship between capital flows and investment.

Notes

1   This is done separately for each country and recursively so that at any time, t, only the information in the sample up to time t is utilized in our regressions.

2   One disadvantage of this variable is that it implicitly assumes that while shocks to the supply of capital are positively correlated across countries, shocks to the demand for capital are largely uncorrelated. This is a reasonable assumption, except perhaps during crisis-periods, when demand shocks are more likely to be correlated across borders. In particular a global crisis may trigger sharp declines in investment in a large sample of countries resulting in a decline in flows to developing countries as a whole.

3   The distances were obtained from Boisso and Ferrantino (1997). Gaps in the data were filled using the authors' calculations.

4   The standard least-squares estimator is biased in dynamic panels and more generally when the explanatory variables are predetermined. Anderson and Hsiao (1982) suggest using lagged observations of the regressors as instruments. Specifically, the dependent variable lagged twice is a valid instrument for the first difference of the

lagged dependent variable, while a lagged value of the regressors can serve as an instrument for the first difference of the regressors, when they are predetermined. Arellano and Bond (1991) propose a more efficient estimator which instruments for endogenous and predetermined variables using an increasing sequence of lagged values, thus making use of more information in the sample.

5 The *IFS* data includes short-term flows, whereas the *GDF* allows a distinction between short-term and long-term flows (the *GDF* definition of short-term debt is the debt with an original maturity of less than one year). The *GDF* data reports only those transactions denominated in foreign currencies.

6 This is the opposite of the convention of treating a 1 as a restriction and a 0 as the lack of restrictions.

7 An important change occurred in the measurement of the intensity of controls on the capital account starting in 1996, when the IMF's *Exchange Arrangements and Restrictions* stopped reporting the summary measure and started reporting details on several aspects of the capital account, which permitted the construction of a graded index of capital account restrictions rather than a dichotomous variable, as in the past. Thus the financial integration index from 1996 onward is not entirely comparable to earlier years. It is, moreover, the case that in 1996 the average value of the financial integration index shows a marked decline (Figure 8.1). However closer scrutiny reveals that this drop in financial integration is driven not by the capital accounts measure but almost entirely by a sharp decrease in the current account transactions measure, which had earlier risen sharply in 1995. Moreover, sensitivity analysis using a sample truncated in 1995 did not qualitatively change our results.

8 Quinn (1997) has also constructed a continuous measure of capital controls based on the details provided in the IMF publication. However, this index is available only for a few years. Moreover, Chinn (2002) regresses the Quinn index on the four measures used to construct our index and finds that they explain 71 percent of the variation in that index.

9 See Country Policy and Institutional Assessment 2001 Questionnaire for a detailed discussion (http://www.worldbank.org/ida/cpiaq2001.pdf).

10 Bosworth and Collins (1999) use two lags of growth rates in their specification. However, our approach is to treat each variable as endogenous and estimate the resulting model using an appropriate set of instruments. Consequently none of the variables enter with lags. Nevertheless, if we employ a specification identical to that in Bosworth and Collins (1999), our results remain largely unaltered.

11 Our sample of developed countries consists of the original OECD member nations, with the exception of Turkey, which enters in our sample of developing countries. In addition, our sample includes the following countries: Australia, Finland, Japan and New Zealand, which are also presently members of the OECD, and Norway, which is not a member. Data were obtained primarily from *International Financial Statistics* and the *World Development Indicators*.

12 First-order serial correlation is to be expected as this simply an artifact of first-differencing.

13 This measure was originally proposed by Lane and Milesi-Ferretti (2002).

Appendix

Appendix Table A1 Country list

East Asia and the Pacific	*South Asia*
Fiji	Bangladesh
Indonesia	India
Korea, Rep.	Nepal
Malaysia	Pakistan
Papua New Guinea	Sri Lanka
The Philippines	
Thailand	
	Sub-Saharan Africa
	Benin
Latin America and the Caribbean	Burkina Faso
Argentina	Burundi
Belize	Central African Republic
Bolivia	Chad
Brazil	Cote d'Ivoire
Chile	Gambia
Colombia	Ghana
Costa Rica	Kenya
Dominican Republic	Malawi
Ecuador	Mali
Grenada	Mauritania
Guatemala	Mauritius
Guyana	Niger
Jamaica	Nigeria
Mexico	Rwanda
Peru	Senegal
St. Vincent and the Grenadines	Seychelles
Trinidad and Tobago	Sierra Leone
Uruguay	South Africa
	Uganda
Middle East and North Africa	Zambia
Algeria	Zimbabwe
Egypt, Arab Rep.	
Jordan	
Morocco	
Syrian Arab Republic	
Tunisia	
Turkey	

Appendix Table A2 Descriptions of variables and data sources

Variable	Description
Investment	Gross domestic fixed capital divided by GDP. Missing values were extrapolated based on gross domestic investment. Source: *World Development Indicators*, NE.GDI.FTOT.ZS.
Growth rate	Annual growth of real GDP at market prices. Source: *World Development Indicators*, NY.GDP.MKTP.KD.ZG. Change in terms of trade: log difference in net barter terms of trade. Missing values were interpolated. Source: *World Development Indicators*, NE.TRM.TRAD.XU.
Real interest rate	Short-term nominal interest rate *minus* inflation rate. Short-term interest rates refer to lending rates, otherwise money market rates or discount rates. Source: *International Financial Statistics* CD ROM series 60, 60B, and 60M.
Broad money	Deviation in M2/GDP from three-year trend. Source: *World Development Indicators*, FM.LBL.MQMY.GD.ZS.
Policy	Country Policy Institutional Assessment Index. Source: World Bank. See text.
Financial integration	Constructed with data from *Exchange Arrangements and Agreements*. See text.
Long-term flows	Gross private flows net of amortizations on account of principal repayment. Data were normalized by GDP. Source: *Global Development Finance* (2001), DT.NFA.PRVT.CD
Foreign direct investment	Foreign direct investment divided by GDP. Source: *Global Development Finance* (2001), BX.KLT.DINV.CD.
Loans	Sum of PPG and PNG loans from private banks and other private financial institutions divided by GDP. Source: *Global Development Finance* (2001), DT.NFL.PCBK.CD and DT.NFL.PNGC.CD. Missing values filled using *IFS* data, when these data were unavailable, missing values were interpolated.
Portfolio flows	Sum of bond and equity investments, divided by GDP. Source: *Global Development Finance* (2001), BX.PEF.TOTL.CD.DT and DT.NFL.BOND.CD. Missing values filled using *IFS*, when these data were unavailable, missing values were interpolated.
Global capital flows	Sum of gross long-run flows to our sample of countries divided by the GDP aggregated across our sample. A similar variable was calculated for FDI, bank loans and portfolio flows.
Regional capital flows	Weighted average of capital flows relative to GDP in other countries in the same region. See text. A similar variable was calculated for FDI, bank loans and portfolio flows.

References

Agosin, M.R., and Mayer, R. (2000) Foreign investment in developing countries. Does it crowd in domestic investment? UNCTAD Paper 146.

Anderson, T.W., and Hsiao, C. (1982) Estimation of dynamic models with error components. *Journal of the American Statistical Association* 76: 598–606.

Arellano, M., and Bond, S.R. (1991) Some tests of specification for panel data: Monte Carlo evidence and an application to employment equations. *Review of Economic Studies* 58: 277–97.

Blanchard, O., and Giavazzi, F. (2002) Current account deficits in the euro area: the end of the Feldstein-Horioka puzzle? *Brookings Papers on Economic Activity* 2: 147–210.

Boisso, D., and Ferrantino, M. (1997) Economic distance, cultural distance, and openness: empirical puzzles. *Journal of Economic Integration* 12: 456–484.

Borenzstein, E., De Gregorio, J., and Lee, J.-W. (1998) How does foreign direct investment affect growth? *Journal of International Economics* 45: 115–135.

Bosworth, B., and Collins, S.M. (1999) Capital flows to developing economies: implications for saving and investment. *Brookings Papers on Economic Activity* 1: 143–169.

Calvo, G., Leiderman, L., and Reinhart, C. (1993) Capital inflows to Latin America: the role of external factors. *IMF Staff Papers* 40: 108–151.

Chinn, M. (2002) The compatibility of capital controls and financial development: a selective survey and empirical evidence. Santa Cruz Center for International Working Papers 02–10.

Grilli, V., and Milesi-Ferretti, G.M. (1995) Economic effects and structural determinants of capital controls. *International Monetary Fund Staff Papers* 42: 517–551.

International Monetary Fund. *International Financial Statistics*. IMF, Washington.

International Monetary Fund (1996) *Exchange Arrangements and Agreements*. IMF, Washington.

International Monetary Fund (2001) *World Economic Outlook*. IMF, Washington.

Kraay, A., and Ventura, J. (1999) Current accounts in debtor and creditor countries. *Quarterly Journal of Economics* 115: 1137–1166.

Lane, P., and Milesi-Ferretti, G.M. (2002) International financial integration. Working Paper prepared for the IMF Third Annual Research Conference.

Mody, A., Razin, A., and Sadka, E. (2003) The role of information in driving FDI flows: host-country transparency and source country specialization. Forthcoming IMF Working Paper.

Quinn, D. (1997) The correlates of change in international financial regulation. *American Political Science Review* 91: 531–551.

Servén, L. (1998) Macroeconomic uncertainty and private investment in developing countries: an empirical investigation. World Bank Policy Research Working Paper 2035.

Tytell, I., and Wei, S.-J. (2003) Does financial globalization induce better macroeconomic policies? Forthcoming IMF Working Paper.

World Bank (2001) *Global Development Finance*. World Bank, Washington.

World Bank (various issues). *World Development Indicators*. World Bank, Washington.

9 How foreign participation and market concentration impact bank spreads

Evidence from Latin America

With Maria Soledad Martinez Peria

1. Introduction

The market structure of the banking industry in many developing countries has recently undergone significant changes. In particular, the ongoing and, often, extensive entry of foreign banks has been the source of a far-reaching transformation. Between 1994 and 1999, the share of assets held by foreign banks (i.e., those banks that are at least 50 percent foreign) increased from 7.8 percent to 52.3 percent among countries in Eastern Europe (IMF 2000). For countries in Latin America, the increase in foreign bank participation over the same period was from 13.1 percent to 44.8 percent. At the same time, the rise in foreign bank participation often occurred in the context of already high and, in some countries, rising levels of bank concentration. Among a sample of 33 developing countries, the level of bank assets held by the three largest banks averaged 64 percent during 1995–99.[1]

Growing foreign bank presence and high levels of bank concentration in developing countries have been the consequence of a number of factors, some of them interrelated. A facet of the larger process of financial liberalization and international integration, foreign entry was encouraged by local banking authorities following financial crises as they sought to minimize the costs of recapitalizing domestic financial systems. The high levels of concentration have also, in part been the consequence of crises, as banks closed, merged or were acquired. In some cases, foreign bank entry contributed to bank concentration where foreign banks mainly acquired existing domestic banks. Foreign competition, moreover, induced domestic bank consolidation and concentration.

A question that of interest to policy makers and academics alike is the impact of foreign bank entry and bank concentration on bank spreads—the difference between the rate charged to borrowers and the rate paid by depositors.[2] Spreads are commonly interpreted as a measure of the cost of financial intermediation (see Saunders and Schumacher (2000) and Brock and Rojas-Suarez (2000)). High spreads can hinder the growth of savings and investment and imply that the cost of using the financial system may become prohibitive for certain borrowers. Furthermore, the impact of high spreads is likely to be more severe for developing countries where, given that capital markets are generally small and underdeveloped, a larger percentage of firms and individuals tend to depend on banks to meet their financial needs.

A number of recent articles investigate the impact of foreign entry on bank spreads and other variables (see for example Claessens, Demirgüç-Kunt, and Huizinga (2000), Barajas, Steiner, and Salazar (2000), and Denizer (2000)). Demirgüç-Kunt, Laeven, and Levine (2004), in turn, examine the implications of concentration and bank regulation on spreads.[3] Yet, few studies have examined the parallel trends towards more foreign entry and consolidation in the sector. None has examined how different types of foreign bank entry affect spreads.

This chapter investigates the impact of foreign bank participation and concentration on bank spreads in a sample of Latin American countries during the late 1990s. Using bank level data for Argentina, Chile, Colombia, Mexico, and Peru over the late 1990s, we examine a number of hypotheses. First, we investigate whether foreign banks are able to operate with lower spreads, directly benefiting borrowers. We refer to this effect as the "own-effect" of foreign bank presence.

Second, we examine whether the type of foreign bank entry influences how big the "own effect" might be. In other words, among the foreign banks we distinguish between those that entered or increased their presence in the system by acquiring domestic banks and those that established de novo operations. Dell'Ariccia and Marquez (2004) suggest that even if all banks are equally cost efficient, they may charge different spreads, based on their specialization in different market segments. Alternatively, newly established foreign banks may be more aggressive in their pricing strategies to gain market share. Though we are not be able to formally test whether variations in market segments or in pricing strategies account for differences in spreads across banks, to our knowledge, our study is the first to examine whether all forms of foreign entry have the same impact on spreads.

Third, we analyze whether there is a "spillover effect" as a result of foreign bank participation. That is, once we control for the origin (domestic or foreign) of individual banks, we test whether the overall level of foreign bank participation in the banking system raises or lowers spreads across the board, and, in particular, among domestic banks. A priori the spillover effect of foreign bank participation is indeterminate. Spreads would be lowered if foreign banks competed directly with domestic banks, forcing them to reduce their spreads.[4] Alternatively, faced with foreign bank competition, domestic banks may redirect their lending to segments that are more opaque, where they have an informational advantage and greater market power, allowing them to charge higher spreads (Dell'Ariccia and Marquez, 2004).

Finally, we study the impact of bank concentration on bank spreads by including several measures of system-wide bank concentration in our estimations. At the same time, we control for banks' market share and for cases of bank consolidation.

We believe this chapter contributes to the existing literature not only by testing some hypotheses that have been overlooked before, but also by focusing on a region that has been at the forefront of the recent changes in bank market structure in developing countries and that has traditionally been characterized by high spreads. Latin America makes for an interesting case study for a number of reasons. First, perhaps after Eastern Europe, Latin America has been the region to witness the sharpest increase in foreign bank participation (IMF 2000). Second, despite embarking on a process of financial market liberalization during the late 1980s and early 1990s—which included the elimination of interest rates and direct credit controls—spreads in the region remained high even in the mid-1990s.[5] Third, concentration rose or remains high (depending on the country) in part because many foreign banks increased their participation by acquiring domestic banks. Also, in many of these countries, there has been a trend towards consolidation among domestic banks.

Our empirical analysis yields a number of interesting results. We find that foreign banks are able to charge lower spreads and have lower costs than domestic banks. Moreover, those foreign banks that acquired domestic institutions have higher spreads than those that established de novo operations, suggesting either some market segmentation or differences in pricing strategies to gain market share. However, we do not find consistent evidence of a direct spillover effect on spreads. Instead, the degree of system wide foreign bank participation (as measured by the share of total loans) appears to influence spreads through its effects on costs. Greater participation of foreign banks lowers costs all around. On the other hand, a higher degree of concentration in the banking system has a positive and economically significant impact on both spreads and costs.

The remainder of the chapter is organized as follows. Section 2 describes the structure of the banking sector and the behavior of bank spreads in Argentina, Chile, Colombia, Mexico, and Peru over the late 1990s. Section 3 discusses the empirical methodology and data used to study the determinants of bank spreads in Latin America. Section 4 presents the empirical results and section 5 concludes.

2. Foreign bank participation, concentration, and spreads in Latin America

As in many developing economies, countries in Latin America experienced a significant increase in foreign bank participation during the late 1990s (see Table 9.1). In Argentina, foreign bank participation increased from 18.9 percent in 1995 to 49.4 percent of outstanding loans in 2000. In Chile, Mexico, and Peru the share of bank loans held by foreign banks rose from below 15 percent in 1995 to exceed 40 percent by the end of the decade.[6] Colombia is the only country in our sample where foreign banks consistently accounted for one-fourth of the loans during the period under consideration.

Table 9.1 Bank market structure and spreads in Latin America, 1995–2000

Country	Variables	1995	1996	1997	1998	1999	2000
Argentina	Total number of banks	141	122	115	106	96	90
	Number of foreign banks	32	32	35	38	38	40
	Foreign bank share (percent)	18.9	24.2	30.4	40.9	47.4	49.4
	Top 3 banks share (percent)	30.0	29.9	29.5	30.8	32.1	33.9
	Top 5 banks share (percent)	40.9	41.7	40.9	43.8	46.7	49.4
	Herfindahl index	483.3	489.6	482.6	545.3	605.5	656.7
	Average annualized spreads—all banks	15.2	11.4	10.6	11.9	12.7	12.3
	Average annualized spreads—domestic banks	16.7	12.8	12	13.5	15.2	14.2
	Average annualized spreads—foreign banks	11.3	8.2	7.6	9.4	9.4	10.2
Chile	Total number of banks	31	31	29	29	29	28
	Number of foreign banks	17	17	17	17	18	18
	Foreign bank share (percent)	13.7	16.7	20.3	21.5	37.7	45.0
	Top 3 banks share (percent)	36.6	35.7	42.5	42.1	41.5	41.1
	Top 5 banks share (percent)	51.9	52.6	62.5	62.1	61.9	61.5
	Herfindahl index	788.8	796.3	982.8	973.1	961.2	949.8
	Average annualized spreads—all banks	4.8	4.5	4.6	4.6	4.5	5.1
	Average annualized spreads—domestic banks	4.8	4.5	4.5	4.3	4.5	6
	Average annualized spreads—foreign banks	4.7	4.4	4.6	4.9	4.5	4.6
Colombia	Total number of banks			33	33	28	27
	Number of foreign banks			13	14	12	10
	Foreign bank share (percent)			27.6	27.6	26.0	24.9
	Top 3 banks share (percent)			29.5	31.5	32.3	29.9
	Top 5 banks share (percent)			44.1	47.4	50.2	47.3
	Herfindahl index			584.7	644.4	714.4	691.6
	Average annualized spreads—all banks			17	15.9	13.3	11.3
	Average annualized spreads—domestic banks			18.7	17.4	14.7	13
	Average annualized spreads—foreign banks			14.2	13.6	11.6	9.1
Mexico	Total number of banks				39	39	40
	Number of foreign banks				18	18	20
	Foreign share (percent)				13.2	14.0	25.8
	Top 3 banks share (percent)				50.0	49.2	47.5
	Top 5 banks share (percent)				63.8	62.7	60.8
	Herfindahl index				1,108.0	1,055.5	1,078.2
	Average annualized spreads—all banks				4.3	8.8	7
	Average annualized spreads—domestic banks				4.2	8.0	7.3
	Average annualized spreads—foreign banks				4.4	9.8	6.7
Peru	Total number of banks	29	27	27	27	24	20
	Number of foreign banks	15	14	14	14	13	11
	Foreign bank share (percent)	14.1	16.4	19.1	21.9	31.1	39.2
	Top 3 banks share (percent)	60.6	61.2	58.2	54.2	53.3	55.7

Top 5 banks share (percent)	74.4	74.8	70.7	67.0	68.2	72.5
Herfindahl index	1468.9	1517.3	1356.5	1203.9	1226.8	1316.4
Average annualized spreads— all banks	15.7	17.7	15.6	12.8	10.5	9.5
Average annualized spreads— domestic banks	17	16.6	14.5	12.2	10.9	10.5
Average annualized spreads— foreign banks	13.3	19.4	17	13.6	9.9	8.4

Despite the dramatic increase in foreign bank participation, the total number of banks in the region dropped in four of the five countries and concentration levels increased or remained high (see Table 9.1). In Argentina and Peru, the number of banks declined by more than 30 percent between 1995 and 2000. The total number of banks in Argentina fell from about 141 in 1995 to 90 in 2000. While Peru had 29 banks in 1995, this number dropped to 20 by 2000. For Colombia and Chile, the number of banks fell by 18 and 11 percent, respectively, during this period. The one exception is Mexico, where the number of banks increased from 39 to 40 between 1997 and 2000.

In all five countries, the share of loans held by the top three (five) banks exceeded 30 (40) percent for most of this period and the Herfindahl index was above 650. Concentration levels rose significantly for Argentina and Chile between 1995 and 2000. In Argentina, the share of loans held by the top five largest banks increased from 40.9 percent in 1995 to 49.4 percent in 2000. Similarly, this share increased from 51.9 percent to 61.5 percent for the case of Chile between 1995 and 2000.

The drop in the number of banks and the high or rising concentration levels can be ascribed to several reasons. First, there were many bank closures during this period. Such closures typically followed periods of financial distress in the countries, like the Tequila crisis in Argentina in 1995, when 32 banks closed, and the 1998–99 period of financial turmoil in Colombia, when 4 institutions were liquidated.

Second, much of the increase in foreign bank participation resulted from purchases of domestic banks. Thus, foreign entry did not typically add to the number of banks. In Argentina, sixteen foreign banks acquired domestic financial institutions during the period 1995–2000. The Spanish banks BBVA and Santander, the British bank HSBC, and the Canadian Scotiabank were among the most significant entrants in Argentina. During the same period, foreign banks acquired five domestic banks in Chile, two in Colombia, and three in Mexico. As in Argentina, Santander, BBVA, and Scotia were important players in these countries. Though there were also some truly *de novo* entries, i.e., cases of foreign banks that started their own operations without any affiliation with domestic banks, these were not the norm.[7] Six foreign banks set up *de novo* operations in Argentina, while two banks settled in Peru over this period. This explains why the total number of foreign banks in these countries did not increase at the same pace as the increase in foreign bank participation in the system.

At the same time, many domestic banks also consolidated with other domestic banks due to financial distress or as a strategy to compete with foreign banks, bringing down the total number of institutions. Thirty-seven such transactions took place in Argentina, four in Chile, three in Colombia, and three in Peru during the late 1990s.

What has been the impact of foreign bank participation and concentration on bank spreads? While a detailed econometric analysis is required to answer this question, it is interesting to note some trends in these variables. In Argentina, Colombia, and Peru, spreads have dropped during most of the late 1990s (see Table 9.1). A cursory look at the data for these countries suggests that spreads tended to decline in periods when foreign participation increased, but concentration levels remained constant. In Chile and Mexico, the increase in foreign participation appears to have had little effect on spreads perhaps because both countries had high levels of concentration at the start of the period and throughout. Note, however, that by the mid-1990s spreads in Chile and Mexico were already quite low by regional standards.

Foreign and domestic bank spreads appear to move very much in tandem across countries in the region. This behavior could signal the influence of macroeconomic factors and/or similar cost structures that affect all banks in the system, as well as the possibility that in general or at least in certain markets foreign and domestic banks compete with each other for customers. However, in Argentina, Colombia, and Peru, throughout most of the sample, and in all countries by the end of the period, foreign banks seemed to be able to operate with lower spreads.

3. Empirical methodology and data

In this section, we turn to an econometric analysis of the impact of concentration and foreign bank presence on bank spreads. In particular, we study the effect of market structure changes on bank spreads, while controlling for a host of bank characteristics and macroeconomic variables, by estimating regressions of the following form:

$$
\begin{aligned}
Spread_{i,j,t} = {} & a_0 + a_1 Liquidity_{i,j,t} + a_2 Administrative\ Cost_{i,j,t} + a_3 NPls_{i,j,t} + \\
& a_4 Equity_{i,j,t} + a_5 Bank\ Market\ Share_{i,j,t} + a_6 Foreign\ Bank_{i,j,t} \\
& a_7 Foreign\_M\&A_{i,j,t} + a_8 Foreign\_M\&A \times Age_{i,j,t} + \\
& a_9 Other\_M\&A_{i,j,t} + a_{10} Other\_M\&A \times Age_{i,j,t} \\
& a_{11} Foreign\_De\ novo_{i,j,t} + a_{12} Foreign\_De\ novo \times Age_{i,j,t} + \\
& a_{13} Foreign\ Bank\ Participation_{j,t} + a_{14} Bank\ Concentration_{j,t} + \\
& a_{15} * Real\ Output\ Growth_{j,t} + a_{16} * Inflation_{j,t} + a_{17} * Short\text{-} \\
& Term\ Real\ Interest\ Rate_{j,t} + \\
& a_{18} * Argentina_{i,j,t} + a_{19} * Chile_{i,j,t} + a_{20} * Colombia_{i,j,t} + a_{21} \\
& * Mexico_{i,j,t} + \varepsilon_{i,j,t}
\end{aligned}
\tag{1}
$$

where i is the bank id, j identifies the country, and t refers to the time period considered.

Equation (1) is motivated by the dealership model of bank spreads developed by Ho and Saunders (1981), extended by Allen (1988), Angbazo (1997) and others, and the firm-theoretical framework developed by Zarruck (1989) and Wong (1997).[8] Both models predict that operating costs, regulatory costs, credit risks, and the market structure of the banking sector can affect spreads.[9]

In equation (1), the variable *Spread* is the difference between the implicit average interest charged on loans and the implicit average interest paid on deposits. In other words, the spread is calculated by taking the total interest received by banks on loans during one quarter divided by the average loans for that period and subtracting from it the total interest paid on deposits throughout the quarter divided by average deposits. *Liquidity* is measured as the ratio of liquid to total assets. Liquid assets refer to cash and deposit balances in other banks (including reserve requirements at the central bank). High liquidity ratios, either self-imposed for prudential reasons or as a result of regulation (e.g., reserve or liquidity requirements), inflict a cost on banks since they have to give up holding higher yielding assets. To the extent that banks are able to transfer this opportunity cost to borrowers, spreads will rise with liquidity ratios.

Administrative Cost refers to the ratio of administrative expenses (including payroll and overhead) to average assets. If banks incur high administrative costs in the process of providing their services as intermediaries, they are likely to increase the spread they charge their customers. *NPls* is the ratio of non-performing loans to total loans. This variable is intended to capture credit risk. Faced with higher credit risk, banks are likely to charge higher rates on their loans, as equity holders demand risk-adjusted returns. *Equity* refers to the share of bank equity to total assets. Holding large equity ratios either on a voluntary basis or as a result of regulation can be costly for banks. We would expect bank spreads to rise with this variable. *Market Share* is the ratio of each banks' loans to total system loans. To the extent that market shares get translated into market power, banks with higher shares of the market may be able to charge higher rates on loans. On the other hand, larger banks may be able to reap economies of scale and may pass on some of these benefits to their customers in the form of lower spreads.

Foreign Bank is a dummy that takes the value of 1 if a bank is foreign at each point in time. By introducing this variable, we can test whether the average spread for foreign banks is significantly different from the average spread for domestic institutions. That is, this variable allows us to test for the "own effect" of foreign bank presence. *Foreign M&A* is a dummy variable that identifies those transactions where foreign banks increased their size or began operations within our sample by acquiring domestic banks. *Foreign_De novo*, on the other hand, is a zero/one variable that captures those foreign banks that set up *de novo* operations in a given country. The purpose of including the latter two variables is to determine how the spreads for these banks compare with those that have been foreign since the start of the sample and how different modes of foreign bank entry and/or strategies to increase participation in local markets affect bank spreads.

We also control for other types of mergers and acquisitions, namely those involving domestic banks or foreign banks, by including the variable *Other_M&A*, which takes the value of 1 for those domestic or foreign banks that acquired an institution of the same type. Both M&A variables (i.e, *Foreign* and *Other*) plus the dummy identifying foreign *de novo* entry are interacted with *Age*, the time since entry (measured in years), to allow for the possibility that there is an adjustment period until banks can attain their desired level of spreads after they enter a new market or purchase/merge with a bank.

Foreign Bank Participation is the share of loans in the hand of foreign banks. This variable captures the dynamic impact of changes in the relative importance of foreign banks on the overall level of spreads. In other words, this variable is included to test whether there is a "spillover effect" arising from the presence of foreign banks in the system. *Bank Concentration* measures the extent to which loans are concentrated on the hands of few banks within a system. In most of the estimations, we include three different measures of concentration, namely, the Herfindahl index—defined as the sum of squared loan market shares—plus the share of loans held by the top three and top five largest banks, respectively. We expect concentration measures to have a positive impact on bank spreads, once we control for differences in cost ratios across banks. Furthermore, contrary to the literature on bank concentration and profitability, where a positive association between these variables can signal different things, we interpret a positive sign on bank concentration as an indication of greater market power and less competition in the banking sector.[10]

Given that the level of bank spreads can be affected by the macroeconomic environment in which banks operate, we control for the *Inflation* rate, the *Real Output Growth,* and a measure of the money market *Short-Term Real Interest Rate*. Following Smith (2001), we include the inflation rate for two reasons. First, given that bank spreads are the difference between two nominal rates, if inflation shocks are not passed through to both rates equally fast, then spreads should reflect this. Second, Cottarelli and Kourelis (1994) have found that inflation can affect the flexibility of loan rates and therefore of bank spreads. The real growth of output variable could help pick up business cycle effects as those discussed by Bernanke and Gertler (1989) and Kiyotaki and Moore (1997). These studies suggest that changes in output can affect lending rates, and consequently spreads, because borrowers' creditworthiness is countercyclical. As output growth slows down, creditworthiness deteriorates and, other things equal, this is likely to be reflected in higher bank loan rates and, consequently, spreads. Finally, we include a measure of the short-term money market real interest rate to control for the marginal cost of funds faced by banks.

We obtained bank-level balance sheet and income statement data from the Superintendency of Banks in each of the countries in our sample. For Argentina, Chile, and Peru the data covers the period 1995–2000. For Colombia, we obtained data for 1997–2000. For Mexico, where a change in accounting standards does not allow us to use data before 1997, the sample studied is 1998–2001. The data frequency is quarterly in all cases. The corresponding bank authorities also provided detailed accounts on the foreign banks operating in each country at each point in time along with information on their mode of entry (e.g., via acquisitions or by *de novo* entry). They also supplied us with the list of mergers and acquisitions among domestic banks and between existing foreign banks.

Data on inflation, output growth, and the real short-term interest rate came from the IMF International Financial Statistics database. Table 9.2 contains a detailed description of the variables used in this paper together with means and standard deviations for each of them.[11]

4. Empirical Results

Table 9.3 presents the estimation results for equation (1), analyzing the determinants of loan-deposit spreads for private banks in Latin America.[12] In particular, results are reported for all private banks and, separately, for domestic and foreign banks, respectively. Throughout, the *t*-statistics shown were calculated allowing standard errors to be correlated for observations corresponding to the same bank within a country (i.e., using clustered standard errors as described by Rogers, 1993).

The estimates reported in Table 9.3 were obtained pooling all countries in our sample (Argentina, Chile, Colombia, Mexico, and Peru). However, they are not intended to explain variations across countries. Instead, because they include country fixed-effects, they explain changes in spreads over time within a country. The purpose of pooling observations in this context is to increase the power of our estimations.[13] At the same time, pooling assumes that the relation between bank spreads and its determinants can be characterized by the same coefficients for all countries. Thus, as part of our sensitivity analysis, we report and discuss below results in which we do not include all countries in the estimation.

The determinants of spreads may be categorized into three groups. First, bank-specific variables that include operational characteristics (such as liquidity, non-performing loans, and administrative costs), the bank's market share, whether it is foreign or domestic, whether the formation of the bank was the result of a merger or acquisition (M&A) or whether the bank was a new (*de novo*) entrant, and the interaction of bank's age with the foreign and M&A dummies.[14] Second, system-wide measures of market structure, including the degree of foreign bank participation and concentration.[15]

Table 9.2 Definition of variables used and data descriptive statistics

Variable	Definitions	Source of original data	Mean	Standard deviation
Spread	Interest income received on loans (over total loans) minus interest expenses paid on deposits (over total deposits)	Bank superintendencies	0.025	0.016
Liquid assets (over total assets)	Cash and deposits with other banks (including the central bank)	Bank superintendencies	0.108	0.077
Non-performing loans (over total loans)	Loans considered to be non-performing by the banking authorities (in most cases 90 days overdue)	Bank superintendencies	0.109	0.151
Administrative costs (over total assets)	Includes payroll and other operating expenses	Bank superintendencies	0.016	0.0128
Foreign bank	Dummy equal to 1 when bank is at least 50% foreign owned	Bank superintendencies	0.412	0.492
Equity (over total assets)	Bank capital plus reserves	Bank superintendencies	0.145	0.116
Bank market share	Share of loans held by each bank to total loans	Bank superintendencies	0.024	0.043
Foreign M&A	Dummy equal to 1 for cases when a foreign bank acquired a domestic bank	Bank superintendencies	0.062	0.289
Foreign M&A×Age	Interaction of foreign M&A with time (in fraction of years) since acquisition of a domestic bank by a foreign bank	Bank superintendencies	0.048	0.263
Foreign *de novo*	Dummy equal to 1 for foreign banks that entered the country by setting up *de novo* operations	Bank superintendencies	0.002	0.044
Foreign *de novo*×Age	Interaction of foreign *de novo* with time (in fraction of years) since entry	Bank superintendencies	0.002	0.044

Table 9.2 (*continued*)

Variable	Definitions	Source of original data	Mean	Standard deviation
Other M&A	Dummy equal to 1 for domestic banks that acquired other domestic banks, or for foreign banks that acquired other foreign banks	Bank superintendencies	0.113	0.439
Other M&A×Age	Interaction of other M&A with time (in fraction of years since entry)	Bank superintendencies	0.091	0.432
Foreign bank participation	Share of loans held by foreign banks (those that are at least 50% foreign owned)	Bank superintendencies	0.273	0.119
Top 3 bank share	Share of loans held by the top 3 banks in the system	Bank superintendencies	0.385	0.105
Top 5 bank share	Share of loans held by the top 5 banks in the system	Bank superintendencies	0.526	0.114
Herfindahl index	Sum of squared bank market shares	Bank superintendencies	794.405	325.403
Inflation	Rate of growth of the consumer price index	IMF International Financial Statistics	0.011	0.015
Real output growth	Rate of growth of industrial/manufacturing production	IMF International Financial Statistics	−0.011	0.054
Real interest rate	Money market rate—inflation	IMF International Financial Statistics	13.189	8.222

Note: The spreads reported here are quarterly spreads as opposed to those shown in Table 9.1, which are annualized spreads.

Table 9.3 Panel estimations for bank spreads including all countries

Variables	All banks			Domestic banks			Foreign banks		
	(3.1)	(3.2)	(3.3)	(3.4)	(3.5)	(3.6)	(3.7)	(3.8)	(3.9)
Liquid assets	0.028 (3.75)***	0.029 (3.86)***	0.028 (3.68)***	0.053 (4.77)***	0.054 (4.85)***	0.052 (4.72)***	0.02 (2.41)**	0.02 (2.50)**	0.02 (2.35)**
Non-performing loans	−0.001 (0.25)	−0.00113 (0.29)	−0.00095 (0.24)	0.000331 (0.08)	0.000179 (0.04)	0.000435 (0.11)	−0.0009 (0.08)	−0.0010 (0.09)	−0.0009 (0.08)
Administrative costs	0.653 (7.88)***	0.656 (7.94)***	0.652 (7.87)***	0.569 (7.73)***	0.573 (7.79)***	0.568 (7.71)***	0.74 (5.82)***	0.74 (5.85)***	0.74 (5.83)***
Foreign bank	−0.005 (3.92)***	−0.005 (3.93)***	−0.005 (3.93)***						
Bank market share	−0.014 (1.38)	−0.014 (1.37)	−0.014 (1.41)	−0.023 (2.00)**	−0.024 (2.01)**	−0.024 (2.02)**	0.05 (1.86)*	0.05 (1.85)*	0.05 (1.85)*
Equity	0.01 (1.59)	0.01 (1.61)	0.01 (1.60)	0.019 (1.35)	0.019 (1.37)	0.019 (1.35)	0.01 (0.85)	0.01 (0.87)	0.01 (0.86)
Foreign M&A	0.002379 (2.54)**	0.002377 (2.55)**	0.002439 (2.61)***				−0.00024 (0.16)	−0.00023 (0.16)	−0.00021 (0.14)
Foreign M&A×Age	0.000209 (0.22)	0.000228 (0.24)	0.000159 (0.17)				0.00 (1.35)	0.00 (1.39)	0.00 (1.33)
Foreign de novo	−0.022 (2.08)**	−0.022 (2.08)**	−0.022 (2.07)**				−0.02 (2.05)**	−0.02 (2.06)**	−0.02 (2.05)**
Foreign de novo×Age	0.007 (1.06)	0.008 (1.08)	0.007 (1.06)				0.01 (1.22)	0.01 (1.25)	0.01 (1.22)

Other M&A	0.000195 (0.25)	0.000152 (0.19)	0.000207 (0.26)	0.000599 (0.82)	0.000579 (0.79)	0.000616 (0.84)			0.00 (1.07)
Other M&A×Age	0.000016 (0.03)	0.000048 (0.08)	0.000001 (0.00)	−0.00025 (0.37)	−0.00026 (0.38)	−0.00027 (0.40)			
Foreign share	0.002 (0.71)	0.002 (0.46)	0.001 (0.22)	0.005 (1.12)	0.003 (0.56)	0.003 (0.64)	0.00 (1.02)	0.00 (0.67)	
Top 3 bank share	0.038 (3.03)***		0.05 (3.26)***				0.02 (1.16)		
Top 5 bank share		0.018 (1.83)*			0.032 (2.76)***			0.002 (0.11)	
Herfindahl index			0.000011 (2.82)***			0.000015 (3.17)***			0.00 (0.97)
Inflation	−0.002 (0.07)	0.005 (0.14)	−0.005 (0.13)	−0.023 (0.57)	−0.017 (0.41)	−0.027 (0.67)	0.01 (0.21)	0.02 (0.33)	0.01 (0.20)
Real growth of production	0.002 (0.78)	0.002 (0.67)	0.003 (0.96)	0.004 (0.98)	0.004 (0.37)	0.005 (1.14)	0.00 (0.26)	0.00 (0.30)	0.00 (0.18)
Real market interest rate	0.000014 (0.23)	−0.000004 (0.06)	0.00003 (0.48)	0.000068 (1.20)	0.000056 (0.36)	0.000089 (1.52)	−0.000034 (0.26)	−0.000055 (0.42)	−0.000027 (0.2)
Argentina	0.007 (1.78)*	0.002 (0.54)	0.007 (1.59)	0.014 (3.10)***	0.01 (2.45)**	0.013 (3.01)***	0.00 (0.35)	0.00 (0.56)	0.00 (0.21)
Chile	0.000009 (0.00)	−0.00442 (1.91)*	−0.00157 (0.63)	0.003479 (1.10)	−0.00104 (0.40)	0.001457 (0.54)	0.00 (0.16)	0.00 (1.18)	0.00 (0.46)
Colombia	0.02 (4.68)***	0.015 (3.95)***	0.018 (4.55)***	0.028 (5.79)***	0.023 (5.50)***	0.026 (5.78)***	0.01 (1.84)*	0.01 (1.25)	0.01 (1.73)*

(continued overleaf)

Table 9.3 (continued)

Variables	All banks			Domestic banks			Foreign banks		
	(3.1)	(3.2)	(3.3)	(3.4)	(3.5)	(3.6)	(3.7)	(3.8)	(3.9)
Mexico	-0.013 (4.47)***	-0.014 (4.92)***	-0.013 (4.75)***	-0.009 (3.29)***	-0.01 (3.76)***	-0.009 (3.58)***	-0.02 (2.94)***	-0.02 (3.19)***	-0.02 (3.10)***
Constant	-0.00651 (0.85)	0.002967 (0.39)	0.000417 (0.07)	-0.0198 (2.21)**	-0.01382 (1.59)	-0.01089 (1.60)	-0.0004 (0.03)	0.01 (0.95)	0.004 (0.48)
Observations	2618	2618	2618	1539	1539	1539	1079.00	1079.00	1079.00
R-squared	0.52	0.52	0.52	0.53	0.53	0.53	0.48	0.48	0.48
F-test, Foreign + Foreign M&A=0	5.39	5.41	5.19						
p-value	0.02	0.02	0.02						

Notes: Estimations include Argentina, Chile, Colombia, Mexico and Peru. Robust t-statistics (calculated allowing for clustered standard errors by bank) are in parentheses. *significant at 10%; **significant at 5%; ***significant at 1%.

And, finally, variables that control for the macroeconomic environment are inflation, real growth of production, and the real market interest rate.

For the sample including all banks, among the bank-specific variables, bank liquidity and administrative costs have a positive and significant impact on bank spreads in all three specifications, corresponding to the different measures of concentration. Banks that either decide or are required by regulation to hold a high proportion of their assets in the form of liquid assets seem to charge higher spreads. This can be interpreted as the banks' response to the fact that in holding higher liquidity ratios, banks forego a return on such assets. However, the impact of higher liquidity on bank spreads seems to be quantitatively small: a one standard deviation increase in liquidity raises spreads by 0.14 standard deviation. On the other hand, administrative costs have a larger impact on bank spreads: a one standard deviation change in administrative costs results in an almost 0.6 standard deviation change in spreads. As discussed below, administrative costs are influenced by macro country characteristics (inflation, growth, and domestic interest rates) and subsume their effects in these regressions, as a consequence of which the macro variables do not appear to have a direct influence on spreads.

Foreign banks, on average, charge lower spreads (0.5 percent lower per quarter) than their domestic counterparts. For foreign banks that enter through an M&A process, the full effect on spreads is the sum of the *Foreign Bank* dummy (which has a negative sign) and the *Foreign M&A* dummy (which has a positive sign). This sum is negative and statistically different from zero, as noted in the F-test reported at the bottom of Table 9.3. The estimated coefficients indicate that spreads for foreign banks that entered the system through acquisitions of domestic banks are 0.26 percent per quarter lower than those for domestic banks. Since the *Foreign_De novo* dummy is also negative, its sum with the *Foreign Bank* dummy is a large negative, implying that while both types of foreign banks charge lower spreads than domestic banks, the *de novo* foreign banks charge much lower spreads (around 2.7 percent per quarter lower than those for domestic banks). The interactions between the mode of entry by foreign banks and the time since entry (Age) are never significant.[16]

Two factors could explain why the spreads charged by foreign banks that entered the market by acquiring domestic banks might differ from those of *de novo* entrants. First, *de novo* banks, interested in gaining market share, may be more willing to charge lower rates to reach their desired size. Second, the two types of foreign banks may be targeting different market segments. Dell'Ariccia and Marquez (2004) suggest that differences in the information available to banks influence who they lend to and the spreads they are able to charge. By virtue of being newcomers to the sector, *de novo* banks are likely to possess the least information about domestic borrowers and, hence, would have an incentive to focus on the more transparent segments of the market (i.e., where information about borrowers is most accessible). At the same time, since transparent market segments are likely to be more competitive, *de novo* banks would be required to charge lower spreads relative to those possible in other market segments. In contrast, foreign banks acquiring or merging with domestic banks would inherit proprietary customer information, allowing them to serve somewhat less transparent firms, in less contestable markets, where they might have some market power and the ability to charge higher spreads. Since both types of foreign banks charge lower spreads than their domestic competitors, it is possible that domestic banks are forced to increase their lending to the least transparent borrowers from whom they are able to obtain the highest spreads.[17]

Beyond their incentive and ability to charge lower spreads, do foreign banks have a "spillover effect" on the overall level of spreads? We test this possibility by investigating if the foreign bank participation variable (i.e., the share of loans held by banks that are at least 50 percent foreign owned) influences spreads. In our basic estimations on Table 9.3, the coefficient on this variable is statistically insignificant. This result could imply either that no spillover effect exists (lower spreads charged by foreign banks do not create sufficient pressure on other banks to lower their spreads, perhaps, because of market segmentation) or that the spillover effect operates mainly in an indirect manner, for example, through the impact of foreign competition on administrative costs, as we examine below. It is possible, of course, that because foreign bank participation is rising over time, the variable picks up mainly a time trend and does not speak to the issue of "spillovers." We also explore this possibility below.

Finally, for the sample including all banks, higher bank concentration raises spreads significantly. Regardless of the measure of concentration included, spreads rise as a response to increases in bank concentration. A one standard deviation increase in concentration results in a 0.13 to 0.25 standard deviation change in bank spreads.[18]

In the rest of Table 9.3, we present estimations for the determinants of spreads among domestic banks only (columns 4–6) and foreign banks only (columns 7–9). We continue to find that liquidity and administrative costs have a positive impact on bank spreads, with administrative costs exercising the stronger influence, especially among foreign banks. Within the sample of domestic banks, we also find that those with higher market shares are able to charge lower spreads. This may point to the presence of economies of scale among large domestic banks. Within the group of foreign banks, the evidence for lower spreads charged by the new entrants is reaffirmed. Once again, changes in foreign bank participation do not seem to directly affect the overall level of spreads for domestic or foreign banks. Finally, as before, a rise in bank concentration leads to higher spreads, with the effect being particularly high and significant for domestic banks.

The spread estimations reported in Table 9.3 make three assumptions. First, by pooling observations across countries we are forcing the coefficients in the spread equations (except for the constant) to be the same for all countries. Second, we are also assuming that there are no structural shifts (over time) in the relation between bank spreads and their determinants. Finally, we are ignoring possible common shocks or time trends.

Because of the short-time series at our disposal, we are unable to run separate regressions for each country and formally test the pooling assumption.[19] However, we conduct alternative estimations to analyze the sensitivity of our results to this assumption. In particular, we obtain results excluding Mexico and Colombia, the countries with the shortest time series and with the lowest levels of foreign bank participation (see Table 9.4).[20] Reassuringly, the results are virtually the same for this smaller sample. Also, to mitigate the concern that our findings are driven by Argentina, the country with the longest time series, Table 9.4 also reports estimations excluding this country. Again, results remained largely unchanged.

Table 9.4 Panel estimations for bank spreads excluding some countries

Variables	Excluding Mexico and Colombia			Excluding Argentina		
	All banks	Domestic banks	Foreign banks	All banks	Domestic banks	Foreign banks
Liquid assets	0.031 (2.73)***	0.0603 (4.89)***	0.0056 (0.38)	0.021 (2.67)***	0.042 (2.66)**	0.018 (2.03)**
Non-performing loans	−0.0002 (0.04)	0.0012 (0.28)	0.0013 (0.10)	−0.011 (0.59)	0.005 (0.31)	−0.037 (1.75)*
Administrative costs	0.611 (5.71)***	0.5251 (7.28)***	0.713 (3.67)***	0.815 (5.81)***	0.922 (4.10)***	0.854 (5.53)***
Foreign bank	−0.0047 (3.26)***			−0.004 (2.68)***		
Bank market share	−0.027 (2.65)***	−0.034 (2.81)***	0.0209 (0.85)	−0.005 (0.45)	−0.014 (1.10)	0.065 (2.22)**
Equity	0.009 (1.35)	0.0245 (1.58)	0.0012 (0.21)	0.007 (0.91)	0.004 (0.21)	0.007 (0.97)
Foreign M&A	0.0023 (2.60)***		0.0004 (0.32)	0.002 (1.99)**		−0.002 (1.15)
Foreign M&A×Age	0.0001 (0.09)		0.0012 (1.02)	−0.00042 (0.55)		0.001 (0.67)
Foreign *de novo*	−0.0223 (2.15)**		−0.0184 (2.28)**			
Foreign *de novo*×Age	0.0073 (1.05)		0.0069 (1.24)			
Other M&A	0.0006 (0.76)	0.001 (1.46)		−0.003 (2.65)***	−0.001 (0.85)	
Other M&A×Age	−0.0001 (0.19)	−0.0004 (0.65)		0.001 (0.58)	0.001 (0.59)	
Foreign share	0.0046 (1.33)	0.0087 (1.71)*	−0.0034 (0.88)	−0.006 (1.52)	−0.007 (1.15)	−0.005 (1.23)
Top 3 bank share	0.0565 (4.16)***	0.0648 (3.83)***	0.0497 (2.39)**	0.027 (2.25)**	0.031 (2.26)**	0.015 (0.82)

(*continued overleaf*)

Table 9.4 (continued)

Variables	Excluding Mexico and Colombia			Excluding Argentina		
	All banks	Domestic banks	Foreign banks	All banks	Domestic banks	Foreign banks
Inflation	0.1036	0.0572	0.1425	−0.02	−0.03	−0.003
	(3.52)***	(1.45)	(3.72)***	(0.52)	(0.71)	(0.04)
Real growth of production	0.000469	0.000805	−0.00125	0.002	0.003	−0.00009
	(0.18)	(0.21)	(0.43)	(0.65)	(0.82)	(0.02)
Real market interest rate	0.0001	0.0002	0.0001	−0.00011	−0.0001	−0.0001
	(1.93)*	(2.23)**	(1.12)	(1.45)	(1.57)	(0.79)
Argentina	0.0152	0.0206	0.0113			
	(3.12)***	(3.93)***	(1.73)*			
Chile	0.0039	0.0075	0.0038	−0.002	0.002	−0.003
	(1.30)	(2.15)**	(0.81)	(0.49)	(0.60)	(0.53)
Colombia				0.02	0.027	0.012
				(4.42)***	(5.37)***	(1.74)*
Mexico				−0.014	−0.009	−0.018
				(4.87)***	(3.65)***	(3.28)***
Constant	−0.0211	−0.0332	−0.0173	0.003	−0.006	0.006
	(2.54)**	(3.23)***	(1.42)	(0.42)	(0.71)	(0.48)
Observations	2188	1303	885	1342	695	647
R-squared	0.57	0.55	0.58	0.56	0.64	0.53

Notes: The estimations excluding Colombia and Mexico include: Argentina, Chile, and Peru. Those excluding Argentina, include: Chile, Colombia, Mexico, and Peru. Robust *t*-statistics (calculated allowing for clustered standard errors by bank) are in parentheses. * significant at 10%; ** significant at 5%; *** significant at 1%.

To test for structural shifts in the relation between spreads and their determinants over time, we try two possibilities (see Table 9.5). First, we interact administrative costs (the most consistently significant variable across all spread specifications) with a dummy that equals one for the period 1999 and beyond. Second, to assess whether the impact of administrative costs on bank spreads changed with the increase in foreign bank presence, we interact administrative costs with the foreign bank share. All interaction terms are always insignificant and our main results do not change.

To control for possible time trends, we repeat our spread estimations including quarterly time dummies (see Table 9.6). Most of our results remain unchanged, except that among domestic banks, the foreign bank share has a positive impact on spreads. One possible explanation for this result is that competition from foreign banks causes domestic banks to redirect their lending to more opaque borrowers to whom they can charge higher spreads. However, this finding does not imply that the net effect of foreign bank participation on domestic banks is to increase their spreads,

Table 9.5 Panel estimations for bank spreads allowing for structural shifts

Variables	Interacting administrative costs with a dummy post 1999			Interacting administrative costs with foreign bank share		
	All banks	Domestic banks	Foreign banks	All banks	Domestic banks	Foreign banks
Liquid assets	0.0281 (3.74)***	0.0522 (4.70)***	0.0187 (2.32)**	0.028 (3.79)***	0.0514 (4.62)***	0.0198 (2.55)**
Non-performing loans	−0.0009 (0.23)	0.0005 (0.12)	−0.0002 (0.02)	−0.001 (0.25)	0.0004 (0.11)	0.0007 (0.06)
Administrative costs	0.6418 (6.24)***	0.5485 (7.35)***	0.7748 (3.98)***	0.6502 (4.60)***	0.4609 (3.98)***	0.8745 (3.56)***
Administrative costs x Dummy 1999–2000	0.0319 (0.39)	0.1051 (1.66)*	−0.0783 (0.46)			
Administrative costs x Foreign bank share				0.0099 (0.03)	0.4513 (1.37)	−0.5312 (0.87)
Foreign bank	−0.0052 (3.91)***			−0.0051 (3.95)***		
Bank market share	−0.0141 (1.39)	−0.0235 (1.99)**	0.0469 (1.79)*	−0.014 (1.38)	−0.0234 (1.98)**	0.0451 (1.69)*
Equity	0.0095 (1.59)	0.019 (1.36)	0.0043 (0.76)	0.0095 (1.58)	0.0194 (1.38)	0.0037 (0.65)
Foreign M&A	0.0025 (2.52)**		−0.0003 (0.22)	0.0024 (2.50)**		−0.0003 (0.20)
Foreign M&A× Age	0.0001 (0.11)		0.0018 (1.50)	0.0002 (0.22)		0.0018 (1.52)
Foreign de novo	−0.0215 (2.07)**		−0.0195 (2.06)**	−0.0217 (2.08)**		−0.0193 (2.17)**
Foreign de novo× Age	0.0073 (1.05)		0.0083 (1.26)	0.0075 (1.07)		0.0078 (1.23)
Other M&A	0.0002 (0.28)	0.0007 (0.90)		0.0002 (0.25)	0.0006 (0.86)	
Other M&A×Age	−0.000007 (0.01)	−0.00029 (0.42)		0.000015 (0.03)	−0.00029 (0.42)	
Foreign share	0.0009 (0.18)	−0.000027 (0.00)	−0.001 (0.15)	−0.0128 (4.45)***	−0.009 (3.35)***	−0.0159 (2.97)***
Top 3 bank share	0.0391 (3.06)***	0.0516 (3.37)***	0.018 (0.87)	0.0382 (3.01)***	0.0513 (3.36)***	0.0175 (0.90)
Inflation	−0.0012 (0.03)	−0.0213 (0.52)	0.0053 (0.09)	−0.0024 (0.07)	−0.0267 (0.66)	0.0046 (0.08)
Real growth of production	0.0017 (0.52)	0.0019 (0.46)	0.0002 −0.04	0.0023 (0.77)	0.0028 (0.72)	−0.0006 (0.16)
Real market interest rate	0.000013 (0.22)	0.000064 (1.13)	−0.00003 −0.24	0.000014 (0.23)	0.000068 (1.19)	−0.000029 (0.22)

(continued overleaf)

Table 9.5 (*continued*)

Variables	Interacting administrative costs with a dummy post 1999			Interacting administrative costs with foreign bank share		
	All banks	Domestic banks	Foreign banks	All banks	Domestic banks	Foreign banks
Argentina	0.0078	0.0151	0.0009	0.0021	−0.003	0.0032
	(1.70)*	(3.26)***	(0.11)	(0.39)	(0.44)	(0.42)
Chile	0.0002	0.0038	−0.0012	0.0074	0.0143	0.0013
	(0.06)	(1.21)	(0.24)	(1.75)*	(3.15)***	(0.19)
Colombia	0.0207	0.0292	0.0118	0.0000	0.0035	−0.0011
	(4.60)***	(5.91)***	(1.61)	0.00	(1.12)	(0.23)
Mexico	−0.013	−0.0095	−0.0151	0.0204	0.0287	0.012
	(4.75)***	(3.48)***	(2.96)***	(4.65)***	(5.92)***	(1.70)*
Constant	−0.0067	−0.0195	0.0011	−0.0065	−0.0183	0.0002
	(0.87)	(2.20)**	(0.09)	(0.85)	(2.10)**	(0.02)
Observations	2618	1539	1079	2618	1539	1079
R-squared	0.52	0.53	0.48	0.52	0.53	0.49

Notes: These estimations include all countries: Argentina, Chile, Colombia, Mexico, and Peru. Robust *t*-statistics (calculated allowing for clustered standard errors by bank) are in parentheses. * significant at 10%; ** significant at 5%; *** significant at 1%.

since as discussed above, the presence of foreign banks can affect spreads indirectly through its impact on administrative costs. We turn to this issue next.

Table 9.7 presents the determinants of administrative costs (expressed as a ratio of total assets) for all banks and separately for domestic and foreign banks.[21] The macro variables are now seen to be significant among domestic banks, unlike in the spreads equations. Inflation is negatively signed, suggesting that bank costs do not respond immediately to general inflation. Higher interest rates, which are a proxy for the marginal cost of capital, raise administrative costs.

In general, foreign banks appear to operate with lower costs relative to domestic banks. However, in the estimations including all banks, different types of foreign bank entry (via M&As or through *de novo* entry) do not seem to have differential effects on costs. On the other hand, in the specification for foreign banks, we find that those that entered through merger and acquisitions with domestic banks have higher costs than other foreign banks.

Regardless of their origin, the overall level of foreign bank presence seems to exert a downward pressure on the administrative costs of all banks. Thus, despite evidence consistent with the hypothesis of market segmentation in our spreads results, foreign bank presence apparently generates sufficient competitive pressure to induce an all round lowering of costs.

However, if foreign bank entry is also associated with increased

Table 9.6 Panel estimations for bank spreads including quarterly time dummies (not shown)

Variables	All banks			Domestic banks			Foreign banks		
	(6.1)	(6.2)	(6.3)	(6.4)	(6.5)	(6.6)	(6.7)	(6.8)	(6.9)
Liquid assets	0.0272 (3.59)***	0.0275 (3.64)***	0.027 (3.56)***	0.0525 (4.65)***	0.0531 (4.69)***	0.0523 (4.63)***	0.0181 (2.12)**	0.0185 (2.18)**	0.0181 (2.10)**
Non-performing loans	-0.0005 (0.12)	-0.0005 (0.13)	-0.0004 (0.09)	0.0012 (0.30)	0.0012 (0.29)	0.0013 (0.33)	-0.001 (0.09)	-0.001 (0.09)	-0.0009 (0.08)
Administrative costs	0.6424 (7.28)***	0.6446 (7.29)***	0.6424 (7.27)***	0.5498 (7.19)***	0.5506 (7.20)***	0.5488 (7.18)***	0.7338 (5.64)***	0.7372 (5.65)***	0.7347 (5.64)***
Foreign bank	-0.0051 (3.90)***	-0.0051 (3.91)***	-0.0051 (3.90)***						
Bank market share	-0.0141 (1.40)	-0.0141 (1.39)	-0.0143 (1.42)	-0.0239 (1.99)**	-0.0241 (2.00)**	-0.0242 (2.01)**	0.0467 (1.82)*	0.0468 (1.82)*	0.0467 (1.82)*
Equity	0.0095 (1.57)	0.0096 (1.59)	0.0095 (1.58)	0.0185 (1.29)	0.0186 (1.30)	0.0185 (1.29)	0.0049 (0.90)	0.005 (0.92)	0.005 (0.91)
Foreign M&A	0.0023 (2.50)**	0.0023 (2.50)**	0.0024 (2.57)**				-0.0001 (0.06)	-0.0001 (0.07)	-0.0001 (0.05)
Foreign M&A×Age	0.0002 (0.26)	0.0003 (0.34)	0.0002 (0.21)				0.0015 (1.31)	0.0016 (1.39)	0.0015 (1.30)
Foreign de novo	-0.0211 (2.04)**	-0.0214 (2.05)**	-0.0213 (2.06)**				-0.0185 (1.92)*	-0.0189 (1.94)*	-0.0187 (1.93)*
Foreign de novo×Age	0.0071 (1.00)	0.0075 (1.05)	0.0072 (1.01)				0.0075 (1.16)	0.0079 (1.22)	0.0076 (1.18)

(continued overleaf)

Table 9.6 (continued)

Variables	All banks			Domestic banks			Foreign banks		
	(6.1)	(6.2)	(6.3)	(6.4)	(6.5)	(6.6)	(6.7)	(6.8)	(6.9)
Other M&A	0.0004 (0.45)	0.0003 (0.41)	0.0004 (0.47)	0.0007 (1.02)	0.0007 (0.98)	0.0008 (1.05)			
Other M&A×Age	−0.00002 (0.04)	0.000018 (0.03)	−0.000051 (0.09)	−0.000251 (0.36)	−0.000227 (0.33)	−0.000293 (0.42)			
Foreign share	0.0099 (1.51)	0.0109 (1.70)*	0.0077 (1.23)	0.0201 (2.64)***	0.0204 (2.72)***	0.0166 (2.30)**	−0.0071 (0.66)	−0.0057 (0.55)	−0.0076 (0.74)
Top 3 bank share	0.0386 (3.18)***			0.0489 (3.46)***			0.0216 (1.03)		
Top 5 bank share		0.0198 (2.09)**			0.0312 (3.03)***			0.0034 (0.20)	
Herfindahl index			0.000011 (2.99)***			0.000015 (3.49)***			0.000005 (0.78)
Inflation	−0.0048 (0.12)	0.0022 (0.05)	−0.0078 (0.19)	−0.0489 (1.04)	−0.0425 (0.90)	−0.054 (1.14)	0.0474 (0.67)	0.0538 (0.76)	0.0475 (0.68)
Real growth of production	−0.0056 (1.71)*	−0.0057 (1.70)*	−0.0046 (1.37)	−0.0057 (1.34)	−0.0058 (1.33)	−0.0046 (1.06)	−0.0037 (0.71)	−0.0039 (0.74)	−0.0033 (0.61)
Real market interest rate	0.000003 (0.04)	−0.00002 (0.28)	0.000019 (0.27)	−0.000003 (0.04)	−0.000019 (0.26)	0.000023 (0.30)	0.000014 (0.10)	−0.000012 (0.09)	0.000016 (0.11)
Argentina	0.0066 (1.70)*	0.0015 (0.41)	0.006 (1.55)	0.0112 (2.60)**	0.0067 (1.81)*	0.0111 (2.65)***	0.0037 (0.57)	−0.0014 (0.23)	0.0024 (0.36)

Chile	-0.0004	-0.0048	-0.002	0.002	-0.0027	0.0004	-0.0005	-0.0039	-0.0018
	(0.15)	(2.17)**	(0.80)	(0.67)	(1.08)	(0.14)	(0.09)	(1.01)	(0.42)
Colombia	0.0199	0.0146	0.0177	0.0288	0.0236	0.0265	0.0107	0.0058	0.0087
	(4.53)***	(3.70)***	(4.44)***	(6.06)***	(5.69)***	(6.27)***	(1.41)	(0.86)	(1.25)
Mexico	-0.0108	-0.012	-0.0111	-0.0047	-0.0057	-0.005	-0.0172	-0.0186	-0.0177
	(3.10)***	(3.40)***	(3.18)***	(1.52)	(1.88)*	(1.64)	(2.59)**	(2.76)***	(2.65)***
Constant	-0.0091	-0.0012	-0.0028	-0.0265	-0.0207	-0.0191	0.0044	0.0142	0.0094
	(0.88)	(0.12)	(0.30)	(2.51)**	(2.03)**	(2.09)**	(0.24)	(0.75)	(0.58)
Observations	2618	2618	2618	1539	1539	1539	1079	1079	1079
R-squared	0.53	0.53	0.53	0.54	0.54	0.54	0.49	0.49	0.49

Notes: These estimations include all countries: Argentina, Chile, Colombia, Mexico, and Peru. Quarterly time dummies are included in all regressions, but not shown to save space. Robust *t*-statistics (calculated allowing for clustered standard errors by bank) are in parentheses. * significant at 10%; ** significant at 5%; *** significant at 1%.

Table 9.7 Panel estimations for administrative costs including all countries

Variables	All banks			Domestic banks			Foreign banks		
	(7.1)	(7.2)	(7.3)	(7.4)	(7.5)	(7.6)	(7.7)	(7.8)	(7.9)
Foreign bank	-0.0029 (2.57)**	-0.0029 (2.57)**	-0.0029 (2.57)**						
Bank market share	-0.0546 (4.57)***	-0.0548 (4.58)***	-0.0549 (4.58)***	-0.0321 (3.12)***	-0.0322 (3.13)***	-0.0323 (3.14)***	-0.085 (2.76)***	-0.0853 (2.75)***	-0.0856 (2.77)***
Foreign M&A	0.0017 (1.52)	0.0017 (1.50)	0.0018 (1.56)				0.003 (2.31)**	0.003 (2.29)**	0.0031 (2.34)**
Foreign M&A×Age	0.000397 (0.16)	0.000353 (0.14)	0.000316 (0.13)				0.000027 (0.01)	-0.000046 (0.02)	-0.000029 (0.01)
Foreign de novo	0.0116 (0.70)	0.0115 (0.70)	0.0115 (0.70)				0.0133 (0.81)	0.0132 (0.80)	0.0132 (0.80)
Foreign de novo×Age	0.0035 (0.39)	0.0035 (0.39)	0.0035 (0.39)				0.003 (0.33)	0.003 (0.33)	0.003 (0.34)
Other M&A	0.0015 (2.83)***	0.0015 (2.79)***	0.0015 (2.87)***	0.0011 (2.06)**	0.001 (2.03)**	0.0011 (2.12)**			
Other M&A×Age	-0.001 (2.24)**	-0.001 (2.24)**	-0.001 (2.28)**	-0.0007 (1.41)	-0.0007 (1.40)	-0.0007 (1.48)			
Foreign share	-0.0165 (4.97)***	-0.0183 (5.51)***	-0.0185 (5.67)***	-0.0209 (4.45)***	-0.0226 (4.80)***	-0.0233 (5.01)***	-0.009 (2.02)**	-0.0113 (2.46)**	-0.0104 (2.41)**
Top 3 bank share	0.0448 (5.75)***			0.0411 (4.10)***			0.0503 (4.08)***		

	(1)	(2)	(3)	(4)	(5)	(6)	(7)	(8)	(9)
Top 5 bank share	0.0278 (4.79)***			0.0249 (3.18)***			0.0338 (3.81)***		
Herfindahl index		0.000014 (5.72)***			0.000014 (4.56)***			0.000013 (3.34)***	
Inflation	−0.026 (1.57)	−0.0185 (1.12)	−0.0285 (1.69)*	−0.0698 (3.47)***	−0.0623 (3.18)***	−0.0748 (3.59)***	0.0314 (1.08)	0.0387 (1.32)	0.0323 (1.09)
Real growth of production	−0.0106 (3.99)***	−0.0109 (4.05)***	−0.0098 (3.77)***	−0.0173 (4.46)***	−0.0178 (4.48)***	−0.0164 (4.29)***	−0.0029 (0.81)	−0.0031 (0.85)	−0.0023 (0.64)
Real market interest rate	0.000113 (3.16)***	0.0001 (2.85)***	0.000135 (3.59)***	0.000167 (3.55)***	0.000154 (3.37)***	0.000193 (3.97)***	0.000027 (0.54)	0.000013 (0.27)	0.000042 (0.79)
Argentina	0.015 (4.78)***	0.011 (3.79)***	0.015 (4.87)***	0.019 (6.29)***	0.0151 (5.42)***	0.0204 (6.83)***	0.0099 (1.75)*	0.0061 (1.17)	0.0077 (1.42)
Chile	−0.0075 (3.09)***	−0.0119 (5.62)***	−0.0089 (3.95)***	−0.0056 (2.76)***	−0.0097 (6.22)***	−0.0061 (3.41)***	−0.0105 (2.31)**	−0.0151 (3.66)***	−0.0132 (3.12)***
Colombia	0.003635 (1.37)	−0.00146 (0.64)	0.001709 (0.72)	0.004937 (1.88)*	0.00041 (0.02)	0.004434 (1.94)*	0.002926 (0.62)	−0.00211 (0.51)	−0.00107 (0.26)
Mexico	0.0026 (0.85)	0.001238 (0.40)	0.002388 (0.82)	−0.000028 (0.01)	−0.00139 (0.74)	0.000251 (0.13)	0.004398 (0.78)	0.003138 (0.55)	0.003509 (0.66)
Constant	−0.0025 (0.49)	0.0039 (0.81)	0.0043 (1.03)	−0.0033 (0.56)	0.0031 (0.55)	0.0008 (0.18)	−0.006 (0.70)	−0.0005 (0.06)	0.005 (0.70)
Observations	2982	2982	2982	1752	1752	1752	1230	1230	1230
R-squared	0.36	0.36	0.37	0.40	0.40	0.40	0.36	0.36	0.36
F test, Foreign + Foreign M&A=0	0.86	0.85	0.74						
p-value	0.36	0.36	0.39						

Notes: These estimations include observations for Argentina, Chile, Colombia, Mexico, and Peru. Robust *t*-statistics (calculated allowing for clustered standard errors by bank) in parentheses. * significant at 10%; ** significant at 5%; *** significant at 1%.

concentration, there may be an offsetting effect. Our results indicate that costs, indeed, go up with concentration. Note that unlike for spreads, where the influence of concentration was especially large for domestic banks, more concentration seems to raise costs all around in similar measure. This result is consistent with the notion that in more concentrated systems there is less pressure for banks to lower their administrative costs in order to offer more competitive spreads. Since bank concentration was also seen to raise spreads, it has a particularly powerful effect on the costs of intermediation.

As with the spreads estimations, we repeated the regressions dropping Argentina, Mexico and Colombia and adding time dummies. The results remain the same. To save space we do not report these results here, but they are available upon request.

5. Conclusions

Our results show that foreign participation and concentration influence the spreads charged to borrowers—and hence the process of financial intermediation—in a complex manner. The overall effect depends on three different channels of influence: the spreads charged by foreign banks relative to domestic banks, the "spillover" effects from the presence of foreign banks on both spreads charged and on operating costs, and the concentration in the banking sector that has accompanied foreign entry. Consider each in turn.

First, foreign banks charge lower interest margins and potentially foster financial intermediation. New establishments (i.e., *de novo* banks) appear to operate with particularly low spreads. Whether such entry generates welfare gains is unclear since that will depend on whether the lower spreads charged are the consequence of a more aggressive pricing strategy or because *de novo* banks choose to lend only to the most transparent segments with high market contestability.

Second, greater foreign presence does not imply a general decline in spreads, but appears to influence the intermediation through lowering costs of operation. More widespread foreign bank presence is associated with cost reduction throughout the banking system. Possibly, a combination of demonstration effects and potential competition, with banks threatening to encroach on each others' customer base, generates the pressures for cost reduction that ultimately benefit bank clients. Thus, long-term benefits of foreign entry are likely to come from lower cost structures in the banking system.

Third, greater concentration raises spreads in an economically important manner. This is so especially for domestic banks. At the same time, concentration is also associated with higher administrative costs all around. The implication is that some part of the benefits from foreign entry may be offset where concentration levels also increase. As noted in the introduction, the consolidation that did occur in the banking sectors of the countries concerned was not necessarily related to foreign entry, although the fact that much of the entry was in the form of takeovers, rather than new establishments, did not help create more competition. For policy makers, this creates a challenge since more competition is desirable for lowering spreads, but could generate vulnerability where the "franchise" value of domestic banks is seriously eroded.

Finally, while we believe this chapter adds to our understanding of the impact of foreign participation and concentration on the costs of financial intermediation in developing countries, more work in this area is clearly needed. Given the limited number of countries and short sample period we study, there is a need to extend the analysis in both of these directions. Also, further research linking bank-level data with the banks' customer profiles would help to explain the apparent differences in the spreads charged by foreign and domestic banks, something which this chapter speculates on but cannot answer definitively.

Notes

1 Figures obtained from Demirgüç-Kunt, Laeven, and Levine (2004).
2 For a review of the potential consequences of foreign bank participation see Levine (1996). For a discussion of the impact of bank concentration on profitability see Berger (1995). For a test of whether bank consolidation and concentration has worsened competition in developing countries see Gelos and Roldós (2002).
3 For a broader discussion of the implications of consolidation, see Gelos and Roldós (2002) for developing countries and Berger (1995) for a review of the U.S. evidence.
4 Domestic banks may lower spreads either because they are driven to become more efficient following bank entry (by, for example, imitating some of the practices introduced by foreign banks) or because they are forced to give up some of the margins they were able to charge before. In other words, lower spreads could be the result of lower costs or lower revenues.
5 Brock and Rojas-Suarez (2000) study spreads in Latin America during 1990–1996 and conclude that they have not gone down significantly (perhaps with the exception of Mexico) and in many cases are still three times higher than those observed for industrial countries (though less so for Chile). In general, the study finds that high operating or administrative costs are particularly significant in explaining the behavior of bank spreads in the region.
6 In the case of Mexico, the foreign bank share exceeded 40 percent by 2001.
7 Following the lifting of restrictions on foreign entry, fifteen foreign banks initiated operations in Mexico during 1995 and 1996. These entrants were small relative to the existing domestic banks, and the main increase in foreign bank participation occurred through the acquisition of domestic banks after 1998.
8 According to the dealership approach, banks are risk-averse dealers trying to balance loan and deposit markets, where loan requests and deposit flows are not necessarily synchronized. In this set up, bank spreads are interpreted as fees charged by banks for the provision of liquidity under transactions uncertainty. The firm theoretical model of banks assumes these operate in a static framework where the demand and supply for loans and deposits clears both markets.
9 A common limitation of the empirical applications of these frameworks is that market structure differences across countries have been modeled by including

country dummies (see Saunders and Schumacher (2000)), that is they have been implicitly assumed to be constant over time.

10 An extensive literature exists studying the impact of concentration on bank profitability (see Berger 1995 for a review). While the literature unanimously predicts a positive association between concentration and profitability, different theories exist explaining what is behind this result. The structure–conduct–performance theory argues that bank concentration signals market power and that a positive association between profits and concentration is unambiguously bad for the economy. A related theory is the relative market power hypothesis, which claims that only firms with large market share and differentiated products can obtain market power and are able to earn profits above normal. On the other hand the efficiency–structure hypothesis contends that larger concentration levels and market shares could reflect greater efficiency by the largest banks, which in turn are able to lower costs and obtain higher profits. While a problem of observational equivalence exists in interpreting the relation between bank concentration and profits, this issue should not arise in analyzing bank spreads. Relatively more efficient banks should be able to charge lower spreads, as a result of having lower costs. Consequently a positive association between bank spreads and concentration should signal greater market power and less competition in the banking sector.

11 Note that while Table 9.1 reports annualized spreads, Table 9.2 presents quarterly spreads, since the regressions are conducted with quarterly observations.

12 Because the spreads charged by public banks may be subject to constraints due to direct subsidies and other political considerations, we do not include these banks in our sample. Also, since implicit bank spreads calculated from quarterly income and balance sheet data can be quite volatile, we exclude those observations in the top and bottom 5 percentile of the distribution of the change in bank spreads. The purpose of doing so is to avoid the possibility that outliers drive our results. However, eliminating these observations does not change the results described below.

13 For example, we are interested in analyzing if and how the mode of foreign bank entry, by merger and acquisition or by *de novo* entry, affects bank spreads. However, there are few such transactions in each country to study this question on a country by country basis.

14 To address the concern of possible reverse causality from spreads to bank's operational characteristics (such as liquid assets, non-performing loans, and market share), we also estimated similar regressions using one-quarter lags of these variables as regressors with virtually identical findings. To save space, this results are available upon request.

15 Because bank origin might be correlated with the degree of foreign bank participation (i.e., the larger the number of foreign banks, the more likely it is that foreign bank participation will be high) and bank market share might be positively associated with the level of system wide concentration, we reestimated the equations after excluding these bank level variables to confirm the robustness of our findings. Our main findings remain unchanged. These results are available upon request.

16 Excluding these interaction terms does not change our results.

17 To test these speculations would require specific data on the portfolio of the different banks, which are not available at the present time in the detail that is necessary. As a second best alternative, we tried controlling for the share of loans to assets and the ratio of non-interest expenses to assets to take into account that some *de novo* banks might be investing in bonds and/or securities rather than lending. However, these variables never proved to be significant and in some cases reduced our sample size. Thus, these results are not reported here, but are available upon request.

18 In particular, a one standard deviation change in the share of loans held by the top three banks (top five banks) results in a 0.25 (0.13) standard deviation change in bank spreads. At the same time, a one standard deviation change in the Herfindahl index leads to a 0.20 standard deviation rise in bank spreads.

19 Argentina is the exception, given its large number of banks. Results for Argentina yield the same results and conclusions as those for the panel. These results are available upon request.

20 To save space in Tables 4 and 5 we only report estimations including the loan share of the three largest banks as a measure of concentration. However, regressions using the top 5 bank share and the Herfindahl index produce virtually the same results. These are available upon request.

21 Again, recognizing the possibility of reverse causation from costs to market share, we reestimated the regressions with lagged values of the market share, with results that are the same as those described here. However, these estimations are available upon request.

References

Allen, Linda (1988). "The Determinants of Bank Interest Margins: A Note." *Journal of Financial and Quantitative Analysis* 23: 231–235.

Angbazo, Lazarus (1997). "Commercial Bank Net Interest Margins, Default Risk, Interest-Rate Risk, and Off-Balance Sheet Banking." *Journal of Banking and Finance* 21: 55–87.

Barajas, Adolfo, Roberto Steiner, and Natalia Salazar (2000). "The Impact of Liberalization and Foreign Investment in Colombia's Financial Sector." *Journal of Development Economics* 63: 157–96.

Berger, Allen N. (1995). "The Profit-Structure Relationship in Banking-Tests of Market Power and Efficient Structure Hypotheses." *Journal of Money, Credit, and Banking* 27: 404–456.

Bernanke, Ben, and Mark Gertler (1989). "Agency Costs, Net Worth, and Business Fluctuations." *American Economic Review* 79: 14–31.

Brock, Philip L., and Liliana Rojas-Suarez (2000). "Understanding the Behavior of Bank Spreads in Latin America." *Journal of Development Economics* 63: 113–34.

Claessens, Stijn, Asli Demirgüç-Kunt, and Harry Huizinga (2000). "The Role of Foreign Banks in Domestic Banking Systems." In *The Internationalization of Financial Services: Issues and Lessons for Developing Countries*, edited by Stijn Claessens and Marion Jansen, pp.117–138. Boston: Kluwer Academic.

Cottarelli, Carlo, and Angeliki Kourelis (1994). "Financial Structure, Bank Lending Rates, and the Transmission Mechanism of Monetary Policy". *International Monetary Fund Staff Papers* 41: 587–623.

Dell'Arricia, Giovanni, and Robert Marquez (2004). "Information and Bank Credit Allocation." *Journal of Financial Economics*. Forthcoming.

Demirgüç-Kunt, Asli, Luc Laeven, and Ross Levine (2004). "Regulations, Market Structure, Institutions, and the Cost of Financial Intermediation." *Journal of Money, Credit, and Banking*. Forthcoming.

Denizer, Cevdet (2000). "Foreign Entry in Turkey's Banking Sector, 1980–1997." In *The Internationalization of Financial Services: Issues and Lessons for Developing Countries*, edited by Stijn Claessens and Marion Jansen, pp. 389–406. Boston: Kluwer Academic.

Gelos, Gastón, and Jorge Roldós (2002). "Consolidation and Market Structure in Emerging Market Systems," IMF Working Paper No. 02/186.

Ho, Thomas, and Anthony Saunders (1981). "The Determinants of Bank Interest Margins: Theory and Empirical Evidence." *Journal of Financial and Quantitative Analysis* 4: 581–600.

IMF (International Monetary Fund) (2000). *International Capital Markets: Developments, Prospects, and Key Policy Issues.* Washington, D.C.

Kiyotaki, Nobuhiro, and John Moore (1997). "Credit Chains." *Journal of Political Economy* 105: 211–248.

Rogers, William H. (1993). "Regression Standard Errors in Clustered Samples". *Stata Technical Bulletin Reprints* 3: 88–94.

Saunders, Anthony, and Liliana Schumacher (2000)."The Determinants of Bank Interest Rate Margins: An International Study." *Journal of International Money and Finance* 19: 813–832.

Smith, R. Todd (2001). "Bank Spreads and Business Cycles." Mimeo. IMF.

Zarruck, Emilio R. (1989). "Bank Margin with Uncertain Deposit Level and Risk Aversion." *Journal of Banking and Finance* 14: 803–820.

Wong, Kit Pong (1997). "On the Determinants of Bank Interest Margins under Credit and Interest Rate Risks." *Journal of Banking and Finance* 21: 251–271.

10 The role of cross-border mergers and acquisitions in Asian restructuring

With Shoko Negishi

1. Introduction

This chapter is motivated by four principal objectives:

- To describe recent trends in cross-border mergers and acquisition (M&A) activity in developing countries (section 2).
- To review the literature on the role that M&A can play in enhancing economic efficiency (section 3).
- To provide an empirical assessment of the role played thus far by cross-border M&A in the restructuring of corporate sector in East Asia following the recent crisis (sections 4 and 5).
- And, finally, to draw policy lessons on mechanisms that facilitate M&A and hence permit their efficient execution while also recognizing the need for complementary measures to enhance competition and improve corporate governance (section 6).

Cross-border M&A activity has been on the rise worldwide, driving the upsurge in foreign direct investment (FDI) over the past decade, and especially over the past few years. While industrialized countries account for a dominating 90 percent share of the value of world cross-border M&As, Latin America and East Asia developing countries have, is significant and the value of cross-border M&As in these countries is on the rise. The benefits of such M&A activity remain controversial. By enhancing the competition for corporate control, mergers can improve efficiency. Some studies show that acquisitions can be especially useful in restructuring underperforming firms.

Before-and-after comparisons of cash flow returns of acquired firms conclude that acquisitions bring higher wealth gains for insolvent firms than those under independent work-out, and that those gains are higher in cross-border transactions than domestic M&As. At the same time, mergers can also destroy value where the projected synergies do not materialize and/or the corporate cultures clash (see Ghemawat and Ghadar 2000, Economist 2000)

In this context, cross-border mergers in the East Asian crisis countries are of special interest.[1] Though financial reengineering of debt owed by troubled firms, including under government-sponsored voluntary work-out schemes, has made progress, severely distressed firms, particularly in the non-tradable sectors, have been compelled to seek buyers for their assets. The Korean and Thai governments, in particular, have introduced a series of policy reforms to create a better environment for foreign investment as well as domestic and cross-border mergers and acquisitions to enhance asset reallocation.

This chapter empirically examines the sectoral patterns of cross-border merger and acquisition activity and their relationship to recovery in East Asia. The main findings are:

- Cross-border M&A activity has occurred primarily in the most distressed sectors, such as non-tradable sectors. On the other hand, the sectors that are performing relatively well have less M&A activity.
- There is insufficient evidence to suggest so-called "fire-sales" of distressed assets.
- But, equally, we found little sign of immediate contributions of cross-border M&As to the restructuring of the troubled economies. Our evidence is, however, tentative since we use industry averages rather than firm-level data. However, the lack of an impact is not implausible. Given the gravity of problems, especially in the non tradable sectors, it is not surprising that the restructuring effects of cross-border M&As have not yet materialized. The most significant role for cross-border M&As, therefore, lies ahead in the longer-term processes such as operational restructuring and reallocation of assets.
- Government policies to enhance domestic mergers and acquisitions, greater competition, and improved corporate governance will reinforce the beneficial effects of foreign mergers and acquisitions.

2. Cross-border M&A: trends, motives, and impacts

This section reports on cross-border M&A trends and, in particular, compares them with trends in FDI. In doing so, however, one important caveat needs to be noted. M&A is a form of FDI. However, the balance of payments data does not distinguish between M&A and "greenfield" FDI (new projects). Hence the comparison has to be made on reported values of cross-border M&As; these reported values, unfortunately, include amounts that are not components of the balance of payments reporting of FDI data. As such, the two series cannot be directly compared. The amount recorded as FDI refers to funds channeled through the capital account of a country in relation to both M&As and new projects; these transferred amounts can either be equity, reinvested earnings, or intercompany debt (i.e., debt issued by the parent to the subsidiary company). In contrast, cross-border M&A data refer to transaction values. If, for example, the foreign acquiring company raises debt within the domestic market to purchase the target company, that amount is also included in the reported values. In practice, such amounts are not likely to be large. Additionally, and perhaps more importantly, the acquiring company may borrow internationally to finance the purchase of the target company. Unlike domestic debt, such international debt financing does represent a transfer of resources to the recipient country. However, the comparison with FDI flows breaks down since, as noted, those flows include only inter-company debt. In practice, it is difficult to judge how important even this difference is. For FDI also it is possible that the international firm may borrow internationally and then on-lend on its own account to its foreign subsidiary.

Cross-border M&As have increased significantly in industrialized as well as developing countries over the past decade. Although developing countries' share of cross-border M&As is still small relative to industrialized countries, transactions in Latin America (primarily through privatization) and East Asia (post-crisis asset sales) have led an upsurge among developing countries. In East Asia, Korea and Thailand in particular have attracted large volumes of M&A activity since 1997. In analyzing these flows, it is helpful to distinguish between two different motives for the M&A activity: creating opportunities for the future (strategic partnering) and resolving past problems (corporate restructuring). Most M&A activity occurring in developed countries is in the industries under competitive pressure as a result of deregulation, technological renovation, or large R&D expenditures, and is thus intended for strategic repositioning. In developing countries, cross-border M&As can immediately provide liquidity and prevent asset losses, and enhance resource allocation. In the long-term, M&As potentially introduce new management and operation systems, thereby improving efficiency and competitiveness.

Trends and principal sectoral characteristics

According to data assembled by the United Nations Conference on Trade and Development (UNCTAD), global cross-border acquisitions (in which a foreign purchaser acquired more than a 10 percent stake) reached $720 billion in 1999, up by 35 percent from $532 billion in 1998, whereas the majority cross-border M&A value was $411 billion.[2] Despite the rise in dollar values, developing country M&As declined from $81 billion (15 percent of total M&As) in 1998 to $63 billion (9 percent) in 1999. Cross-border M&As in developing countries grew at an annual average rate of 81 percent during the period of 1991–1999, compared with 26 percent annual average growth of FDI flows in developing countries. These decade averages, however, mask the sharp jump in recent years, such as 132 percent from 1996 to 1997.

Within developing countries, Latin America has been the largest target region of cross-border M&As, most of which have been through privatization programs (Figure 10.1). Though smaller in M&A size, East Asia has been the fastest growing target region, growing at an annual average rate of 106 percent (Table 10.1), again with the big absolute jump occurring after the 1997 crisis.

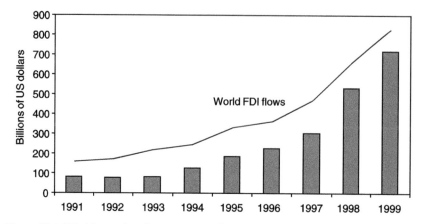

Figure 10.1 World cross-border mergers and acquisitions, 1991–1999*.

Note: *Involves acquisitions of a more than 10 percent equity.

Source: World Bank GDF 2000 and UNCTAD.

Unlike in Latin America, cross-border M&A activity in East Asia has been largely through sales of private firms.

The recent cross-border M&As in industrialized countries and, to a lesser extent, in developing countries are characterized by large-scale transactions (Ghemawat and Ghadar 2000, Economist 2000). The mega deals in industrialized economies in 1999 include acquisitions of AirTouch Communica-

Table 10.1 Cross-border mergers and acquisitions in developing countries (billions of US$)

		1991	*1992*	*1993*	*1994*	*1995*	*1996*	*1997*	*1998*
East Asia and the Pacific	*FDI*	14.3	22.0	39.1	45.1	52.0	59.9	64.1	64.2
	M&A	0.2	0.3	1.2	2.1	1.3	2.0	6.7	10.1
Europe and Central Asia	*FDI*	3.4	4.6	6.3	7.0	16.9	15.8	22.8	24.4
	M&A	1.1	3.9	2.4	2.4	4.3	2.1	7.8	1.9
Latin America and the Caribbean	*FDI*	12.8	15.0	13.7	28.4	29.8	43.6	64.7	69.3
	M&A	1.0	6.1	3.8	3.1	6.0	11.2	25.6	31.2
Middle East and North Africa	*FDI*	2.8	3.6	3.8	3.4	−0.2	3.3	5.9	5.1
	M&A	0.0	0.3	0.2	0.4	0.03	0.2	1.1	1.2
South Asia	*FDI*	0.4	0.8	1.1	1.6	3.0	3.5	4.9	3.7
	M&A	0.05	0.01	0.1	0.4	0.2	0.2	0.3	0.8
Sub-Saharan Africa	*FDI*	1.6	1.6	1.9	3.4	4.2	4.7	7.7	4.4
	M&A	0.08	0.07	0.5	0.1	0.3	3.0	1.6	1.5
Developing Countries Total	*FDI*	35.3	47.5	66.0	88.9	105.6	130.8	170.3	170.9
	M&A	2.4	10.8	8.2	8.5	12.1	18.6	43.2	46.8

Note: * Involves acquisitions of a more than 50 percent equity.

Source: World Bank (1999a) and UNCTAD (1999).

tions of the United States by Vodafone Group PLC in the United Kingdom for $65.9 billion and Atlantic Richfield Co. of the U.S. by BP Amoco PLC in the UK for $33.7 billion. Mega transactions in developing countries, notably in Latin America, have been closely related to privatization projects, such as the sale of Brazil's Telebras for $19 billion in 1998 and Argentina's petroleum company YPF SA for $19 billion in 1999.

What drives M&As?

M&A activity creates competition for corporate control, motivated by both private and regulatory incentives. Private incentives include imperfections and asymmetries in domestic product and capital markets (Kindleberger 1969, Caves 1971, Hymer 1976, Froot and Stein 1991), competitive environment of the market, differences in tax systems (Scholes and Wolfson 1990). The imperfections and costs motivate firms to pursue mergers and acquisitions to capitalize on monopoly rents or internalize operations. Regulatory incentives include variations in corporate governance (Jensen 1986), and policy frameworks towards foreign investment.[3] Management that acts in its own interest may cause financial losses to shareholders, which provides a potential for other firms to intervene. Liberalization of foreign entry and ownership will open up more opportunities for cross-border M&A activity.

Though the distinction is not always clear-cut, M&A activity can be broadly classified into two categories (Table 10.2). The first type of M&As is mainly motivated by past problems and attempts to create value through restructuring. The second type is forward looking, seeking to create value through creative partnerships. Negative features of M&As arise if the first type is driven by "fire-sales" of distressed firms, and the second type of M&As is triggered by firms seeking for market monopoly. In both cases, mismanagement may destroy shareholder value.

The upsurge of M&As in the United States in the 1980s reflected the need to revitalize domestic firms to a new reality of increased global competition. Acquisitions by foreign firms were significant. During the 1985–1989 period, foreign acquisitions of U.S. firms amounted for over $170 billion, 17 percent of total U.S. takeover activity (Harris and Ravenscraft 1991). Japan was one of the major investors, with a $13 billion outlay in 1988 for acquisitions of 132 U.S. firms (Kang 1993). Motivated largely by the value of restructuring

Table 10.2 Why M&As occur?

	PAST	*FUTURE*
POSITIVE	Overcome capital market imperfections	Build value through strategic partnering
NEGATIVE	Fire-sale/monopoly	Monopoly

the acquired firms, these early U.S. M&As were similar to the M&As in post-crisis East Asia. In the U.S. M&As of the 1980s, the firms were under competitive pressure to rationalize and raise profitability, whereas East Asian firms have been struggling to recover from severe financial distress and also improve their long-term competitiveness.

In contrast, the recent mega mergers have been largely driven by incentives for strategic partnerships to share costs of the innovation process and extend product variety. Strategic partnering through M&As can lead to new forms of oligopolistic competition based on knowledge networks. Strategic M&A activity can increase the operational flexibility of firms to meet new demands that are constantly generated under the continuous process of innovation (UNCTAD 1999). The sectoral examples of M&As demonstrate the pressures for consolidation and rationalization of assets. The telecommunication and banking industries, having gone through a series of deregulatory measures, are dealing with a complex mix of greater competition arising from technological change and the need to supply a worldwide market. The oil and chemical industries are similarly facing the challenge of technological renovation. Firms in the pharmaceutical industry, a major target of M&As in industrialized countries, rely heavily on R&D, which makes strategic mergers advantageous. As these examples show, globalization heightens competition, which forces firms to rationalize internal resources and increase access to wider markets as well as to achieve economies of scale through M&As. Meanwhile, internationalization of operation, management and financial assets can make firms more resistant to external shocks and volatility as a result of rapid globalization in developing countries.

In developing countries also, deregulation and liberalization of trade and services has opened up more opportunities for foreign investors. However, this first stage of M&A is being driven either by privatizations of state-owned enterprises, which need significant upgrading, or by M&As of troubled private firms.

The increased M&A activity in the crisis-afflicted economies has been driven by exchange rate depreciations and lower domestic asset prices, which provided foreign investors with greater scope for acquiring assets. Meanwhile policy frameworks towards foreign entry have been liberalized in those economies. On the other hand, domestic firms are faced with large debt repayments in rising interest rates and thereby forced into restructuring. This has particularly been the case for those firms in the non-tradable sectors that could barely benefit from the export growth as a result of currency depreciation. For some financially troubled firms the only alternative to bankruptcy has been to sell their assets. This has let to a concern in East Asia that the current wave of cross-border M&As represents "fire-sales" of domestic assets, which will result in substantial transfer of domestic wealth to foreigners, thereby involving little prospect of restructuring the troubled sectors.

Benefits of M&A

We focus here on two questions. First, are cross-border M&As different from domestic M&As? Second, do M&As play a special role in restructuring?

Cross-border M&As Whether cross-border M&As bring benefits to host countries has not yet been empirically clarified. Consolidation and rationalization of resources as a result of M&As—domestic or cross-border—can resolve over-capacity and improve efficiency. Nevertheless the immediate impact of M&A activity may be negative as consolidation and rationalization result in reduced employment and, possibly, reduced competition.

Cross-border M&A activity can be beneficial to a host country when it prevents potentially profitable assets from being wiped out, which is specifically applicable to M&As involving either privatization of state-owned enterprises in transition economies or sales of financially distressed firms in developing countries. Highly indebted, loss-making companies—state-owned or private—often have no option but to go insolvent unless they can be sufficiently financed by external resources, most probably coming from foreign investors given domestic financial constraints. Various examples from the transition economies in Central and Eastern Europe suggest that privatization-related cross-border M&As have played a key role in restructuring domestic firms. A study of the Czech Republic, Poland, and Hungary during the 1992–1995 period indicates that foreign investment enterprises had a higher propensity to invest, were more export-oriented, and also were faster in restructuring, than domestic firms (Hunya 1997).

Other evidence suggests that in Hungary's banking sector, where the major privatization program has been completed, foreign investors have provided technical expertise as well as financial support, and have demonstrated greater independence from domestic political influence than domestic firms. Moreover the new entry of foreign investors into the retail market of the banking sector has increased competition, thereby promoting the development of innovative services as well as improving personnel training and marketing (World Bank 1999a).

Empirical analyses of M&As and corporate restructuring are, however, limited because of the lack of availability of financial information of acquired firms. Financial information of firms whose majority stake is acquired by other operating firms will be replaced by the consolidated information of the acquirers shortly after the transactions are completed. Therefore very few studies examine the long-term impact of M&A activity on restructuring. Some analyses of U.S. firms suggest that cross-border M&As bring larger wealth gains than domestic transactions, by comparing short-term stock returns (a few days before and after the announcement of mergers) of acquired firms. A comparative study of 1273 U.S. firms acquired during the period 1970–1987 by foreign and domestic firms shows that wealth gains for target firms observed 1–4 days after the announcement of mergers (approximated by cumulative abnormal stock returns) are significantly higher in cross-border transactions than in domestic acquisitions by around 10 percentage points (Harris and Ravenscraft 1991). Similarly, a study of Japanese M&A activity in the United States during the 1975–1988 period concluded that the sale of a majority stake to Japanese firms leads to significantly higher target returns than the sale of a majority interest to U.S. firms (Kang 1993).

Role in restructuring   Some evidence suggests that M&As can facilitate efficient redeployment of assets of insolvent firms in the longer-term. Hotchkiss and Mooradian (1998) focused on 55 post-merger performance of insolvent firms that were acquired by other operating firms, in comparison to matching non-bankrupt transactions. The study found that post-merger cash flow returns of acquired insolvent firms improved in the first and second years by around 6 percent each, whereas post-merger cash flow returns of non-bankrupt firms showed no statistically significant improvements. They also suggested that potential sources of operating gains for the acquisitions of insolvent firms were reductions in operating expenses.[4]

In the long-term, however, not only can M&As induce new investment, domestic or foreign, by the acquirers and their suppliers, but they can also introduce new managerial, production and marketing resources to target firms, thereby improving efficiency and productivity (UNCTAD 1999). Eventual integration with the corporate networks of the acquirers can further expand opportunities. Moreover, cross-border M&As bring foreign exchange and help the developing host countries fill the gaps in their current accounts.

3. East Asian financial distress and recovery

More than two years since the onset of the East Asian crisis a strong cyclical recovery is ongoing but large parts of the corporate and financial sectors in the crisis economies remain in distress. In late 1999, non-performing loans (NPLs) in their banking systems, though lower in some countries than their historical peaks, were still at considerably high levels. In Indonesia, the Republic of Korea, Malaysia and Thailand respectively, NPLs were 25 percent, 18 percent, 45 percent, 41 percent of gross domestic product (GDP), and an estimated 50 percent, 15 percent, 21 percent and 39 percent of total loans.[5] Recovery has been strongest in Korea, which along with Malaysia, has benefited especially from the strong international demand for electronics products. And while such a recovery is likely to continue, the after-effects of the financial shock will persist, and continued restructuring is essential both to reinforce that recovery and to reduce future vulnerabilities.

Summary of events

The East Asian crisis has exposed financially weak firms in the corporate sector that have operated on thin margins, and their subsequent inability to pay interest has aggravated their debt burden. Since their ability and incentives to invest are limited—and since such firms constitute a significant portion of the crisis economies—they will continue to act as a drag on investment and growth until the financial claims are resolved, and either their operations return to adequate profitability or their assets are redeployed. Meanwhile the distressed banking sector itself requires further recapitalization or consolidation to avoid continued systemic risks and growing fiscal liabilities for governments.

The East Asian crisis has driven many marginal firms into illiquidity, and resulted in a high level of accumulated debt and associated interest payments. Consequently, many firms that have recently emerged from the worst effects of the crisis are still in a precarious situation and are vulnerable to further shocks. Furthermore, non-performing loans by banks and non-bank financial companies have remained exceptionally high.

- Investment rates have fallen sharply since the onset of the crisis (Figure 10.2). Relative to the average of 1992–1997, the investment rates in the second quarter of 1999 were down by about 57 percent in Indonesia, 40 percent in Thailand, and by 30 percent in Korea.
- The government has borne the brunt of bank restructuring. Bank recapitalization costs are significantly large in relation to existing public debt; estimated at 48 percent, 4 percent, 8 percent, and 8 percent of GDP in Indonesia, Korea, Malaysia, and Thailand respectively (World Bank

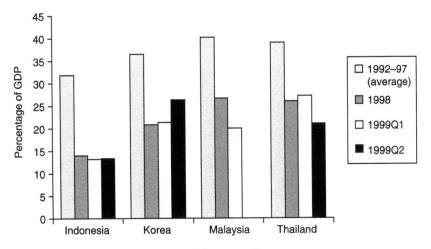

Figure 10.2 Total investment in East Asia (percent).

Source: IFS, IMF.

Table 10.3 Illustrative post-crisis policy reforms in crisis countries

	Loss allocation and transfer	Resource mobility	Corporate governance
Indonesia	Tax exemptions for loan-loss reserves held by banks (March 1998)	Relaxation of foreign ownership restrictions (September 1997) Tax exemptions of up to 8 years for new investments in 22 industries (January 1999)	Presence of a corporate secretary to improve disclosure Bankruptcy Law updated (August 1998) Code of best practice for corporate governance (in progress)
Korea	Revaluation and adjustment of capital and foreign exchange losses (August 1999)	Introduction of Foreign Investment Promotion Act (November 1998)	Restrictions on cross-debt guarantees (April 1998) Enhancing institutional voter rights (June 1998) Introduction of international accounting standards (August 1999) Lowering the minimum equity holding requirement to exercise shareholder's rights (1999)
Malaysia	Reduction of corporate tax rate from 30 percent to 28 percent (October 1997) Tax exemption on interest from non-performing loans (effective for 1999 and 2000)	Reduction of real property gains tax rate from 30 percent to 5 percent for nonresidents on the sale of a property held for a minimum of five years (October 1997) Exemption of real property gains tax on mergers of financial institutions (October 1998)	Creation of High-Level Finance Committee on Corporate Governance Code on takeovers and mergers with stricter disclosure standards (January 1999)

| Thailand | Elimination/deferral of income tax and taxes on asset transfer and unpaid interest (January 1999) Introduction of new asset depreciation method (March 1999) | Alien Business Law August 1998, revised in October 1999) Tax-free M&As in cases of 100 percent mergers (January 1999) Introduction of Equity Fund, Thailand Recovery Fund for large- and medium-scale companies, and Venture Capital Fund for small and medium-size enterprises (March 1999) Reduction of real estate transfer fee from 2 to 0.01 percent of the appraised value (March 1999) | Financial statements of public companies and financial institutions to be in accord with international best practices (1999) Requirement of board audit committees (1999) Bankruptcy and foreclosure laws amended (March 1999) |

1999b). Without the ability to collect on non-performing loans, debt levels will show a higher than reported increase.

* In corporate restructuring in contrast, the proper role for governments is to facilitate resolution of financial claims and foster the reallocation and mobility of assets.

In the absence of effective bankruptcy regimes, governments in all the crisis countries have instituted out-of-court mechanisms to speed up financial settlements. At the same time, bankruptcy procedures, where needed, have been reformed, which may also help resolution of financial claims in the short run and may provide a sounder basis for improved corporate governance in the long run. Once financial property rights have been clarified, the market system and the private sector should be in a position to undertake the required reallocations of productive assets, but governments can play an important role in permitting greater asset mobility. Reforms following the crisis also included short-term tax regime changes to facilitate asset transactions and, more importantly from a long term perspective, better accounting standards, which should contribute to improved corporate governance through better evaluation of financial assets and liabilities (Table 10.3).

Sectoral distress and recovery

The crisis had a disproportionate impact on firms with pre-existing structural weaknesses, and this has also consequently resulted in uneven recovery. Signs of distress and recovery become apparent through the examination of various indicators. Industrial production in manufacturing has shown significant recovery in Korea and, to a lesser extent, also in Malaysia (Figure 10.3). This faster recovery reflects in part their greater strengths in sectors such as electronics, computers, and telecommunication equipment. Korean firms have also shown resilience in the transport equipment sector (Figure 10.4a). Similarly Thai firms in the transport equipment sector have made a strong bounce back after a sharp decline in output, whereas Malaysian firms are still on the way to returning to the pre-crisis level (Figure 10.4b, 10c). In Korea, Malaysia and Thailand traditional manufacturing sectors such as chemical products, cement products, metals, and machinery have only shown a limited recovery, but in some cases a decline significantly predated the crisis.

More importantly, the most distressed sectors appear to be non-tradable/ services sectors where production remains below pre-crisis levels (Figure 10.5). In particular gross domestic product in the wholesale and retail trade as well as the finance and real estate sectors show signs of severe distress, with a sharp decline and/or slow recovery (Figure 10.6a–c). Currency depreciations, which favor traded goods, have reduced the incentive to invest in the non-tradable sectors. The share of insolvent firms is significantly higher in the non-tradable sectors than in the tradable sectors, for instance, in Malaysia about three-quarters of the non-performing loans are to enterprises in the

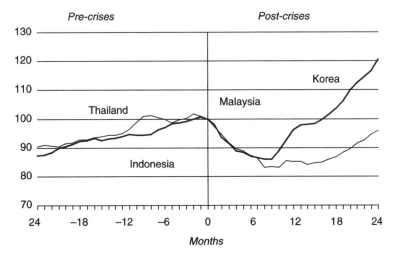

Figure 10.3 Industrial production before and after the crisis (index = 100 at the start of the crisis).

Note: * 3 month moving averages.
Source: Datastream.

non-tradable sectors. The high level of distress reflects prevalent problems in the non-tradable sectors, which, even prior to the crisis, had been characterized by overcapacity and low productivity (Crafts 1999), reflecting local monopolies in sectors such as retail trade and distribution. Low productivity in the real estate sector also reflects excess capacity. The Japanese experience shows that deregulation of domestic trade is an important spur to competition and to increasing productivity (Alexander 1999).

The share of firms unable to pay their debts is significantly higher in the non-tradable sectors than in the tradable sectors. The estimates show that, in the second quarter of 1999, distress was especially high in the non-tradable sectors of services and real estate, as could be expected from the trends in non-tradable production (Table 10.4). For Malaysia, where the sectoral distribution of non-performing loans is available, the data shows that the problems have worsened especially for the non-tradable sectors (Table 10.5). Non-performing loans as a share of GDP by sector rose more rapidly in the non-tradable sectors than for manufacturing overall during the period of March 1998 and September 1999.

4. Cross-border M&As in East Asian restructuring

As noted, cross-border mergers and acquisitions (M&As) can be a useful—and, unlike most other initiatives, a private-sector driven—restructuring tool for host economies when distressed firms have limited alternatives for their survival. However, a concern with respect to the possibility of "fire-sales" has

a. Korea

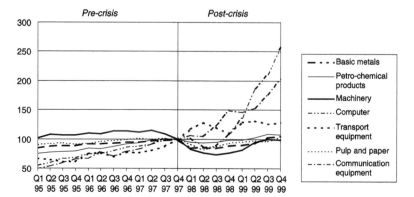

b. Malaysia

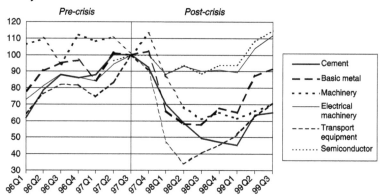

c. Thailand

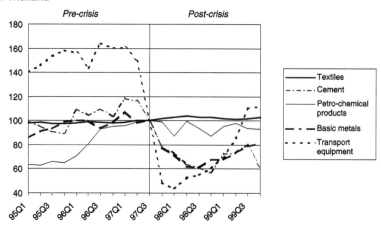

Figure 10.4 Production index before and after the crisis by industry (index = 100 at the start of the crisis).

Note: *3 quarter moving averages.

Source: a and b, Datastream; c, Bank of Thailand.

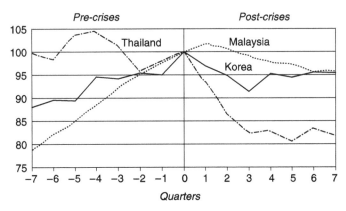

Figure 10.5 Non-tradable production before and after the crisis (index = 100 at the start of crisis).

Note: 3 quarter moving averages.

Source: Datastream.

Table 10.4 Financial distress, 1999, 2nd quarter (percentage of firms unable to meet current debt repayment)

Country	1999 (Q2)			
	All	Manufacturing	Services	Real estate
Indonesia	63.8	41.8	66.8	86.9
Korea	26.7	19.6	28.1	43.9
Malaysia*	26.3	39.3	33.3	52.8
Thailand	28.3	21.8	29.4	46.9

Note: * For Malaysia, firms in agriculture and utilities bring down the average for all firms in 1999.

Source: Claessens, Djankov, and Klingebiel (1999a).

Table 10.5 Non-performing loans as share of GDP in Malaysia by sector (percent)

	Mar-98	Dec-98	Sep-99	Change, 3/98–9/99
Agriculture, forestry and fishing	6.4	11.7	15.0	58.3
Mining	1.9	9.0	6.6	32.5
Manufacturing	24.3	59.1	56.8	32.7
Utility	7.3	13.1	21.2	63.2
Wholesale and retail trade	21.8	46.0	57.2	58.1
Construction	131.8	328.1	342.2	47.1
Transportation and communications	23.4	63.3	52.5	23.5
Financial services	50.5	136.7	210.5	124.2

Source: Bank Negara.

a. Korea

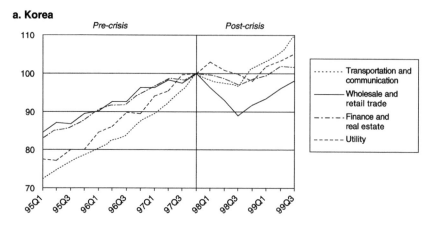

b. Malaysia

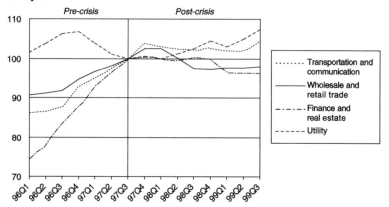

c. Thailand

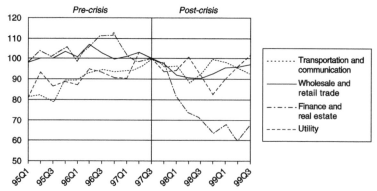

Figure 10.6 Non-tradable production before and after the crisis by industry (index = 100 at the start of crisis).

Note: *3 quarter moving averages.

Source: a, Bank of Korea; b, Datastream; c, Bank of Thailand.

been prominent in the policy discussions. "Fire-sales" of domestic assets can result in substantial transfer of domestic wealth to foreigners. Nevertheless whether they do so depends on how "fire-sales" are defined (Krugman 1998). If pre-crisis asset values had been inflated by implicit guarantees that ultimately fail, and the crisis returns the values to their appropriate level, purchases by foreigners may reflect their greater liquidity or their superior management skills, but properties are sold at equilibrium prices and there is no transfer of wealth. Alternatively, if an excessive exchange rate depreciation, perhaps the result of contagion in international markets, forces domestic firms to liquidate to pay off short-term debt, foreign firms that are not liquidity-constrained can purchase these domestic firms or projects, which will generate a stream of profit above the liquidation value once the exchange rate recovers. The domestic economy will lose because of the wealth transfer, more so if foreigners are less efficient at running domestic investment projects than local firms (see Krugman 1998). Though the evidence is not clear-cut, we do not find "fire-sales" to be a significant phenomenon. However, neither do we find obvious evidence for the positive effects of restructuring.

FDI and cross-border M&As

Majority-owned cross-border M&A sales in the crisis countries reached $7.3 billion in 1998, compared with $3.6 billion in 1997, largely due to significant increases in M&A activity in Korea and Thailand. In 1999, the cross-border M&A value (including both majority and minority acquisitions) in East Asia's crisis four countries were $20 billion, up from $17 billion in 1998, with $12 billion in Korea and $3 billion in Thailand (compared to $9 billion and $5 billion in 1998 respectively) (Figure 10.7). Malaysia received a high level of cross-border M&A deals prior to the crisis, but levels did not rise after the crisis. M&As in Indonesia, traditionally at the miniscule level, doubled in 1999 to $2.7 billion from 1998.

Figure 10.8 shows the sectoral distribution of cross-border M&As in the crisis countries during the period of 1997–1999. Indonesia had half the number of transactions in light manufacturing (mainly food products), and petro-chemicals (mainly oil refining). In Korea and Malaysia, the wholesale and retail trade sector had the largest number of transactions, 24 percent and 30 percent of their respective totals. Korea also had a large share of sales in the petro-chemicals industry. Other sectors that sold a large number of assets in Malaysia are the finance and real estate and the light manufacturing sectors (comprising the paper and pulp, textiles, and cement industries). In Thailand, the transactions have taken place mostly in the finance and real estate and the wholesale and retail trade sectors, accounting for more than 50 percent of total sales.

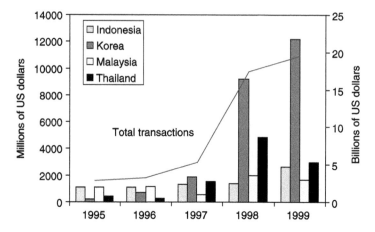

Figure 10.7 Cross-border mergers and acquisitions in crisis countries, 1997–1999*.

Note: * Includes both majority and minority ownership.
Source: Thomson Financial Securities Data.

Cross-border M&As and financial distress

Though it is early to judge the impact of M&As in East Asia, certain conclusions can be drawn. The existing literature on U.S. firms, as noted earlier, compares pre-merger cash flow performance of target firms with post-merger performance of acquirer firms. In cross-border M&A transactions in East Asian countries, on the other hand, the size of the acquired firms is not significant relative to foreign firms to affect the performance of acquirer firms after the mergers, which means that the post-merger performance of acquired

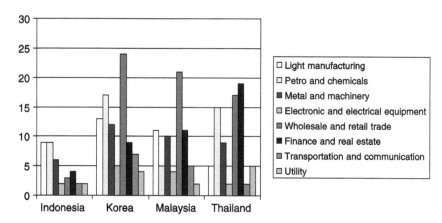

Figure 10.8 Cross-border mergers and acquisitions in crisis countries by sector 1997–1999 (number).

Source: Thomson Financial Securities Data.

firms will not be measured by the performance of surviving entities, unlike the studies of the U.S. cases. We focus, therefore, on industry aggregates, recognizing that this reduces the confidence in the findings since those aggregates may mask individual firm performance.

Some descriptive pictures are presented in Figure 10.9, comparing the average recovery rate in production since the crisis with the number of cross-border M&A sales by sector. Cross-border M&A sales tend to take place in larger numbers in the sectors showing deeper distress and slow recovery. In Thailand, 30 percent of mergers and acquisitions occurred in finance and real estate, where GDP has declined most sharply with the slowest recovery, followed by the wholesale and retail trade sector. The petrochemicals industry has also stagnated, as seen in Figure 10.4c, whereas foreign investors have shown considerable interest in acquiring assets among the manufacturing sectors. On the other hand, the transport equipment sector required less asset sell-offs due to its strong upturn (Figure 10.4c). In Malaysia, foreign investors have bought majority stakes largely in the wholesale and retail trade and the finance and real estate sectors, those that have suffered most from fallen production and sluggish recovery. The average rate of growth in production in the finance and real estate sector still remains negative. There has been a relatively small number of cross-border M&A sales in the utility (electricity, gas, and water) sector which has shown the fastest recovery among the non-tradables. The ratio of the average post-crisis growth rate of production (where there has been a positive growth) to the pre-crisis rate is 0.09 for the wholesale and retail trade sector, whereas for the utility, food, and basic metal sectors, the ratios are 1.53, 2.21 and 2.31, respectively.

In comparison, Korea's picture is somewhat ambiguous partly because production has not only declined by a smaller magnitude, but also it has recovered more rapidly than the other crisis economies. Nevertheless, the wholesale and retail trade sector, with the severest fall in production in the economy, has had by far the largest number of asset sales. As also observed for Thailand, in the transport equipment sector, which shows resilience and recovery, there has been a relatively small number of asset sales. In Korea's petro-chemicals industry, 10 out of 17 cases have taken place with major chemical and allied products companies in Europe, which appears to be part of increased global oligopolistic competition in the industry since 1998. Meanwhile, overall demand growth prospects for petroleum products in the region augment the high volume of asset acquisitions by foreign investors.

Inferences on production efficiency can also be tentatively drawn from inventory trends in Korea, where such data is available (Figure 10.10). The patterns in inventory appear to be somewhat associated with cross-border M&A activity: the industries with low inventory level—textile, metal, and transport equipment—show the least M&A activity, whereas machinery and petro-chemical industries have the largest numbers of M&As among the tradable sector.

a. Korea

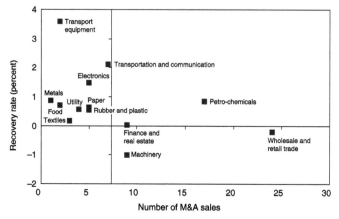

b. Malaysia

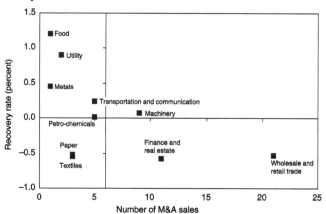

c. Thailand

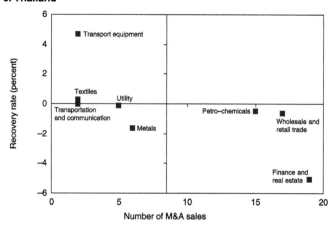

Figure 10.9 Cross-border mergers and acquisitions and recovery in production by sector, 1997–1999 (number).

Note: Recovery rate is the average quarterly change in production between the crisis period and end-1999. The X axis crosses at the average number of M&As.

Source: Thomson Financial Securities Data.

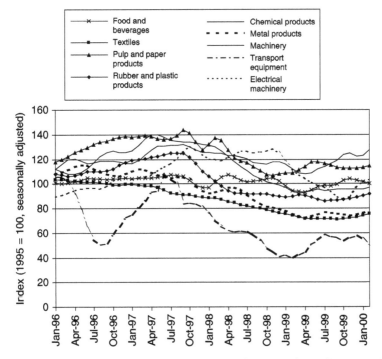

Figure 10.10 Inventory index by industry in Korea (three-month moving average).
Source: Datastream.

Table 10.6 shows selected companies in the wholesale and retail trade and the finance and real estate sectors, whose majority stakes were sold to foreign acquirers during 1998–1999. The last three columns indicate return on equity (a ratio of net income to shareholder's equity) of the companies; two years, one year, and at the most recent date available, prior to the announcement of sales. The return on equity in acquired companies had sharply deteriorated

Table 10.6 Return on equity of acquired companies

Company		Sector	Sale value ($mil)	Return on equity		
				2 years	1 year avail.	Last avail.
Korea First Bank	Korea	Finance and real estate	415.0	−1.8	−162.0	−1587.6
Shangri-La Hotels	Malaysia	Wholesale and retail trade	94.6	7.1	3.5	–
Bank of Asia	Thailand	Finance and real estate	181.5	15.9	−4.6	−78.8
Nakornthon Bank	Thailand	Finance and real estate	319.3	−4.0	−341.9	–
UOB Radanasin Bank	Thailand	Finance and real estate	382.5	−29.0	−283.0	–
Shangri-La Hotel	Thailand	Wholesale and retail trade	34.7	0.5	−13.9	–
Golden Land Ppty Dvlp	Thailand	Finance and real estate	76.3	−1.6	−62.0	–

Source: Thomson Financial Securities Data.

prior to the transactions in all cases. Among the wholesale and retail trade sector in Thailand, the hotel industry is considered to have a stronger potential to recover through the involvement of foreign capital. Investors from Europe, the United States and Asia's newly industrialized economies have been attracted by long-term growth prospects in the industry, as well as to assets made available in the market at lower prices as the new bankruptcy law forces the highly indebted owners to sell them off.

Besides the urgent need of distressed firms for liquidity, coupled with overall policy measures to encourage cross-border M&As, the large number of asset sales in the finance and real estate sector has been partly driven by the recent efforts of the East Asian governments to recover assets of the nationalized banking institutions. Since, through their direct takeovers and recapitalization initiatives, governments of the crisis countries have become substantial owners of the banking systems, the reprivatization of these institutions has remained a priority that will influence the long-term structure and performance of the financial sectors. So far, efforts at privatization have been partially successful, particularly in Korea and Thailand, albeit with problems partly as a result of the continued growth of non-performing loans, which new acquirers have difficulty in valuing.

The sale of a 51 percent stake in Korea First Bank, one of the country's largest commercial banks, to a US investment fund, Newbridge Capital, was finally settled in September 1999 after nine months of negotiations. The protracted negotiations centered around the valuation of non-performing loans that had not been carved out or revealed and on the extent of continued government obligations to assume non-performing loans following the privatization. The issues were particularly serious since Korea First Bank was a principal creditor to the second largest *chaebol*, Daewoo where a creditor-led restructuring is ongoing as a result of the continued increase in debt. The final terms of agreement require the government to be responsible for any loans that are non-performing over the next two years. There have been a number of smaller-scale acquisitions of Korean banks by foreign investors, including a 17 percent stake in Kookmin Bank by a Goldman Sachs-led investment fund, and a 31 percent stake in Korea Exchange Bank by Commerzbank of Germany (EIU 1999).

In Thailand, continued concerns over the scale of the non-performing loans and of asset quality, has delayed sales of the nationalized banks to foreign investors, although the slow but steady progress in the asset resolution process appears to some regaining of foreign investor confidence. ABN-Amro Bank of the Netherlands acquired a 75 percent stake in Bank of Asia, while the Development Bank of Singapore bought 51 percent of Thai Danu Bank in 1998. Nakornthon Bank (NTB) followed when Britain's Standard Chartered bought a 75 percent stake for $319 million in September 1999 after two years of negotiations. The government is expected to reimburse Standard Chartered for any loss of interest revenue resulting from the bank's non-performing loans. Numerous minority acquisitions include a 15 percent stake in Thai Farmers Bank to the Government of Singapore Investment Corporation for $258 million.

As discussed previously, some argue that the post-crisis asset acquisitions in East Asia by foreign investors are often based on "fire-sale" pricing, although evidence has been insufficient to support this argument. Limited information of cross-border M&A transactions in Thailand suggests that prices paid by acquirers per share have been around 70 percent of book value per share (Table 10.7). In contrast, non-performing assets in Thailand have been auctioned at values that are considerably lower than the acquisition values of local firms. The average auction price of non-performing assets in Thailand has been 25 percent of the book value (Table 10.8). The case of Korea also indicates that foreign acquisitions of assets have not been "fire-sales". Korea suffered least from domestic liquidity constraint among the crisis-hit countries. Nevertheless total cross-border M&A transactions shot up to $9 billion in 1999, five times higher than the level in 1998. M&A activity in Korea continued to rise by 32 percent in 1999 despite the considerable appreciation of the won by 15 percent from 1998. This suggests, therefore, that foreign acquisitions of assets have been driven by not only their greater liquidity from foreign exchange depreciation, but also new opportunities as a result of improved policy environment towards M&As.

In summary, financial and corporate restructuring is not a short process, and clear outcomes have largely yet to materialize. East Asia's financially distressed firms have so far made major progress in the rescheduling of debt as a short-term agenda item of restructuring. Once the troubled firms stabilize their liquidity position, further steps would be needed towards longer-term restructuring measures—such as re-organization, changes in management, and reductions in excess capacity—which often require new investments.[6] Successful firms in market economies restructure continuously in order to reposition their businesses and thus remain competitive to survive in the long term. Restructuring occurs when a firm shifts its product mix and cost structure and positions itself dynamically to remain competitive in response to

Table 10.7 Transaction value of selected cross-border M&A activity in Thailand

Effective Date	*Company*	*Industry*	*Book value per share (US$)*	*Transaction value as share of book value (%)*
March 29, 1998	Carpets International	Textile Products	1.3	70.0
September 24, 1999	Shangri-La Hotel	Wholesale and retail trade	0.9	72.2
February 3, 2000	United Motor Works	Transport Equipment	3.7	72.7

Source: Thomson Financial Securities Data.

Table 10.8 Auction results of non-performing assets (as of end-1999)

FINANCIAL SECTOR RESTRUCTURING AUTHORITY, THAILAND*

Bid date	Items	Book value (baht)	Auction value as % of book value
June 25, 1998	Auto hire purchase contracts	52 billion	48 %
August 13, 1998	Residential mortgage loans	24.6 billion	47 %
December 15, 1998	Business loans	155.7 billion	25 %
March 19, 1999	Business loans	221.5 billion	18 %
July 6, 1999	Construction loans	1.3 billion	8 %
August 11, 1999	Business loans	129.0 billion	24 %
November 10, 1999	Business loans	17.8 billion	30 %

Note: * Excludes sales of non-core assets.

Source: Financial Sector Restructuring Authority.

KOREA ASSET MANAGEMENT CORPORATION

Bid date	Items	Book value (won)	Auction value as % of book value
September 1, 1998	Business loans	207.5 billion	12 %
October 30, 1998	Real estate assets	6.0 billion	–
December 9, 1998	Loans secured by real estate assets	564.6 billion	36 %
May 27, 1999	Business loans	772.4 billion	17 %
June 22, 1999	Loans secured by real estate assets	1.04 trillion	51 %
November 11, 1999	Business loans	811.1 billion	21 %
December 8, 1999	Loans secured by real estate assets	1.02 trillion	62 %

Source: Korea Asset Management Corporation www.kamco.or.kr/engl.html

DANAHARTA

Bid date	Items	Book value (US$)	Auction value as % of book value
July 1, 1999	Foreign loans	94.95 million	55 %

Source: Danaharta www.danaharta.com.my

changes in technology and public policies. Alongside those measures of so-called operational restructuring, the firms' assets need also to be rationalized. Reallocation of assets requires effective methods for asset pricing, which in turn requires credible bankruptcy procedures and a market for mergers and acquisitions, including liberal foreign investment rules.

5. Policy implications

Cross-border M&A activity can bring most benefit to the host country when facilitated by certain policy frameworks. After a crisis, once the first step of loss allocation and transfer is complete, liberalization of foreign investment and ownership as well as tax incentives can amplify resource mobility. Introduction of institutional bankruptcy laws and accounting standards, alongside reinforcement of shareholders' rights will improve corporate governance. Meanwhile, the potential downside of M&A activity, such as higher market concentration and immediate unemployment effects, can be avoided by removing bureaucratic barriers to competition and increasing the flexibility of labor market.

Loss allocation and transfer   East Asian governments have taken several steps to achieve the above agenda, as summarized in Table 10.3. To facilitate debt restructuring, corporate tax rates have been reduced and tax exempted on interest from non-performing assets in Indonesia and Malaysia. Korea and Thailand adopted new methods of capital valuation as well as asset depreciation towards the same goal.

Resource mobilization   The second step of resource mobilization includes measures that are directly related with M&A activity, both international and domestic, such as liberalization of foreign investment and ownership as well as tax reduction and exemption on real estate transfer. Success of M&As depends heavily on procedural simplicity and clarity.

Since their crises in 1997, both Korea and Thailand have introduced various measures to encourage business consolidation involving M&As, which have led to the rapid rise in cross-border M&As in these two countries. Korea has been providing tax exemption and deferral on capital gains from so-called "big deals," that is, exchange of businesses through the transfer of shares. The Korean government also released a new legislative framework in July 1999 to reduce transaction-related taxes incurred in corporate mergers, acquisitions, and divisions. Thailand approved a set of new measures in January 1999, including provisions for tax-free mergers and noncash acquisition of assets in cases of 100 percent mergers, and for the elimination of all taxes on asset transfers from debtors to creditors. Moreover new bankruptcy procedures introduced in March 1999 allow creditors to force business restructuring on insolvent firms. As a result, firms with high liabilities have no other choice but to sell their assets as banks push them to repay their debts.

In addition to these measures, Korea and Thailand have also taken effective steps to deregulate and liberalize their foreign investment policies since late 1997. Korea has opened several sectors to foreign investors since April 1998, including various property businesses, securities dealings, and other financing businesses. The ceiling on foreign stock investment was abolished as of May 1998, granting foreign investors the right to purchase all the shares of a domestic firm. Meanwhile, the Foreign Investment Promotion Act of November 1998 affords protection for foreign direct investment through national treatment, the reduction and exemption of certain corporate taxes, the provision of financial support for local governments to attract foreign direct investment, and the establishment of foreign investment zones. In Thailand, the Board of Investment has eased its regulations to promote foreign participation in the economy. The twenty-year old Alien Business Law was replaced in August 1998 (and has since been revised again in October 1999) to incorporate sectoral liberalization measures. Under the August 1998 provisions, foreign firms are allowed to hold up to 100 percent equity in banks and in finance companies for up to ten years, and 39 sectors have been opened up to increased foreign participation, including transportation and pharmaceuticals production. Policy liberalization includes a temporary measure introduced in November 1998 (expiring in December 1999) allowing foreign firms to own a majority stake in joint ventures that received favorable policy treatment, and authorizing them to distribute their products domestically. In the meantime, the proposed cutback of import tariffs is expected to help reduce production costs for both domestic and foreign firms dependent on imported raw materials and intermediate products.

Unlike in Korea and Thailand where cross-border mergers have shot up, in Malaysia, cross-border M&As have been low compared to its own historical performance. Malaysia has, however, had high levels of domestic M&As.[7] Malaysia's Promotion of Investment Act 1986 and other measures provide various tax incentives, including investment tax allowances in the services sector. The high level of domestic merger and acquisitions activity in Malaysia suggests that the regime is basically a friendly one. However, cross-border activity could remain low, on account of restrictions on the repatriation of earnings. More recently, Malaysia has endorsed an extensive merger program of the banking system, in which all the banking institutions have submitted their merger proposals by end-January 2000. In contrast, the Indonesian system appears not to favor M&As. Gains from transfers of assets in corporate reorganizations are taxable, and companies cannot transfer tax losses in a liquidation process, merger, or acquisition (Asia Law 1998). Certain exceptions apply only to banks, financial institutions, and companies going public. The sales of banking institutions have been deterred, due also to difficulties in valuation of non-performing loans as in the other crisis countries. Overall merger and acquisition activity has remained at extremely low levels.

Corporate governance   Finally, the third step of enhancing corporate governance can also be highly effective in encouraging market-driven M&As. Some studies of ownership structures in East Asian firms suggest large family control disadvantaging shareholders (Claessens, Djankov, Fan, and Lang 1999 and Claessens, Djankov, and Lang 1999). Good corporate governance can improve distribution of control.

Improvement of enterprise monitoring, disclosure of information, accounting practices, and equity issuance processes are essential to strengthen corporate governance frameworks. Korea and Thailand have taken steps to enhance institutional voter rights and increase the number of shareholders to exercise their rights. The amendment to the bankruptcy code in Thailand, which came into effect in March 1999, is an example of an effective measure to encourage M&As through market forces. In Thailand, as previously discussed, financially distressed sectors such as the hotel industry have been attracting a high level of foreign interest for its long-term growth prospects since the bankruptcy laws have been amended. The new codes allow creditors to enforce resolution of assets on debtors for repayments. Meanwhile, Korea's movement towards international accounting standards has been welcomed by foreign investors whose concerns over the acquisition of Korean assets were centered around the valuation of non-performing loans. Korea also introduced new requirements for domestic companies to increase the involvement of non-insiders on their boards On the other hand, efforts to improve corporate governance in all crisis countries. Those measures have been important to increase transparency and accountability, though further progress has yet to be made.

Competition policy and labor mobility   Certain policy measures should be taken to avoid any potential downsides and induce utmost benefit of cross-border M&As. Consolidation and rationalization through M&As may lead to a higher degree of concentration as well as employment reduction in the host market, which particularly will apply to sectors with excess capacity. To maintain the right balance between competition and cooperation has been an important concern for East Asian policy makers (Stiglitz 1996 and Mody 1999). In so doing, market-oriented measures need to be taken by reducing bureaucratic restraints to competition and monitoring market shares. Moreover, domestic firms could be provided with incentives to invest in research and development and to form strategic alliances with advanced companies, which will increase competitiveness through continuous technological renovation. Meanwhile social security systems could be improved, e.g. by tentatively extending the coverage of unemployment insurance, to support the laid-off due to M&A activity, whereas vocational training could be provided to enhance flexibility of the labor market.

Lessons from M&A activity in Japan   The Japanese case also gives a good example where improved regulations governing M&As have contributed to the restructuring process. According to Alexander (1999) and UNCTAD (1999), M&As are occurring in numbers unprecedented for Japan, though their importance to the economy is still a small fraction of that in the United Kingdom or the United States. The value of foreign takeovers in Japan rose from US$1.1 billion in 1997 to US$6.9 billion in 1998, and then shot up to US$24.2 billion in 1999, accounting for 32 percent of the country's total

M&A activity. Major transactions include sales of a majority stake in Yamai-chi Securities to Merrill Lynch (the United States) in 1998, and in Japan Leasing to General Electric for $6.6 billion, as well as a 37 percent stake of Nissan Motors to Renault (France) for $5.4 billion. Similarly, domestic M&As have also risen briskly as M&As are becoming acceptable business transactions among Japanese firms, a fundamental change from the previously held view that M&As are predatory actions.

The rise in Japanese M&A is partly explained by the elimination of cross-shareholdings, as the returns on these equity holdings have been persistently low or negative. At the same time, many regulatory constraints on business activities are being removed, and specific measures to facilitate M&As are being instituted. For instance, a 1997 amendment of the Commercial Code by the Japanese Diet reduces the number of shareholder meetings required to approve mergers. The Holding Company Law of 1997 removes constraints on carving out subsidiaries for sale and allows buyers more freedom in structuring their acquisitions. The securities transaction tax formerly required when an acquisition involved share purchases was discarded in April 1999. In addition, the moves to implement international accounting principles and, in particular, consolidated reporting, are bringing more transparency to the operation of subsidiaries.

6. Conclusion

Foreign investors, who see opportunities in corporate distress, lower asset prices, and more liberal policies towards M&As and FDI in general, have been attracted to the post-crisis East Asia. Cross-border M&A activity in the crisis countries has largely concentrated in the most troubled sectors of the crisis countries. Some non-tradable sectors as well as traditional manufacturing sectors suffer from excess capacity as a consequence of over-investment since the early 1990s, and thereby from lower capacity utilization and reduced production. Moreover a large number of firms carry large debt repayments due to rising interest rates, whereas other domestic companies are also financially constrained. East Asian governments have taken several steps to encourage mergers and acquisitions, whereas, albeit to varying degrees, foreign investment has been liberalized.

However, cross-border M&A activity is still in its early phase in East Asia's financially distressed economies, and remains small, relative to the stage of development and the size of their economies.[8] The recent upsurge in M&A activity in East Asia, particularly in Korea, are largely attributed to changes in policy environment that used to work against foreign acquisitions of local assets. Liberalization of foreign entry and ownership restrictions alongside introduction of international accounting standards and shareholding systems has exponentially increased access for foreign investors to the local market and acquire assets.

The immediate role of cross-border M&As has been to provide sufficient funds and to preserve the existing assets that would otherwise have been wiped out. In the long-term, M&As can bring in more FDI by the acquirers and their suppliers and new resources in management and production to host countries. Eventual integration with the corporate networks of the acquirers will expand their opportunities for higher industry diversification. Though M&As have been most prominent in distressed sectors, at this stage there is little evidence to suggest that cross-border M&A activity has made an immediate contribution to the restructuring of troubled sectors. We should, however, highlight that the sectoral aggregates may not reflect the full effect of M&As on recovery of the distressed sectors. It will require some firm-level analysis to draw more robust conclusions.

Given the gravity of problems in some sectors such as the non-tradables, the restructuring effects of cross-border M&As may not materialize in such a short time span. The most significant role for cross-border M&As lies in longer-term restructuring processes such as operational restructuring and reallocation of assets. Foreign participation through M&As could also be more effective in achieving improved efficiency and competitiveness as well as better corporate governance. Under the circumstances, foreign direct investment, in the form of cross-border M&As, has a significant role to play in restructuring and development of financially distressed economies.

"Fire-sales" are also not evident. For the few transactions for which we can compare sale prices to book value, the receipts have been surprisingly high. Moreover, Korea has had the highest level of M&As despite the least liquidity constraint. Also, the levels of M&A activity have continued to remain high despite appreciation of exchange rates from their lower levels, especially but not only in Korea.

Notes

1   All the statistical references to cross-border M&As in this chapter involve acquisitions of more than a 50 percent equity stake by foreign investors unless otherwise noted.
2   UNCTAD introduced a new statistics of acquisitions of a more than 10 percent stake, which is more comparable to FDI statistics. We do not have information of 1999 according to this definition, and hence no comparison is made to the rest of the statistics based on the majority acquisitions of a more than 50 percent stake.
3   A comprehensive summary of the literature is also provided in Kang (1993).
4   There is a study of 344 cross-border and domestic M&A transactions of U.S. firms during the 1980–1990 period, which showed that significantly high cumulative abnormal returns in cross-border acquisitions was also observed in domestic transactions (Blumberg and Owers 1996).
5   These numbers include non-performing loans purchased by asset management companies.
6   Claessens *et al.* (1999b) indicate that concentration of ownership as well as extensive links between financial institutions and corporations are likely to delay restructuring in East Asian crisis economies.
7   The total number of domestic M&As has been about 50 to 70 per quarter in

Malaysia in 1997–99, while it remained low (in the range of 4 to 10) in the other countries (see Securities Data Company 1999).
8   Cross-border M&As account for 0.6 percent of GDP in East Asia in 1998, significantly lower than 1.5 percent of GDP in Latin America.

References

Alexander, Arthur (1999) "Japan Confronts Corporate Restructuring." Background paper for *Global Economic Prospects and the Developing Countries 2000*, World Bank. Washington D.C.

Asia Law (1998) *Cross-border M&A: A guide to global strategic direct investment for Asian companies*. Asia Law & Practice, Ltd., Euromoney Publications.

Blumberg, Aryeh and James E. Owers (1996) "The Convergence of Foreign Direct Investment and Restructuring: Evidence from Cross-border Divestitures." *Global Finance Journal* 7(1): 67–87.

Caves, Richard E. (1971) "International Corporations: The Industrial Economics of Foreign Investment." *Economica* 38: 1–27.

Claessens, Stijn, Simeon Djankov, and Daniela Klingebiel (1999a) "Bank and Corporate Restructuring in East Asia: Opportunities for Further Reform." Financial Sector Discussion Paper 3, World Bank. Washington D.C.

Claessens, Stijn, Simeon Djankov, and Daniela Klingebiel (1999b) "How to Accelerate Corporate and Financial Sector Restructuring in East Asia." *Viewpoint* 200, World Bank. Washington D.C.

Claessens, Stijn, Simeon Djankov, and Larry H. P. Lang (1999) "Who Controls East Asian Corporations?" Policy Research Working Paper 2054, World Bank. Washington D.C.

Claessens, Stijn, Simeon Djankov, Joseph P. H. Fan, and Larry H. P. Lang (1999) "Expropriation of Minority Shareholders: Evidence from East Asia." Policy Research Working Paper 2088, World Bank. Washington D.C.

Crafts, Nicholas (1999) "East Asian Growth Before and After the Crisis." *IMF Staff Papers* 46(2): 139–66.

Economist (2000) "Merger Brief: The Digital Dilemma." July 22.

Economist Intelligence Unit (1999) *Business Asia. September 1999*.

Froot, Kenneth R., and Jeremy C. Stein (1991) "Exchange Rates and Foreign Direct Investment: An Imperfect Capital Market Approach." *Quarterly Journal of Economics* 106: 1191–1217.

Ghemawat, Pankaj and Fariborz Ghadar (2000) "The Dubious Logic of Global Megamergers." *Harvard Business Review* July/August.

Harris, Robert S. and David Ravenscraft (1991) "The Role of Acquisitions in Foreign Direct Investment: Evidence from the U.S. Stock Market." *Journal of Finance* 46(3): 825–844.

Hotchkiss, Edith S. and Robert M. Mooradian (1998) "Acquisitions as a Means of Restructuring Firms in Chapter 11." *Journal of Financial Intermediation* 7: 240–262.

Hunya, Gabor (1997) Foreign Direct Investment and its Effects in the Czech Republic, Hungary, and Poland. The Vienna Institute for Comparative Economic Studies (WIIW). No. 186.

Hymer, Stephen H. (1976) *The International Operations of National Firms: A Study of Direct Foreign Investment*. MIT Press, Cambridge, Massachusetts.

International Monetary Fund. Various issues. *International Financial Statistics.* Washington D.C.

International Monetary Fund. 1998. *World Economic Outlook 1998.* Washington D.C.

International Monetary Fund. 1999. Financial Sector Crisis and Restructuring— Lessons From Asia. August 12, 1999.

Jensen, Michael C. (1986) "Agency Costs of Free Cash Flows, Corporate Finance, and Takeovers." *American Economic Review* 76: 323–329.

Kang, Jun-Koo (1993) "The International Market for Corporate Control: Mergers and Acquisitions of U.S. Firms by Japanese Firms." *Journal of Financial Economics* 34: 345–371.

Kindleberger, Charles P. (1969) *American Business Abroad: Six Lectures on Direct Investment.* Yale University Press, New Haven, Connecticut.

Krugman, Paul R. (1998) "Fire-sale FDI." (http://web.mit.edu/krugman/www/ FIRESALE.htm)

Mody, Ashoka (1999) "Industrial Policy after the East Asian Crisis: From 'Outward Orientation' to New Internal Capabilities?" Policy Research Working Paper 2112, World Bank, Washington D.C.

Scholes, Myron S., and Mark A. Wolfson (1990) "The Effects of Changes in Tax Laws on Corporate Reorganization Activity." *Journal of Business* 63: 141–164.

Stiglitz, Joseph (1996) "Some Lessons from the East Asian Miracle." *The World Bank Economic Observer* 11(2): 151 177.

Thomson Financial Securities Data 1999–2000. SDC Platinum 2.1—Mergers & acquisitions database.

United Nations Conference on Trade and Development (1999) *World Investment Report 1999: Foreign Direct Investment and the Challenge of Development.* Geneva.

World Bank (1999a) *Global Development Finance.* World Bank, Washington D.C.

World Bank (1999b) *Global Economic Prospects and the Developing Countries.* World Bank, Washington D.C.

Index

www.ingramcontent.com/pod-product-compliance
Ingram Content Group UK Ltd.
Pitfield, Milton Keynes, MK11 3LW, UK
UKHW020357010325
455677UK00021B/502